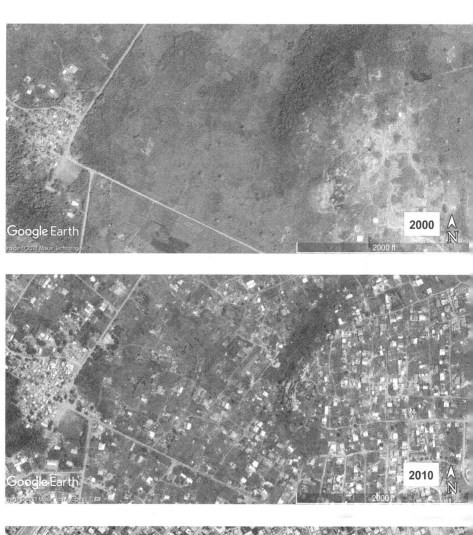

Urban Planning in a World

of Informal Politics

URBAN PLANNING
IN A WORLD OF
INFORMAL POLITICS

Chandan Deuskar

PENN

UNIVERSITY OF PENNSYLVANIA PRESS

PHILADELPHIA

THE CITY IN THE TWENTY-FIRST CENTURY

Eugenie L. Birch and Susan M. Wachter, Series Editors

A complete list of books in the series is available from the publisher.

Published by
University of Pennsylvania Press
Philadelphia, Pennsylvania 19104-4112
www.upenn.edu/pennpress

Printed in the United States of America on acid-free paper

10 9 8 7 6 5 4 3 2 1

Library of Congress Cataloging-in-Publication Data
Names: Deuskar, Chandan, author.
Title: Urban planning in a world of informal politics / Chandan Deuskar. Other titles: City in the twenty-first century book series. Description: 1st edition. | Philadelphia : University of Pennsylvania Press, [2022] | Series: The city in the twenty-first century | Includes bibliographical references and index.
Identifiers: LCCN 2022002172 | ISBN 9781512823066 (hardcover) | ISBN 9781512823103 (eBook)
Subjects: LCSH: City planning—Political aspects—Developing countries. | Urbanization—Political aspects—Developing countries. | Patron and client—Developing countries. | City planning—Political aspects—Ghana. | Squatter settlements—Ghana. | Patron and client—Ghana. | Ghana—Politics and government—2001- Classification: LCC HT169.5 .D48 2022 | DDC 307.1/216091724—dc23/eng/20220203
LC record available at https://lccn.loc.gov/2022002172

Frontispiece: Figure 1. Growth of an informal subdivision on the periphery of Greater Accra (2000, 2010, and 2021). Source: Google Earth (Image © 2021 Maxar Technologies).

CONTENTS

PART III. POLITICALLY ADAPTIVE PLANNING

The Challenge of Planning the Informal City

*T*he residents of Accra, Ghana, were used to their city flooding every rainy season, but June 2015 was worse than normal. Heavy rainfall caused floods in thetreets several feet deep. The city's marketplaces, normally crowded and lively, came to a standstill as stormwater destroyed the goods of traders. Traffic froze as people climbed on top of cars to escape the water coursing through the streets. Twenty-five people died in the floods. Countless others only barely escaped being swept away.

Just when things seemed like they couldn't get any worse, another disaster struck. Near Kwame Nkrumah Circle, the city's busiest interchange, petrol from a fuel station mixed with the floodwater and flowed to a nearby house. A cooking flame ignited the mixture, causing a massive explosion and fire. Firefighters struggled to get through the floods to put out the fire. By the time they finally managed to extinguish the fire, it had killed two hundred more people. Ghana's president called for three days of national mourning for the victims of what came to be known as the "twin disaster" of flood and fire.

City leaders knew that they had to do something to quell public anger over the tragedy. They turned their attention to the informal settlement that straddled Korle Lagoon. Officially named Old Fadama, the settlement was widely referred to as "Sodom and Gomorrah," after the biblical cities that God destroyed as punishment for their sinfulness. Surely the flooding was caused by structures in Old Fadama obstructing the city's drainage, city officials reasoned. Twenty years previously, the government itself had used the site to resettle people fleeing a conflict in the north of the country, and the settlement had grown over time. But these origins were now either forgotten or ignored. As far as city officials were concerned, the residents of the settlement were squatters and had no legal right to be there. The mayor quickly ordered the demolition of structures *along the waterway. Bulldozers soon rolled into the settlement and destroyed the homes of thirty thousand people.*

The residents were distraught. Rumors and conspiracy theories circulated. The demolitions were just a pretext for the mayor and his friends to confiscate and develop the prime land for personal profit, some said. The president of Ghana had awarded his brother a contract for dredging the lagoon, said others, and Old Fadama was the easiest place to do it. Perhaps the mayor was trying to win favor with residents of nearby areas, where he happened to be campaigning to become a member of Parliament. After all, the surrounding community, consisting largely of the ethnic group indigenous to Accra, had made no secret of their desire to see Old Fadama gone.

Residents of Old Fadama rioted in protest of the demolitions. National political leaders from the incumbent party watched footage of the angry protestors on the news and grew nervous. They summoned the mayor to Parliament. He arrived, bringing the city's director of planning with him. The planning director justified the demolitions by explaining that the area was officially intended as the site of recreational facilities, not residences. As proof, he unfolded a fading copy of a 1970 plan for the Korle Lagoon area. Sure enough, the plan depicted a stadium, a yacht club, tennis courts, a cricket ground, an aviary, and botanical gardens laid out picturesquely where the makeshift structures of Old Fadama now crowded together.

The party leaders were unmoved by the plan. They reminded the mayor that the residents of Old Fadama were supporters of their party. The settlement's poverty and precariousness meant that the party had been able to capture its votes with relatively inexpensive handouts. But voters were fickle, and election results in Accra had been getting uncomfortably close. The party could not afford to antagonize the residents of Old Fadama. The mayor, who was appointed to his role by the party, had no choice but to stop the demolitions.

The residents of the demolished structures soon returned and rebuilt their homes along the waterway. Despite this reprieve, their legal status did not change. In the ensuing years, government bulldozers have occasionally arrived to destroy more homes. Residents usually rebuild these homes, and the population of the settlement continues to grow. At other times, campaigning politicians visit to promise the residents paved roads, schools, and public toilets. Meanwhile, the city's planners look on as their official plans for the area, full of green space and public amenities, gather dust. The residents know that as long as political leaders need to maintain their control over them, their existence will remain precarious.

The growth of informal settlements ("slums") like Old Fadama is not simply the result of poverty, rapid rural-to-urban migration, or a lack of technical capacity of governments to make or enforce plans. Informal settlements in low- and middle-income democracies grow and persist because people in positions of political power have an incentive to cultivate the vulnerability and dependency of communities who must provide political support to them in exchange for their survival. In this book, I argue that urban planners must adapt to this political reality in order to produce more inclusive and sustainable outcomes. Trying to emulate practices from different political contexts will not work. Instead, planners and policymakers should identify strategies that are already working in their own cities, even if only partially so far, and try to build on them.

Urban planners are failing to provide adequate shelter, secure land and property rights, and safe and healthy living environments for vast numbers of people in rapidly urbanizing parts of the world. Over a billion people worldwide live in what the United Nations defines as "slums," and this number continues to grow by millions each year.[1] The world's urban population is expected to have nearly doubled between 2015 and 2050.[2] With 90% of new urban growth occurring in low- and middle-income countries, the number of people living in informal settlements is likely to continue to rise dramatically in coming decades.[3]

Though scholars debate definitions of *informality*, the term refers broadly to activities that do not conform to official regulations but are nonetheless widespread. Informality is not a problem as much as it is a poor solution to a problem. The problem is the inability or unwillingness of the formal public or private sectors to provide sections of the population with access to shelter, services, and livelihoods. Informality is a partial solution to this problem to the extent that the poor are able to use informal practices to secure these necessities. However, it is a poor solution because of the challenges that come with it. Informal access to necessities is typically inadequate, inequitable, and precarious, and leaves those who have to rely on it open to exploitation. Urban informality also constrains the ability of planners to regulate urban spatial growth for equity and sustainability. As the window of opportunity to avert catastrophic climate change narrows, the inability to regulate urban growth prevents effective urban climate change mitigation and adaptation, as cities expand in ways that lock in automobile-oriented development and put people's lives at risk.

National governments and international organizations often see informal urbanization as the result of a lack of urban planning and respond to it with calls to build planning capacity. For example, the government of Kenya's 2030 strategy for metropolitan Nairobi aims to "plan, plan, plan."[4] According to the urban sociologist Lisa Björkman, "the notion that slums arise from lack of planning, and must therefore be prevented and upgraded using planning-related tools, has become a veritable battle-cry" across the rapidly growing cities of the "Global South."[5]

However, simply planning *more* is not the solution. Planning as practiced in many low- and middle-income democracies is largely ineffective. At times, it may even cause more problems than it solves and help create or perpetuate informality. When the state tries to assert itself in cities dominated by infor- mality through planned interventions, it often does so in the form of master plans and "mega-projects" that exclude the poor. In rapidly urbanizing coun- tries, there is a legitimate role for the state in performing some urban plan- ning functions. Yet, given past failures and ongoing ineffectiveness, simply adding more resources for urban planning is unlikely to improve outcomes.

Instead, planning theory and practice must adapt to the context of rapid informal urbanization in the twenty-first century. Part of this adaptation in- volves developing a much more sophisticated understanding of the politics of informality and the ways in which it shapes cities in general and informal urban growth in particular. Although urban informality may appear un- planned, haphazard, and chaotic, an underlying order does exist, governed by complex but well-established social and political relationships. Informal- ity has emerged for many reasons: urban populations are growing rapidly, the formal sector lacks jobs, housing markets are exclusionary, and states lack capacity. However, in developing democracies around the world, informal- ity persists because powerful actors—politicians, government officials, busi- ness leaders, and others—have learned to benefit financially and politically from it. This gives them disincentives to effect change. These disincentives, which include corruption and clientelism, undermine formal planning ef- forts. They are arguably more responsible for the limited impact of planning than the lack of technical training, funding, technology, public participation, or "political will."

In this book, I focus on *clientelism*, the provision of benefits to the poor in contingent exchange for political support. For example, when a politician distributes cash to the residents of a poor informal settlement, paves the set- tlement's streets, or protects it from being demolished, but only on the con- dition that the residents vote for him or her, such an exchange is an instance of clientelism. Influencing voters in this manner is typically illegal but remains widespread throughout the world, and so it can be considered a form of "informal" politics. Clientelism among the urban poor is "broadly accepted to be ubiquitous in the Global South."[6] In Africa, Asia, and Latin America, clientelism is so widespread that it may be considered the "normal" form of democracy around the world today.[7]

What does clientelism have to do with urban planning? Clientelism undermines formal urban planning in various ways. It can encourage informal urban growth, as politicians supply land and services for informal settlements or protect informal settlements from removal after they have formed, in exchange for political support from the residents of these settlements. This creates an alternate, informal channel by which political leaders supply the poor with urban land and services. The need to maintain this alternate channel disincentivizes both political leaders and the urban poor from supporting broad-based, formal planning efforts. Planning agencies, therefore, lack the political support needed to implement plans, build financial and technical capacity, and involve the public in planning. Politicians manipulate planning decisions, allocating urban resources in accordance with their electoral calculations rather than broader, long-term public need.

The example of Old Fadama in Accra illustrates these dynamics. Its residents are politically important enough to escape permanent removal and receive some services through clientelism. Arguably, the political importance of Old Fadama is not in spite of but *because* of its informal status. The vulnerability of the residents' situation makes them rely on reprieves and handouts, which political leaders can use to manipulate their loyalties. While politicians may have an incentive to help the residents occasionally, they also have no incentive to help the residents enough for them to no longer need help. Meanwhile, formal plans, no matter how potentially beneficial to the city they may be, remain unimplemented. Politicians have no interest in empowering a planning department that could potentially undermine their ability to benefit politically. Old Fadama's residents alone cannot be blamed for the tragic consequences of the flood and fire in Accra in 2015. What can be blamed is an environment in which political leaders have no incentive to support the kind of urban planning that might allow a city to grow in a way that is, among other things, resilient to such disasters. Versions of these dynamics are playing out across the cities of the Global South.

A danger in focusing on the ways in which clientelism allows some informal settlements to survive and grow is that it may reinforce the narrative, often popular among middle-class and wealthy residents of cities of the Global

South, that informal settlers are somehow "gaming the system," exploiting democracy in order to flout the law. The urban poor are far more vulnerable than that. Not all informal settlements have the political importance that Old Fadama does, and many do not survive. Even in Old Fadama, thirty thousand people were rendered homeless during the demolitions of 2015. Brutal evictions and demolitions in informal settlements are frequent around the world, and they are rightly decried as human rights violations. However, to understand them properly, we must acknowledge that they are neither uniform nor arbitrary. The difference between settlements that are demolished and those that are not is usually informal politics. In addition, the high visibility of confrontations between the powerful and the poor—evictions, demolitions, and the accompanying protests and riots—should not obscure the fact that unequal but stable power relations are more common than confrontations.[8] While this book mentions several such dramatic incidents, its focus is on the unequal stability that clientelism brings, which forms the daily reality of most informal settlements.

Scholars have documented clientelism and related forms of informal politics in cities around the world. However, the impact that these political dynamics have on urban growth, and what planners can do to be more effective in such political environments, has not received as much attention. In this book, I try to fill this gap by exploring the relationships between clientelism, informal urban growth, and urban planning. My aim is to offer insights that might help urban planners and policymakers bring about more inclusive and sustainable outcomes in environments dominated by informal politics.

Of course, generations of urban theorists and planning theorists have examined the interactions between politics and planning in a variety of contexts.[9] Chapter 1 of the American Planning Association's theory textbook is titled "Planning Practice and Political Power," suggesting that the importance of politics to planning has been absorbed into the mainstream, at least in parts of the Global North.[10] Yet, planning theory has offered little practical guidance to planners working within the complex informal politics of the Global South.[11] Planners and policymakers working in the Global South are well aware of informal politics in their own cities and how it interferes with their work, but have not systematically adapted their approach accordingly. The idea that informal politics is a structural problem facing planners in most of the urbanizing world is not yet central to planning practice or planning education in the Global South. This book tries to move beyond simply theorizing planning failure or lamenting the lack of "political will" in the Global South, and instead suggests practical approaches that might allow planners to develop ways to contend with political interference more effectively. While I include plenty of theory, description, and analysis, I do so with the goal of helping to develop a more "politically adaptive" planning approach in the Global South.

I write this book as an urban planner, mostly for other urban planners and policymakers, though I draw on relevant insights from the literatures of other disciplines—political science, anthropology, sociology, and others—as well as from statistical analysis of new global quantitative data. Despite my focus on planning, this book might also contribute to how social scientists in these other disciplines understand the impacts of clientelism. The literature on clientelism in these disciplines is extensive, but this book pays more sustained attention than writings in other disciplines to the impact of clientelism on urban planning, which is a distinct institution within the state apparatus and a specific mode of state-society relations. This book also explores the spatial impacts of clientelism on cities—for example, the ways in which clientelism is correlated with specific forms of urban expansion—in more detail than works in other disciplines tend to do.

Why Bother Planning?

Why bother trying to make planning work better? In much of the Global South, urban planning is a legacy of colonial regimes, and over the last century it has been ineffective at best and destructive at worst. Why not, then, just write off planning as a failed colonial-era experiment and stop interfering in the lives of the urban poor, who have learned to fend for themselves through informal means?

Public-sector urban planning needs to exist for some of the same reasons that government needs to exist: it is required to regulate externalities (the impact of one person's activities on others) and provide public goods (amenities that benefit everyone and from which no one can be excluded, like clean air). Neither the formal private sector nor the informal sector can play these roles. State-led urban planning is the subset of government regulation and public-goods provision that is concerned with the growth and functioning of cities. Urban planning is necessary to make public land available for open space, streets, public transportation, and other amenities. Planning can help protect ecologically sensitive land via environmental regulations. It is needed to support the supply of safe and affordable housing and the construction of large-scale infrastructure to allow the urban economy to function. Crucially, low-carbon and climate risk-sensitive urbanization is impossible without some form of coordination at scales of geography and time beyond those considered by individual households and businesses.

For these reasons, urban planning is necessary. Planning and informality conflict because plans involve regulations and informality is the widespread violation of regulations. However, instead of simply trying to get rid of the most visible manifestations of informality, planners need to rethink how they understand and engage with informality. This involves recognizing the many dimensions of urban informality that may not be as easy to identify and target as "slums," informal street vendors, or unlicensed taxis. These other dimensions include informal dealings of property developers who cater to the middle class and wealthy, informal practices of government officials, and informal patron-client relationships between politicians and the urban poor.

Rethinking how planning engages with informality also involves not just rooting out informality but also identifying which informal practices employed by the poor, politicians, or planners might serve a necessary function, and finding ways to make these practices more inclusive and sustainable, even if doing so means formalizing them to some degree. For example, the quantitative analysis I discuss in Chapter 2 suggests that clientelism creates room for residents of informal settlements, or those who provide them with land, to spatially lay out informal settlements in advance of occupation. This is reinforced in the case study in Ghana, which shows that traditional authorities (chiefs) hire informal, unlicensed surveyors to subdivide their customary landholdings into plots for sale. This suggests that in the absence of state-led planning, alternate, bottom-up forms of spatial planning emerge. Planners in local governments may be able to work with these forms of spatial planning that are more rooted in existing practices and aligned with prevailing politics. Similarly, while clientelism can be unreliable, inequitable, and exploitative, it does also provide the poor with some urban land and services that they would not otherwise have. Urban planners have little power to eradicate this system, at least in the short term, but they can potentially try to work with this system to produce better outcomes. For example, they can help identify and coordinate the benefits that communities receive through clientelism, to make the provision of these benefits more transparent, equitable, and beneficial to the city as a whole.

Grounding Planning Research in the Local and the Present

This book draws on literature from across the Global South and uses global data in its exploration of clientelism and planning. However, it also devotes several chapters to an in-depth case study of Ghana. Ghana is a stable, peaceful democracy with strong economic growth. It is considered one of the best-governed countries in Africa[12] and has institutions and regulations that aim to support urban planning. Yet urban planning has largely failed to influence the growth of its cities. Most urban growth in Ghana ignores urban plans and regulations with impunity, and nearly all recent urban expansion is informal in its disregard for planning permissions and procedures. This includes not just the growth of low-income settlements like Old Fadama, but also middle-class neighborhoods on the urban periphery. The case study examines several possible causes for this failure of planning but demonstrates that the root cause is informal politics. While it is true that planning in Ghana suffers from a lack of financial and human resources and that the mode of planning practiced is often ill-suited to the country's needs, the most binding constraints to effective planning in Ghana are political in nature.

This case study, and the book as a whole, is concerned primarily with local political dynamics, as opposed to the impact of transnational forces such as globalization or neoliberalism. This is not because I believe these forces to be irrelevant. International investment, from an increasing number of countries with a range of ideologies, distorts urban land and property markets around the world.[13] Large cities strive to create a "world-class" image to attract such investment, often at the expense of their poor.[14] Important work from influential scholars has theorized these transnational forces. However, in its focus on the role of transnational forces, the study of urbanization in the Global South has often neglected local forces that are at least as important, even if they fit less neatly into global narratives. A parallel trend, led by scholars with perspectives based in the Global South, has been trying to reassert the importance of the local. These scholars argue that framing urbanization anywhere in the world only in terms of the impact of transnational forces paints an incomplete picture.[15] This book is part of that trend, which one might call the "relocalization" of research on global cities.

This local perspective also involves acknowledging the specificities of present-day institutions and practices, and the agency of present-day local actors, rather than ascribing everything in the cities of the Global South to an undifferentiated legacy of colonialism. It is true that colonialism casts a long shadow over many cities in the Global South. Urban planning was introduced to many countries by colonial governments as a tool for controlling and segregating populations. Many large cities around the world were built as colonial capitals and were designed from the beginning to serve only a small section of the population.[16] Planning regulations in many postcolonial countries have remained unchanged since the colonial era.[17] However, although it is undeniable that postcolonial planning is shaped by its colonial origins, it is also a mistake to assume that planning today operates exactly as it did under colonialism.

For one, assuming that planning in developing democracies is simply an instrument of a state fixated on control, order, and surveillance, like its colonial predecessors, underestimates the extent to which its political context has changed in many places, especially in recent decades. In several postcolonial democracies (e.g., Ghana, India, Indonesia, Kenya, Mexico, South Africa), political competition between multiple political parties has emerged or accelerated since the late twentieth century. In the competitive political environment that prevails in such countries today, the primary concern of political leaders is not imposing order but winning elections by obtaining political support from the public by any means necessary. This sometimes includes suppressing the enforcement of urban plans to selectively benefit potential voters, even if it results in apparent disorder.

The postcolonial democratic state is also not as much of a monolith as the colonial state might have been. Literature on cities of the Global South often perceives "the state" as being unified in its intentions and character, and treats planning as simply an arm of the state apparatus.[18] Studies like this one demonstrate that this is not the case. The incentives of agencies and individuals even within the same local government are not always aligned and may pull the state in different directions simultaneously. The internal relationships among state actors—for example, between planners and local politicians, local and national politicians, or planners and other local bureaucrats—are full of conflicting objectives, power imbalances, and even unexpected alliances. For example, in Ghana, national political leaders might put pressure on a mayor to approve a certain development. Local government planners might oppose the development but fear retaliation from the mayor if they push back openly. Behind the scenes, the planners may enlist the support of their friends in other, more politically insulated local government departments to raise objections in planning meetings on their behalf. All the players in this instance—national leaders, the mayor, local planners, and other local officials—are part of the machinery of the state, but they clearly represent distinct moving parts, with different aims and complex relationships to one another.

The state is also more discontinuous over time than colonial governments, especially in countries where there is high turnover in personnel at all levels after elections. Moreover, in many countries, particularly African countries, traditional nonstate power structures are very influential, which further diminishes the control exercised by the state over the public. All of this means that postcolonial planning cannot operate as colonial planning did, whether it wants to or not.

In taking a more locally focused approach, I also largely ignore the examples of cities such as Singapore, Shanghai, Dubai, and others. Governments in the Global South frequently aspire to emulate these cities, despite the fact that (or perhaps because) these cities have limited or no democratic contestation.[19] I also avoid the global "best practices" in planning that international organizations often promote, which largely ignore political context.[20] As Vanessa Watson argues, every approach to planning is a function of its political and cultural origins, even those that are promoted as being universally applicable. Inappropriately borrowed ideas in planning have "impoverished and limited planning thinking and practice, and have left it open to accusations of irrelevance and of directly worsening urban poverty."[21]

Instead, I aim to develop recommendations by first observing the strategies adopted by players in the context in question, even if the context appears to be one of planning failure, and then proposing practical ways to enhance these strategies that might yield better outcomes. This approach draws inspiration from Bish Sanyal's collection of "hidden successes" in urban management in India[22] and is also similar to John Forester's search for urban planning "practice stories."[23] For example, as previously discussed, planners can build on the informal subdivision of land and the clientelistic provision of benefits to the poor. Strategies that planners themselves use to push back on political interference are also instructive. The practice mentioned earlier, in which planners in Ghana enlist support from more politically insulated colleagues in opposing a mayor, is one such strategy. Planners in Ghana also sometimes appeal to a professional organization, the national planning agency, or the media to help resist political interference. They may also avoid open opposition to political leaders by strategically employing public consultation as a means of discouraging leaders from pursuing actions that they know will be unpopular with the voting public. These strategies are all employed in an ad hoc manner at present, and they are not always successful. However, by demonstrating that they can sometimes be successful in the prevailing political environment, they may contain the seeds of an approach that can be institutionalized. For example, in Ghana, a planning "watchdog" organization might be able to play a more consistent version of the role that professional organizations, the media, and the public already play occasionally.

When it comes to urban planning in a world of informal politics, the picture appears grim. Nothing seems to be working. However, if we look more closely, it turns out that some things *are* working, even if only partially, occasionally, or temporarily. Among the contributions of this book is that it draws attention to how planners are already trying to contend with informal politics, sometimes successfully, and considers how they can build on some of these strategies.

Plan of the Book

The book proceeds as follows. Chapter 1 describes urban clientelism and establishes the conceptual tension between clientelism and urban planning. Chapter 2 presents new insights about the global relationships between clientelism and patterns of urban growth, based on statistical analysis of new global statistical data. The results of this analysis show that clientelism is relevant to issues that are at the core of planning, namely the pace and form of urban growth. Chapter 3 considers whether clientelism will disappear on its own over time as a result of economic growth (and finds that it probably will not). It goes on to explore international examples of instances in which clientelism in low-income urban settlements has declined and discusses whether planners have any role to play in transitions away from clientelism.

The next several chapters explore the case study of Ghana in detail, grounding these theoretical concepts and global trends in the specific, complex context of a lower-middle-income democracy. The case study refines and complicates the understanding of the relationship between clientelism and informality developed in the earlier chapters. Chapter 4 presents the context, with a focus on urban planning and informality in Ghana. Chapter 5 explores the constraints to planning in the country, particularly the impact of clientelism. Chapter 6 discusses other political constraints to planning, including the power of traditional authorities, corruption, and organized violence around the control of peri-urban land, and argues that each of these is related to politics in some way. Chapter 7 expands on the story of Old Fadama, the subject of the opening paragraphs of this introduction, detailing its origins and growth as well as government attempts to demolish it over the years. Chapter 8 examines how past recommendations for planning in Ghana—in government policies, reports from international organizations, and academic studies—respond to the failures of planning in Ghana. It also explores what the future of urban planning in Ghana might be. Chapter 9 concludes the case study by exploring what a "politically adaptive" approach to planning in the context of informal politics might look like. It bases this approach on the strategies that planners in Ghana already use to contend with the political pressures that they face every day. It then proposes a general framework for politically adaptive planning that may be used beyond Ghana. The concluding chapter reflects on the lessons of this study for planning practice and research, and on how future research can proceed from here.

PART I

Global Patterns

CHAPTER 1

The Conflict Between Informal Politics and Urban Planning Around the World

A s elections approached, the neighborhood association president in the informal settlement was busy negotiating with politicians. Two candidates running for positions in the state government made competing offers in exchange for the votes of the residents of the settlement. One offered sets of soccer shirts; the other promised the construction of toilets. The latter was clearly the better offer, but the association president, despite being functionally illiterate, was a skilled negotiator. Now in his sixties, he had arrived in the city as a nine-year-old, when his first job had been selling combs and pens from a stall in a public square. As the neighborhood association president, he had already convinced politicians to pave streets and provide streetlights in his settlement. Now, he bargained with his preferred candidate for six weeks, reminding him that his neighbors were pressing him for directions on whom to vote for. Finally, just ten days before the election, the candidate and the association president agreed on a budget for the construction of toilets. As soon as the candidate handed over a check, the association president publicly endorsed him and accompanied him on door-to-door visits around the neighborhood. The residents of the settlement did not need to know the politician's policies or his party's platform; the candidate's gift and the neighborhood association president's endorsement were enough.

Informal Politics as Normal Politics in the Global South

The sequence of events just recounted occurred in Vila Brasil, a favela in Rio de Janeiro, Brazil, in the 1980s.[1] Residents of informal settlements around the world, from Indonesia to Nigeria to Mexico, could tell countless similar stories of how they access urban services even today. Not every informal settlement has politicians competing to court its residents' votes as enthusiastically as Vila Brasil did, or a political broker as adept at negotiating for benefits as this particular neighborhood association president, but the exchange of benefits for votes is a common phenomenon. It is so common, in fact, that some see this form of informal democratic politics, which political scientists refer to as clientelism, as the "normal" form of democracy today.[2] That residents of informal settlements in democratic countries in the Global South exchange their votes for benefits from politicians is common knowledge among social scientists, as well as among most residents of large cities in these countries, including urban planners. Yet urban planning practice and theory have failed to fully appreciate the ways in which these informal political dynamics affect urban growth and the implementation of plans. As a result, planning remains thwarted by them.

Consider the incentives of the winning politician in the Vila Brasil anecdote. Having come to power through the informal provision of benefits in exchange for votes, he and his affiliates have an incentive to continue to keep the residents of such settlements dependent on their patronage. Continuing to provide small-scale, ad hoc benefits such as a block of toilets is easier than implementing more complex, citywide plans and welfare programs. Besides, why put effort into such plans and programs if they will ultimately make the residents of these settlements so much better off that they stop needing handouts from politicians at all? Better to keep them vulnerable and dependent so that their support remains easy to buy. Of all the things to spend time, money, and political capital on, planning is a low priority.

What this should make clear is that the formation and persistence of informal settlements is not simply about a lack of state capacity to enforce land regulations or to produce and implement urban plans; it is also about political incentives. For planning to have a more positive impact on the urban poor in developing democracies, planners and policymakers must recognize and adapt to the sociopolitical order underlying urban informality, rather than treating informality simply as the outcome of a lack of planning. Clientelism— that is, the provision of benefits to the poor in exchange for political support— is a particularly important aspect of the politics of urban informality across the Global South.[3] Clientelism may benefit the urban poor in some ways, but it interferes with the implementation of formal plans and the reliable and equitable delivery of basic services.

This chapter uses examples from across the Global South to illustrate the conflict between the principles of planning and the realities of clientelism. Because I aim this chapter at readers with prior knowledge of urban planning who may not be as familiar with clientelism, I focus much more on explaining how clientelism works and how it affects planning than explaining how planning itself works. For this reason, I draw more heavily from the literature on political science, sociology, anthropology, and other disciplines than from urban planning literature.

Although informal politics provides powerful political leaders with disincentives against supporting formal planning efforts, the Vila Brasil story and others like it are also cause for hope. They upend assumptions about the state's undifferentiated neglect and hostility toward the urban poor in the Global South, as well as the helpless victimhood of the poor. Clientelism is ultimately a bad deal for the poor, but acknowledging its importance forces planners and policymakers to reckon with the agency that the poor do have, and to craft solutions that work with this agency.

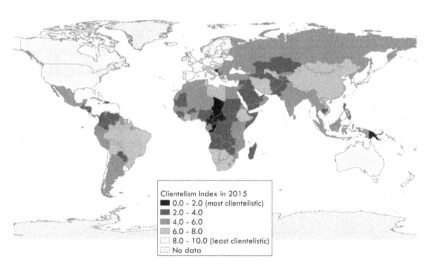

Figure 2. Clientelism by country, 2015. Sources: Author, using data from V-Dem (Coppedge et al., "V-Dem Country-Year Dataset 2018") and country boundaries from UIA World Countries Boundaries (ArcGIS Hub, https://hub.arcgis.com /datasets/UIA::uia-world-countries-boundaries, accessed November 13, 2018).

The map in Figure 2 indicates how widespread clientelism is in the world today. Countries in the map are shaded according to a clientelism index,[4] produced with information provided by country experts around the world. (The Appendix provides more details about how the index is constructed.) Darker shades denote higher levels of clientelism. For reference, at the time of the anecdote related at the beginning of the chapter, Brazil had a clientelism index value of between 4 and 5, putting it in the middle category. As the map suggests, clientelism is a feature of politics in some of the most populous and rapidly urbanizing countries in the world. These include Bangladesh, India, Indonesia, Mexico, Nigeria, Pakistan (which are all among the ten most populated countries in the world), and many others.

At first glance, the exchange of benefits for votes may simply seem like corruption. However, the concept of corruption, defined as the abuse of public office for private gain,[5] is distinct from clientelism. Corruption is the use of public office to gain wealth, whereas clientelism is the use of wealth to gain or retain public office. Wealth from corruption accumulates to the powerful, but in the case of clientelism, wealth is distributed to the less powerful. Corruption around urban land, service delivery, and urban infrastructure projects is an important topic that requires more analysis, especially as countries with high corruption risk urbanize,[6] but it is mostly beyond the scope of this study, which focuses specifically on clientelism.

Although corruption and clientelism may be conceptually distinct, they are not mutually exclusive, and, in fact, are often mutually reinforcing. Politicians may use private wealth to buy their way into public office through clientelism, which office they then abuse through corruption to gain more wealth, some of which they use to retain public office through clientelism, and so on. Studies in developing democracies such as Ghana and Indonesia find that politicians believe that if they do not engage in corruption to gain wealth while in office, they will not be able to keep up with the costs of the clientelism required to compete in future elections.[7]

How Clientelism Operates in Informal Settlements

Clientelism is practically ubiquitous in poor urban settlements across the Global South. Political scientists, anthropologists, sociologists, and others have documented clientelism in poor urban settlements in Asia, Africa, Latin America, the Middle East, and elsewhere.[8] Clientelism involves the provision of *private (or "club") goods to the poor* in *contingent exchange* for *political support*, often mediated *through brokers*. Next, I examine each of these elements of clientelism in the context of low-income urban settlements.

"Private (or 'Club') Goods"

The goods that patrons distribute may be "private goods," such as cash, clothes, or food. However, in dense urban settlements, patrons often distribute "club goods," which benefit several households or an entire neighborhood at once. These may be water pipes, electricity poles, sewerage, or paved roads. Patron-client relationships also provide land to the urban poor, through direct and indirect processes described later in this chapter. The fact that urban clientelism involves the provision of urban land and services makes it a competitor of formal municipal systems of urban land-use planning and service delivery.

In terms of their origin, clientelistic benefits may be private or public. A candidate may use personal funds to pay for patronage or, particularly if already incumbent or supported by an incumbent party, may direct public resources toward clients.

"To the Poor"

Clientelism involves asymmetrical power relationships; those distributing the goods are in positions of greater power or authority than those receiving them. Patrons mostly target the relatively poor, whose needs can be met more affordably at a scale large enough to matter electorally.

"Contingent Exchange"

To be considered clientelism, an exchange must involve mutually contingent reciprocity. In other words, clients provide political support only if the patron has already provided benefits or can credibly commit to providing future benefits, and vice versa: the patron provides benefits only if clients have demonstrated or credibly promised political support. The provision of the same benefits to a poor community that is not directly contingent on political support would be an instance of welfare, "constituency service,"[9] or "pork-barrel politics," rather than clientelism. Nonetheless, despite the contingent nature of clientelism, it typically does not involve a one-off, quid pro quo exchange. Instead, patrons and clients tend to cultivate long-term relationships, gradually building trust through iterative acts of support.

Patrons often monitor voting in poor urban settlements not at the individual level but at the level of the neighborhood or voting booth. Some scholars categorize this kind of exchange as more in the realm of pork-barrel politics than traditional clientelism.[10] However, in their study of clientelism in Indonesia, Edward Aspinall and Ward Berenschot argue that regardless of the scale of the exchange or the difficulty of monitoring reciprocity, as long as an exchange is *intended* to be contingent on reciprocity, it still constitutes clientelism.[11] They note instances in which a candidate will take back a benefit provided to a neighborhood if he or she believes that the community that received the benefit has not fulfilled its end of the bargain at the voting booth. The candidate may go so far as to have new water pipes pulled out, streetlights taken down, and tiles ripped out from mosques after a poor electoral result, suggesting that the exchange was very much a contingent one.[12] Similarly, Shafali Sharma and colleagues describe how a politician in Bengaluru (Bangalore), India, did not fulfill a promise to resettle residents of an informal settlement whose houses had been demolished, because he had been told that some residents of the settlement had not voted for him.[13] In this case, benefits to some members of the community were contingent on political support from the entire community.

Throughout this book, I use the term *clientelism* broadly, to include the provision of club goods and the monitoring of votes at the neighborhood scale. This is in the spirit of Allen Hicken and Noah Nathan's argument that a dogmatic focus on monitoring individual voters as a defining criterion of clientelism misses broad commonalities between similar types of exchange. They argue that distinctions between "real" and "not-quite" clientelism are arbitrary, and that politicians may have reasons to practice clientelism even if they cannot easily monitor votes.[14]

"Political Support"

Clientelism is sometimes described as election-time "vote buying," a reference to a candidate's providing material inducements to voters to switch their vote choice in his or her favor. However, it may also involve "turnout buy-ing," which is inducing voters assumed to already support the candidate to show up to vote, or "abstention buying," which is the opposite of turnout buy-ing.[15] While voting is central to clientelistic exchange, communities may also demonstrate their support in other ways, such as attendance at political rallies in large numbers.

"Through Brokers"

Accounts of clientelism in informal settlements often highlight the role of "brokers" who act as intermediaries between communities and officials. These brokers may be agents of parties or politicians entering informal settlements from the outside. However, they are often the opposite: leaders of poor com-munities selected and promoted from within to forge political connections and channel benefits to the informal settlement. For example, in her study of squatting in Montevideo, Uruguay, sociologist María José Álvarez-Rivadulla describes a community leader of an informal settlement who approached a political contact of hers in the municipality and (as she later recalled) stated bluntly: "The campaign is coming and if you want votes, come down to earth: I need water for my people."[16] When Adam Auerbach and Tariq Thachil surveyed residents in 110 informal settlements in two Indian cities, they concluded that the "bottom-up construction of informal slum leadership demands that we take the agency of residents seriously in explaining the rise and mechanics of patron-client networks."[17]

Depending on how competitive the political landscape is, political can-didates may compete to win the favor of such brokers before elections, as in the Vila Brasil case presented in the opening anecdote of this chapter. Aspi-nall and Berenschot provide the example of another such community leader in Jakarta, Indonesia. They describe how he proactively contacted candidates in a 2014 election so that the residents of his neighborhood could "leverage their voting power to gain benefits for their community."[18] Similarly, Álvarez-Rivadulla describes a broker who, in his own words, "flirted" with many politicians before establishing a relationship with one on behalf of his com-munity.[19] Álvarez-Rivadulla and others describe this as "market clientelism."

Politicians may reward neighborhood leaders working as brokers with personal benefits in various forms, including cash, construction materials, or jobs for themselves or their family members. However, these relationships are not purely transactional either and often persist beyond political campaigns. In their study of clientelism in a low-income settlement in Recife, Brazil, Martijn Koster and Flávio Eiró describe how broker-patron relationships may instead "center upon friendship, care, respect and exchanges of favors," and take on a political dimension only during election times.[20]

Clientelism as the "Poor Country's Welfare State"

For the poor, patron-client relationships are often the only means of accessing the power of an otherwise unresponsive state. Patrons and brokers can be highly receptive to the needs of client communities. They build trust over time by developing personal relationships with households. Describing clientelism in an informal settlement in Buenos Aires, sociologist Javier Auyero relates examples of brokers who distribute food and medicine to residents, hold "office hours" to listen to residents' complaints and requests, and even arrange to take schoolchildren to the beach.[21] In her 1976 study of favelas in Rio de Janeiro, Janice Perlman mentions political brokers who negotiate such collective benefits as sewerage and cement steps.[22] Gerrit Burgwal describes how clientelism gave a settlement in Quito, Ecuador, access to electricity, a paved road, a market, bus service, and sewerage.[23] Sociologist Lisa Björkman, in describing an informal settlement in Mumbai, India, notes how residents rely on assistance or information from leaders to accomplish a range of everyday activities, including accessing municipal water, disposing of garbage, and unblocking drains.[24]

Residents of informal settlements often see political patrons and brokers in positive terms. For example, according to Auyero's study of urban clientelism in Argentina in the 1990s, the urban poor viewed political party–affiliated brokers as "'helpful' and 'sacrificing' and 'good people' with whom problem holders have a personal relationship sometimes described as 'friendship' but always as worth keeping."[25] The personal nature of these relationships is critical. Álvarez-Rivadulla recalls being surprised early in her research to find that the urban poor in Montevideo referred to high-ranking state officials by their first names and had their phone numbers in their home directories.[26] In a study of urban Ghana, the political scientists Mohammed Awal and Jeffrey Paller argue that "everyday interaction is a crucial—but poorly understood—component of how accountability is generated between leaders and citizens in the absence of formal mechanisms."[27] This personal relationship means that a sense of obligation, gratitude, or trust rather than a strictly transactional exchange of votes for services often motivates the support that the poor provide to these political figures.

For these reasons, some scholars dispute critiques of clientelism that dismiss it without regard for its benefits and without adequate consideration as to what could replace it.[28] They defend clientelism as the "poor country's welfare state," the removal of which would deprive the poor of their only networks of support and lead not to programmatic democracy but instead to mass neglect.[29] Clientelism, they argue, can act as a counterweight to elite influence and unrealistic technocratic standards in development,[30] and under certain circumstances can help consolidate democracy.[31] Vanessa Watson describes how poor communities use clientelism opportunistically as one of many "strategies of survival, creating conditions of access to vital resources," which means that they cannot be "wished away."[32]

Clientelism as the "Politics of Vulnerabilization"

Noting the benefits of clientelism just described helps understand why residents of informal settlements may be reluctant to abandon their trust relationships with patrons. The urban poor have seen these relationships work, however imperfectly. This cannot always be said of untested formal systems of service provision, no matter how inclusive or participatory their intent.

However, clientelism clearly does not represent an ideal system for the poor either, for several reasons. Clientelism locks residents of informal settlements into dependency, as political patrons have little incentive to allow the poor to access land and services independently and reliably through formal channels.[33] As a result, state effectiveness and institutional development are undermined when clientelism is the source of legitimacy of political leaders.[34] Clientelism disincentivizes politicians from providing secure property rights in order to maintain this dependency.[35] For example, Ananya Roy describes how politicians in Kolkata (Calcutta), India, promise land to squatters but never deliver secure tenure to them, as a means of keeping them "continuously mobilized" as an electorate.[36] Robert Coates and Anja Nygren refer to this as the "politics of vulnerabilization."[37]

Coercion and violence may mark clientelistic relationships, especially if organized crime is active in the settlement, as studies observe in the case of Latin America,[38] India,[39] Jamaica, South Africa, and Bangladesh.[40] When

clientelism involves protection of residents from land or building regulations, it effectively functions as a type of "protection racket." The promise of
protection for a price comes with an implicit threat of punishment if the
price is not paid. In the case of clientelism, the price is political support, and
the punishment is the strict implementation of regulations. For example, in
parts of Beirut, Lebanon, the militant organization and political party
Hezbollah grants exceptions to planning regulations to its base, allowing the
party's supporters to retain their "illegal" structures as a "favor" pegged to
allegiance to the party.[41]

Clientelism can also be exploitative, helping the powerful achieve their
own ends. Evidence from Mumbai and from Nairobi, Kenya, sheds light on
a specific ploy through which some powerful interests exploit informal settlers to access land. They first encourage the poor to occupy land that formal
plans have deemed unsafe or ecologically sensitive. Once the government has
accepted it as residential land, these interests then force out or price out the
settlers and sell the land to wealthier residents or real estate developers.[42] Roy
quotes an elderly resident of a peri-urban settlement in Kolkata: "You see,
there is an unwritten law here—that the poor like us develop areas, fill in
marshes, build homes, struggle to get infrastructure, and are then evicted to
make way for the rich who move into a now desirable area."[43]

Patrons may distribute clientelistic benefits unequally, with the most dis-
advantaged groups often being the ones least likely to benefit.[44] Clientelism
produces worse outcomes for the poor than formal municipal systems of service delivery, in various ways. Studies of service provision in informal settlements in India[45] and Pakistan[46] find that settlements or households that
are likelier to engage in clientelism are less likely to receive access to public
goods (as opposed to private or club goods). Clientelism can also be associated with lack of completion of infrastructure projects.[47]

Clientelistic benefits are often supply-driven and targeted inefficiently. For
example, a study of urban clientelism in Turkey describes the ruling party's
providing poor households with coal for heating at the peak of summer during an election campaign but not in winter, and distributing washing machines to households that had no running water.[48] In Ghana, politicians paid
for the construction of a large block of public toilets without providing water
for them to function.[49]

Lastly, clientelism stifles political mobilization and activism among the
urban poor. In the absence of state provision of infrastructure and services at
scale, clientelism simply "buys off, co-opts and absorbs pressure and protest

from the urban poor," according to David Satterthwaite and Diana Mitlin.[50] Research on South Africa in particular provides multiple examples of the role of clientelism in undermining political mobilization in this manner. When authorities threatened the eviction of a Johannesburg settlement in 2010, the residents initially sought help from a rights-based nongovernmental organization (NGO). The NGO began to work with them on resisting the eviction. However, when the ruling party stepped in and promised to preserve and refurbish their homes, the residents distanced themselves from the NGO and even denounced it as undermining the nation.[51] Steven Robins explains how local leaders embedded in clientelistic politics and open to patronage thwarted the efforts of Shack/Slum Dwellers International (SDI) to produce horizontal networks of the urban poor in Cape Town.[52] Also in Cape Town, the emergence of competing factions among potential beneficiaries of a resettlement program acted as a boon to authorities who had promised housing to former squatters, as they were able to provide housing only to the best-organized faction and leave the others on a decades-long waiting list.[53]

These observations also echo descriptions of "bossism," the form that clientelism took in the United States in an earlier era. For example, in his account of the Republican political machine or "Organization" in Philadelphia between the 1860s and 1930s, Peter McCaffery observes: "Even though the Organization managed to secure the support of the overwhelming majority of Philadelphia's new immigrant, poor, and black population in return for the 'personal service' it rendered, it exploited those social groups as much as it helped them. . . . [I]t effectively prevented political parties and government from responding to the real needs of the city's poor inhabitants, and also thwarted the emergence of alternative structures grounded in the effective mobilization of mass political power at the grassroots level."[54]

Neighborhood organizations can help strengthen the bargaining power of the poor and make it easier for patrons to engage with communities.[55] However, such mobilization among the urban poor in a clientelistic environment tends to remain highly local, with communities competing with each other to attract patronage.[56] Burgwal acknowledges that, while the community in Quito that he studied was able to use its collective power to successfully negotiate for a range of clientelistic goods, it probably did so at the expense of other neighborhoods.

Even when the poor are aware of the ways in which their political patrons prevent them from independently accessing the benefits of the state, they have little choice but to accept this system. Their situations are too precarious and their reliance on patrons is too great. According to Joop de Wit and Erhard Berner, for the poor, "relations of patronage and reciprocity that offer some security have to be maintained regardless of their long-term costs. To cut off links with exploitative patrons and intermediaries would imply foregoing all claims to emergency assistance."[57] To Geof Wood, remaining poor in exchange for staying secure is a "Faustian bargain": "To be poor means, inter alia, to be unable to control future events because others have more control over them. . . . Securing any kind of longer term future requires recruiting the support of these others, but this only comes at a price: of dependency and the foreclosure of autonomy. Becoming a client, in other words."[58]

Clientelism and Informal Urban Growth

Clientelism contributes to the growth and persistence of informal settlements. Political patrons may own or otherwise control land and distribute it as a private good to clients. For example, politicians and government officials own more than half the land in Kibera, the large informal settlement in Nairobi, and these figures or their brokers allocate plots of land to residents informally.[59] The late activist Perween Rehman explained that, in Karachi, Pakistan, "the government, the political parties, the police, the members of the national assembly, [and] the councilors" are all involved in "land grabbing" to set up organized squatting.[60] In the absence of adequate formal land supply, she argued, these informal land grabbers are really "land suppliers," who provide land, infrastructure, and services to the poor, which in her view makes the municipality and planners redundant.[61]

Politicians may instead simply protect informal settlements from demolition after they have formed, which acts as indirect provision of land. Patronage from powerful politicians and their associates is a large part of the explanation of why informal settlements manage to survive despite their precarious legal status and official antagonism from governments. Old Fadama, the large informal settlement in Accra, Ghana, discussed in the introductory chapter, has faced hostility from neighboring residents and multiple demolition attempts by the government over the years, and yet no political party dares to demolish it entirely because of its political importance. Informal settlers are well aware of these political dynamics, and sometimes plan their actions around them. For example, Burgwal describes how leaders from among the urban poor in Quito waited several months before initiating a planned "land invasion" on vacant private land, so that the invasion would coincide with an election campaign during which they knew they would receive political support.[62] Similarly, informal settlements in Karachi often grow in size and number just before elections.[63]

Clientelism may also result in the "informalization" of settlements, if political leaders are able to prevent them from receiving formal infrastructure and services. This can cause settlements to deteriorate and take on the qualities of an informal settlement, regardless of the circumstances of their origin or their legality. For example, Old Fadama originated partially as a temporary government-provided camp for people displaced by a violent ethnic conflict elsewhere in Ghana, but it is now considered an informal settlement. Similarly, the local government of Mumbai allocated land to households in an area called Shivajinagar-Bainganwadi in the 1970s, but antipathy on the part of subsequent political leaders toward its residents caused it to deteriorate into what is now widely considered an informal settlement.[64]

Clientelism may also lead to informal urban growth in other, less direct ways. Clientelism undermines state capacity in general and urban planning capacity in particular, as mentioned previously. This lack of capacity may restrict the ability of the state to supply or regulate the formal supply of land and services. This leaves poor urban residents, particularly migrants, to resort to informal alternatives. The broader lack of state capacity in a clientelistic country may also result in a weaker economy, leading to more poverty and, therefore, more informality.

Conversely, the prevalence of informal settlements could lead to an increase in clientelism. As discussed previously, some informal communities, particularly those that are internally cohesive and have proactive leadership, may seek out and cultivate patron-client relationships with politicians. Politicians would find clientelism to be a more attractive strategy when faced with densely populated, low-income settlements, which have needs that can be easily met through clientelism.

Chapter 2 returns to this discussion of causal linkages between clientelism and informal urban growth. Later chapters demonstrate that, in Ghana, several of these mechanisms are at work in parallel. There, clientelistic politicians protect informal settlements from demolition, and clientelism also undermines urban planning capacity, resulting in informal growth. Politicians also do not intervene when community leaders, usually traditional authorities (chiefs), informally subdivide and distribute land, possibly fearing that any intervention would result in a loss of political support.

Clientelism as a Barrier to Planning

The responsibilities, legal powers, and institutional location of the state's urban planning function vary from one country or city to another. As discussed earlier, by *planning* I mean the aspects of government regulation and public-goods provision that are concerned with the growth and functioning of cities. In rapidly urbanizing contexts, spatial planning (also referred to as land use planning or physical planning), which involves creating and enforcing land use and building regulations, is particularly important. Spatial planning determines how a city grows, which has a range of long-term environmental and economic implications. However, it is difficult to discuss spatial planning in isolation, as it is linked inextricably to a broader system of urban service delivery. This system usually extends beyond "planning" departments to utilities, transportation departments, and other agencies. Nonstate actors may also perform activities that involve spatial planning.

The approach that urban planners and urban policy experts in international development circles have taken to tackling challenges of informal settlements and housing has also evolved over the last half century. The full history of planning approaches to informal settlements in the Global South is beyond the scope of this discussion, but some key trends are worth recounting briefly. In the 1970s, planners and policymakers began to perceive state provision of public housing for the poor as inadequate, inefficient, and mistargeted. Public-housing provision was also often accompanied by the demolition of existing informal settlements. Influenced by the work of John Turner and others, policymakers came to see the self-construction of housing by the poor in a more positive light. Consequently, many governments, supported by loans and technical assistance from the World Bank and other international organizations, implemented "slum upgrading" projects focused on existing settlements, and "sites-and-services" projects, which provided plots of land connected to utilities which households could build on themselves in incremental fashion.[65] The World Bank moved away from the sites-and-services projects in the mid-1990s,[66] though slum upgrading projects continue. Since the 1980s, the focus has shifted toward creating an "enabling" policy environment for private housing markets and expanding access to housing finance. In the 1990s and 2000s, the argument promoted by econo-mist Hernando de Soto that well-defined property rights would unlock the economic potential of informal housing influenced governments and inter-national organizations to implement land titling programs.[67]

Despite all this, government officials, including urban planners, remain largely hostile toward informal settlements. Most residents of informal settlements live under a constant threat of demolitions and evictions. Even during the COVID-19 pandemic, local governments throughout the Global South carried on demolishing informal settlements, often rendering residents homeless during a public health and economic crisis (e.g., in Ghana,[68] India,[69] and Kenya[70]).

One constant feature of all the approaches to informal settlements by planners in governments and international development organizations is that they treat the issue as apolitical, to be solved through technical means (pro-viding sites and services, upgrading, titling, and financing). Plans and pol-icy documents do complain occasionally about "political interference" in implementation or the need for "political will." However, they do not treat the growth of informal settlements as an essentially political phenomenon.

All of the above is to acknowledge that planning can mean different things for informal settlements, depending on the time and place. However, despite these variations, one can still contrast clientelism with an abstract ideal of planning. Public-sector city planning entails the provision of public (i.e., non-excludable) goods. This, along with the regulation of spatial externalities, is its reason to exist, as it is a function that private individuals or businesses cannot perform. Planning also involves developing a long-term vision and should involve broad public participation in decision-making, which requires transparency. The logic of clientelism—which involves targeting benefits to specific individuals or groups in the short term and in the form of nontrans-parent dealmaking—is incompatible with all these ideals of planning (as summarized in Table 1.)

In more practical terms, clientelism often means that powerful politicians facilitate the occupation of land that planners have reserved for streets, public transportation, parks, or other infrastructure, or land that is too ecologically sensitive or hazard-prone to build on safely. This occupation may be in the form of informal settlements that provide the poor with land and housing they would not otherwise have. However, it may also take the form of busi-nesses or real estate developments that do not benefit the poorest. Similarly, a local government cannot implement medium-term plans for infrastructure

Table 1. Differences between the provision of urban land and services through urban planning and clientelism

Planning (ideal)	*Clientelism*
Provision of public goods (i.e., widely accessible benefits)	Provision of private or club goods, specifically targeting supporters
Long-term vision	Short-term benefits, in order to maintain dependency
Transparent, inclusive decision-making	Illicit dealmaking

if the incumbent mayor unexpectedly diverts municipal resources to neighborhoods with potential supporters in order to secure their votes for reelection. Political interference also prevents local governments from collecting property taxes, especially from politically important residents, which is partly why local governments struggle to generate revenue with which to implement plans.[71]

Once clientelistic land and service provision is established, those who benefit from it often oppose the entry of formal planning or of any program that provides universal access to basic services to formal and informal settlements alike. Diane Davis describes how, in Latin America, when planners turned their attention to informal settlements and tried to formalize them in the late twentieth century, "it was too little too late. . . . [U]rban planners' room for maneuver was highly circumscribed, owing to the prior informal relations of brokerage that had flowered during earlier periods of state neglect. Even when they sought to introduce new urban projects into informal areas, planners were sometimes kept at bay by the local power brokers whose authority rested in the maintenance of a clear distinction between the formal and informal city."[72]

This echoes Perlman's observations about community leaders in Rio de Janeiro's favelas who acted as brokers in the 1960s and 1970s: "If the squatter settlements were to achieve legal rights to their lands and full urban services and facilities, in many cases the usefulness, power, and importance of these leaders would be severely reduced. . . . In order to survive, they must persuade residents to be content with token change and slow progress, and to trust that local leadership is doing its best to deal with the difficult problems of infrastructure and tenure. This may sound Machiavellian, but it is generally true."[73]

Alisha Holland argues that once the post hoc regularization of squatting is established as an informal welfare policy, both the poor and the state are locked into a "forbearance trap."[74] The poor organize their demands around acceptance of informality rather than more involved forms of welfare (e.g., public-housing provision), and the state does not develop the capacity to provide these forms of welfare.

An Unresolved Conflict

There is a conflict between the provision of urban land and services through informal political channels and their provision through formal planning. Planners must develop an understanding of clientelism and its role in the provision of urban land and services. They must also understand why not only politically powerful patrons but also residents of informal settlements themselves may resist change to formal service delivery or land use planning.

Gaps remain in this picture of how planning and clientelism are related. First, how do planners operating in clientelistic environments respond to political interference in their work? Have some planning initiatives or approaches been effective in moving informal settlements away from clientelism toward a more formal, programmatic system of land and service provision? Later chapters in this study begin to address these questions through global examples, as well as through a case study of the relationships between planning, informality, and clientelism in urban Ghana.

Second, though the discussion so far has suggested that clientelistic politics and informal urban growth go hand in hand universally, most of our knowledge of clientelism comes from research in specific cities or settlements. These studies do not provide evidence to confirm the intuition that there is a generalizable relationship between clientelism and informal urban growth. Until recently, lack of data made it impossible to test the global relationships between these phenomena. However, new data now allow these relationships to be analyzed empirically at the global scale, and it is to the results of my analysis of such data that I turn next.

CHAPTER 2

The Global Relationship Between Clientelism and Urban Growth

Q ualitative evidence from around the world suggests that informal politics and urban growth are related. Political patrons provide land informally to the urban poor in exchange for their political support. Informal settlements whose residents are loyal to the incumbent political party seem to escape demolition. More broadly, informal politics might support or encourage informal economic activity, informal transportation services, informal utility connections, or other forms of informality in exchange for political support. In all these ways, clientelism can make urban life viable for residents who do not have the means to adhere to formal regulations but are favored by patrons.

In this chapter, I use statistical modeling to show that this leads to a global relationship between clientelism and urban growth, including informal growth. The fact that clientelism may affect things as fundamental to the core concerns of urban planning as the pace and density of a city's growth and the layout of its neighborhoods reinforces the argument that planners must take clientelism seriously. It emphasizes the notion that planners and policymakers must understand the informal political dynamics that tend to accompany urbanization and adapt their planning approach to account for them.

Scholars across disciplines have been studying the relationships between political dynamics and urban growth for a long time, through theoretical explorations, qualitative studies, and narrative accounts. In recent years, scholars have devoted extensive attention to the role that clientelism in particular plays in poor urban settlements in low- and middle-income countries. Some of these studies discuss the relationship between clientelism and the *growth* of informal settlements.[1] However, attempts to measure this relationship systematically have been rare and specific to one or a small number of countries at a time. Some studies model the growth of informal settlements through simulations, but most of these models do not incorporate the role of politics.[2] No study has yet attempted to identify a statistical correlation between clientelism and urban growth across large numbers of global cities.

This is partly because the kind of consistent data on either clientelism or patterns of urban growth that would be necessary to conduct this analysis on a global scale have not existed until recently. However, the release of new data sets that measure global political behavior and urban growth now allows us to identify statistical relationships between informal politics and urban growth across the world. One such source of data is the Varieties of Democracy (V-Dem) database, which includes a clientelism index. This index uses inputs from country experts to characterize the level of clientelism in each country. The Global Human Settlements (GHS) database and the *Atlas of Urban Expansion* provide data on global urbanization. Among other information, the GHS database includes statistics on the growth from 1975 onward of all urban centers around the world with populations of more than 50,000 people, of which there are several thousand. The *Atlas of Urban Expansion* looks more closely at a global sample of two hundred cities, including at the share of informal growth since 1990. (The Appendix describes these data sets in detail.) Using these global data sets in statistical models provides new insights.[3]

Insights from Statistical Modeling

Clientelism and Urban Population Growth

Do cities that are more clientelistic grow faster than cities that are less so? Clientelism often leads authorities to accommodate some urban residents in ways that a strict enforcement of regulations might not. If this is the case worldwide, we would expect cities in more-clientelistic countries to grow faster (or shrink more slowly). Statistical models find that clientelism is, in fact, significantly correlated with positive population change in cities (i.e., a faster increase or slower decrease in population), when controlling for city-level characteristics, such as population and population density, and country-level characteristics, such as gross domestic product (GDP) per capita and national

population growth rate.[4] When I apply such a model to more than 7,500 urban centers from the GHS data set, it shows that if a country were one point
more clientelistic on a scale of 0 to 10 in 1990, all else remaining equal, the
annual population growth rate of an urban center in that country between
1990 and 2015 would have been higher by 0.1% of its previous value.[5]

When I apply a similar model using 189 cities from the *Atlas* sample
instead,[6] clientelism at the national level is again a significant predictor of
population change at the city level. However, this is only the case when
controlling for the share of the urban extent in 1990 that was in the form of
informal subdivisions. The share of informal subdivisions itself was highly
negatively correlated with population change (a result I discuss later). This
model finds that a one-point increase in clientelism in 1990 results in a 0.2%
proportional increase in an urban center's annual 1990–2015 population
growth rate, larger than the 0.1% in the GHS model.

These may seem like very minor effects, but compounded over twenty-five
years, the estimated impacts are substantial, particularly in the largest cities.
For example, the *Atlas* model estimates that if India had been less clientelistic
by just one point out of ten in 1990, all else being equal, the population of
Mumbai would have been lower by more than a million people in 2015.

Clientelism, Built-Up Area, and Population Density

Since it turns out that clientelism is, in fact, correlated with positive population change, there are two possible ways in which this could occur. One possibility is that clientelism causes urban areas to expand more quickly and thus
accommodate a greater population by facilitating the creation of more urban land. The other is that it causes a greater population to be accommodated
without faster spatial expansion, through higher population density (the ratio of population and built-up area).

When applied to the *Atlas* data, the model shows no significant correlation between clientelism in 1990 and the 1990–2015 rate of spatial expansion.
A model using the GHS urban centers shows that built-up areas actually expanded significantly more slowly, rather than faster, in more-clientelistic
countries. (The GHS data excludes low-density peri-urban growth, which
means that this may not be the most reliable data with which to test urban
expansion.) Regardless, neither result suggests that clientelism accommodates
more urban population through faster urban spatial expansion.

This implies that the faster population growth that is correlated with clientelism must be accommodated through higher population densities. Sure enough, models do find that clientelism is a significant predictor of density change. The effect of clientelism on density is practically the same as the effect on population growth. The model using the GHS urban centers finds that if a country were one point more clientelistic in 1990, the annual rate of change of density in its urban centers between 1990 and 2015 would be higher by 0.1% of its previous value, all else equal. The equivalent figure for the *Atlas* cities is 0.2%. Again, as these are annual growth rates, the effect of these small changes compound and become more substantial over the twenty-five-year period.

Clientelism and Informal Growth

These results suggest that clientelism is associated with changes in density rather than changes in the rate of spatial expansion. This could happen either if clientelism is associated with specific forms of residential growth (e.g., informal settlements) that are denser, or if clientelism facilitates higher population densities across all types of growth.

In each of its two hundred sample cities, the *Atlas of Urban Expansion* estimates the share of recent growth that has occurred in four different forms: "atomistic" settlements (spatially uncoordinated, haphazard informal growth), informal subdivisions (informal settlements that show some signs of spatial planning), formal subdivisions, and housing projects. Examples of these four types of growth are shown in Figure 3. (The Appendix provides more detail on how these types of growth are defined.)

Models using this data set show that the only form of growth that was correlated with clientelism in 1990 was the informal-subdivision type. Informal subdivisions are settlements that appear "informal" based on their low level of infrastructure and small lot dimensions, but they nonetheless appear to have been spatially planned in advance. The evidence of spatial planning is the presence of straight streets and regularly sized plots and blocks. No other category had a share of 1990–2015 growth that was positively or negatively correlated with clientelism in 1990. The fact that clientelism was correlated with more growth in the form of informal subdivisions but not with less growth in the form of any one of the other three categories suggests that the additional informal subdivisions associated with clientelism would not have taken the form of a specific one of the other types of growth in a less clientelistic environment. A

Figure 3. Four types of residential land use in Accra, as identified in the *Atlas of Urban Expansion*: atomistic settlements (top left), informal subdivisions (top right), formal subdivisions (bottom right), and housing projects (bottom left). Source: Google Earth.

combined "informal growth" category, including both atomistic settlements and informal subdivisions, also showed no correlation with clientelism.

The model suggests that if a country were one point less clientelistic on a scale of 0 to 10 in 1990, the proportion of residential growth in the form of informal subdivisions between 1990 and 2015 in its cities would decrease by 16% of its previous value. A country's wealth is also correlated with the share of informal subdivisions in its cities. This means that we can compare the effects of changing the level of clientelism and changing the wealth of a country. The reduction in the share of informal subdivisions that the model predicts would result from reducing clientelism by one point on a ten-point scale is the equivalent of the reduction that would result from increasing GDP per capita (in terms of purchasing power parity) by approximately $2,700.[7] This is substantial, considering that the median country in the *Atlas* sample had a GDP per capita of around $8,000 in 1990.

The example of an individual city helps illustrate the correlation between clientelism and informal subdivisions. The city for which the model predicts the share of informal subdivisions with the highest degree of accuracy is Lahore, Pakistan (the model predicts 31.36%, very close to the observed share of 31.38%). This makes Lahore a useful example. The dashed line in Figure 4 depicts the shares of informal subdivisions in 1990–2015 residential growth in Lahore that the model predicts for every value of the clientelism index for 1990. The version of the clientelism index used in this analysis is constructed such that higher values represent *less* clientelism, with 0 representing the highest possible level of clientelism and 10 representing the lowest. Pakistan's clientelism index score in 1990 was 2.6 on a scale of 0 to 10. If it were one point worse in terms of clientelism, at 1.6 (between Nigeria and Nepal), holding all other variables constant, the model predicts that the share of informal subdivisions would change from 31% to around 37%. This is equivalent to the effect of reducing Pakistan's 1990 GDP per capita from $3,057 to around $360, close to that of the poorest country in the sample (Mozambique). If it were one point better in terms of clientelism in 1990, at 3.6 (between Egypt and the Philippines), the share of informal subdivisions would reduce from 31% to 26%. To achieve the impact of this one-point reduction in clientelism through changes to wealth alone would require increasing Pakistan's 1990 GDP from $3,057 to around $5,760.

Figure 4 also provides the equivalent graph for Accra (the dotted line). Accra's observed share of informal subdivisions is higher than the model

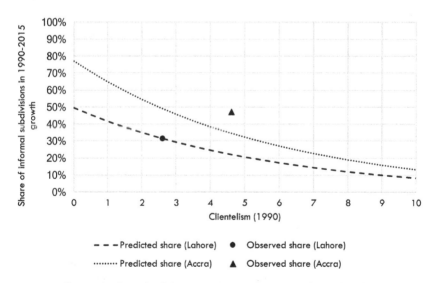

Figure 4. Share of informal subdivisions in 1990–2015 growth, predicted by the model and observed (Lahore, Pakistan, and Accra, Ghana). Source: Modeling by the author, described in this chapter. See Deuskar, "Informal Urbanisation and Clientelism" for more details.

predicts. This may be because customary land rights make it particularly easy for traditional authorities to informally subdivide and sell land (see Chapter 6).

The results show that clientelism is associated with increases in population density as well as with higher shares of informal subdivisions. Does this mean that the higher densities are specifically the result of the higher share of informal subdivisions? This does not appear to be the case. Models show that neither the share of informal subdivisions in 1990 nor the share of informal subdivisions in 1990–2015 growth was significantly correlated with changes in density between 1990 and 2015. Moreover, the share of informal subdivisions in a city was not significantly correlated with its population density either in 1990 or 2015. These results suggest that the increases in population density that are correlated with clientelism are a result of general densification rather than specifically a greater share of informal growth.

Clientelism and National Urbanization

Clientelism is associated with faster urban population growth at the city level. Does this mean that it is also associated with a faster overall shift toward an urban population at the national level? Models using national-level GHS data suggest that this is not the case. Clientelism in 1990 is not significantly correlated with the rate of change in the share of national population living in urban areas between 1990 and 2015. This is the case regardless of whether urban areas are defined as urban centers, urban centers and suburbs, or urban centers, suburbs, and towns.

One possible explanation for this could be that clientelism is associated with faster population growth overall (i.e., in both urban and nonurban areas), which means that the balance between the two need not change. However, models show that this is not the case either, as clientelism is not significantly correlated with national population growth rates.

This suggests that the reason that the correlation between clientelism and faster urban population growth rates at the individual city level does not translate to the national level has to do with the various other characteristics of cities and countries. If two cities were identical in 1990 and were in two countries that were identical apart from their levels of clientelism, the population of the city in the more clientelistic country would grow faster between 1990 and 2015. Of course, no two cities or countries are identical in any regard, and some of their other differences may counterbalance the effect of clientelism such that more-clientelistic countries do not urbanize faster.

Understanding Causality

Given that clientelism at one point in time is correlated with population growth at the city level during a future period might suggest that clientelism *causes* faster urban growth. This does seem plausible, based on the dynamics discussed in the previous chapter. The many ways in which politicians provide benefits or relax regulations in informal exchange for political support might help attract or retain urban residents.

However, it is hypothetically possible that the opposite is the case, that population growth or densification at the city level makes clientelism more attractive to politicians. Scholars have posited that this might be the case, but few studies have directly examined this phenomenon.[8] If this is the only way in which the two are correlated, then any apparent correlation between clientelism in 1990 and population growth in the 1990–2015 period may simply arise from the fact that both are correlated to a higher urban population growth rate in previous periods. It is impossible to test the reverse sequence— namely, whether urban population size or density in 1990 is correlated with changes in clientelism in the subsequent period—at the city level, because clientelism data are only available at the national level.

National-level models using the GHS data find that the share of national population in urban areas in 1990 is not correlated with changes in clientelism between 1990 and 2015. In addition, neither the average population size nor the average population density of urban centers in a country are significant predictors of changes in clientelism. This does not definitely rule out the notion that larger or denser populations cause increases in clientelism at the individual city level. However, it suggests that this is unlikely to be the only way in which the two are correlated. These results, together with the previous results and the broader literature, reinforce the plausibility of clientelism's *causing* population growth and densification at the city level.

It is not possible to test whether the share of informal subdivisions in 1990 caused changes in clientelism in the subsequent period. This is because the *Atlas* data that estimates this share only includes one or a small number of cities per country, whereas clientelism is only available at the national level.

While it is reasonable to expect that clientelism at the country level can be a proxy for clientelism at the city level, and therefore could help determine the prevalence of certain types of urban growth in a specific city, it would be a stretch to claim that the presence of informal subdivisions in one city or a small number of cities in a country could determine the overall level of clientelism across the entire country.

Summary of Findings

The populations of cities in countries that are more clientelistic grow faster and denser, but these cities do not necessarily expand faster in terms of their spatial footprint. Clientelism is correlated with the growth of "informal subdivisions," which are informal settlements that show signs of having been laid out in advance. Clientelism is not correlated with the growth of informal settlements that grow in an ad hoc, spatially unplanned manner. Clientelism is not correlated with faster urbanization at the national level.

Understanding the Relationships Between Clientelism and Informal Subdivisions

The finding that there is a significant relationship between clientelism and informal subdivisions warrants further discussion. What explains the relationship between clientelism and this type of urban growth in particular (i.e., informal settlements that appear to involve prior spatial planning) and the absence of a relationship between clientelism and "atomistic" settlements (i.e., informal settlements that appear spatially unplanned) or informal growth in general? The literature indicates some possible causal relationships.

Causal Mechanisms Inconsistent with the Findings

The specific findings I have presented allow us to eliminate, at least as sole explanations, some of the possible mechanisms by which clientelism and informal growth might be linked. These are mechanisms which would result in a correlation between clientelism and *all* informal growth—informal subdivisions and atomistic settlements—or between clientelism and atomistic settlements specifically, which is not what the analysis finds. In some cases, this correlation would also disappear when controlling for GDP.

Low state capacity independently causes clientelism and informal growth (low state capacity → clientelism; low state capacity → informal growth). An apparent correlation between clientelism and overall informal growth (atomistic settlements and informal subdivisions) may actually result from both being correlated with a variable not included in the models, the omitted variable being state capacity. In a version of events in which low state capacity is the only reason for the correlation between clientelism and informal growth, a weak state fails to provide land and services to the poor, resulting in informal growth, and in parallel, fails to deliver on programmatic policies at the national level, leading to the prevalence of clientelism.[9] This could result in a correlation between clientelism and informality without any direct causal relationship in either direction. However, this would result in a correlation either between clientelism and *all* informal growth, if informal settlers would sometimes subdivide their land even in the absence of clientelism, or between clientelism and atomistic settlements specifically, if they would not. It is unlikely to lead globally to only informal subdivisions and not atomistic settlements. This is inconsistent with the observed correlation, which is between clientelism and informal subdivisions alone.

Clientelism weakens state capacity, which in turn causes informal growth (clientelism → low state capacity → informal growth). In this version of events, the causal relationship between clientelism and state capacity runs in the opposite direction, with clientelistic politics reducing the incentive or ability to build state capacity. Consequently, diminished state capacity to provide formal land and services results in the growth of informal settlements. If the only relationship between clientelism and informal settlements is via state capacity, clientelism would be correlated with the share of urban growth in the form of all informal settlements or with just atomistic settlements. It would not be correlated with just informal subdivisions.

Low GDP independently causes clientelism and informal growth (low GDP → clientelism; low GDP → informal growth). As with state capacity, low GDP could independently cause both informal growth and clientelism, without any direct causal link between clientelism and informal growth. However, a version of events in which this is the only causal link between clientelism and informal growth is not in keeping with the findings. This is because, again, it would likely result in a correlation between clientelism and all informal growth, or just atomistic settlements, in the absence of GDP as a control variable. This correlation would also disappear once the GDP variable is included, which is not what happens in the models previously described.

Clientelism causes low GDP, which in turn causes informal growth (clientelism → low GDP → informal growth). Hypothetically, the causal relationship between clientelism and GDP could run in the opposite direction. Clientelistic politics might prevent conditions conducive to economic growth from arising, and low GDP in turn would result in informal settlements. If the only relationship between clientelism and informal settlements is via GDP in this manner, clientelism would again be correlated with all informal growth, or with just atomistic settlements, in the absence of GDP as a control variable. This correlation would disappear once the GDP variable is included.

Informal growth causes low GDP which in turn causes clientelism (informal growth → low GDP → clientelism). In this version of events, the existence of informal settlements (or an informal land market in general) lowers productivity in the economy as a whole, which creates conditions conducive to clientelism. As previously, if the only relationship between clientelism and informal settlements is via GDP in this manner, clientelism would be correlated with all informal growth, or just atomistic settlements, in the absence of GDP as a control variable. This correlation would disappear once the GDP variable is included.

Causal Mechanisms Consistent with the Findings

The potential causal mechanisms I have just outlined are not consistent with the findings, as they would not explain why clientelism is correlated only with informal subdivisions and not also with atomistic settlements. However, there are some possible causal mechanisms that are consistent with the findings.

To be clear, the finding here is not that clientelism can *only* be associated with informal subdivisions and not with other types of residential urban growth. If this were the case, more clientelism would be correlated with a significantly *smaller* share of the other types of growth. Rather, the analysis simply shows that the other types of growth may or may not be associated with clientelism and so do not necessarily form a larger or smaller share of residential growth in a clientelistic environment. An atomistic settlement may indeed result from clientelism, or may foster clientelism after it forms. Similarly, clientelism may be involved in the provision of land or services to what the *Atlas* describes as formal subdivisions,[10] or in the allocation of public housing to beneficiaries.[11] However, atomistic settlements, formal subdivisions, and housing projects could also arise in the absence of clientelism. By contrast, the discussion that follows suggests certain mechanisms that make informal subdivisions particularly likely to be linked with clientelism and unlikely to form in its absence. These mechanisms might explain the observed correlation between clientelism and the share of informal subdivisions.

Clientelism causes the growth of informal subdivisions through direct provision of land (clientelism → informal subdivisions). Political patrons may own or otherwise control land and subdivide it in order to distribute it to clients. For example, politicians and government officials own more than half the land in Kibera, the large informal settlement in Nairobi, and these figures or their brokers informally subdivide and allocate plots of land to residents.[12] Even if political patrons do not own the land, they may collaborate with informal land brokers to organize the informal settlement of land, as in Karachi, Pakistan.[13] The land may be settled gradually, but brokers may subdivide it informally in advance, resulting in the physical features associated with informal subdivisions. This mechanism would be less likely to operate in the absence of clientelism, in which case land would be less likely to be provided by a single patron or broker.

Clientelism encourages the growth and persistence of new informal subdivisions through postsettlement protection and regularization (clientelism → informal subdivisions). Even if political patrons are not involved in the initial occupation of the land, they may become involved in "regularizing" the settlement after it has formed, by intervening to prevent demolitions[14] and organizing the provision of urban services, such as water and electrical connections, and neighborhood-level infrastructure, such as paved roads, sewerage, or public toilets, often through brokers.[15]

This kind of postsettlement support may happen regardless of whether the built form of the settlement is as an informal subdivision or an atomistic settlement. However, evidence suggests that leaders among the urban poor are likelier to organize "planned" land invasions, in which an entire community settles a site in concert, in clientelistic environments in which they expect future support. For example, in Montevideo, Uruguay, the formation of ad hoc "accretion" informal settlements had always been common. However, "planned" land invasions grew in number during a period of intense political competition, when political parties eagerly courted the votes of the urban poor. Participants in these preplanned invasions were likelier to subdivide land into streets and individual parcels in advance of settlement.[16] In Quito, Ecuador, leaders among the urban poor waited several months in order to carry out a land invasion during campaign season, when they would be less likely to be evicted as political candidates fought for their votes.[17] Similarly, in Karachi, in contrast to "unorganized" land invasions, informal subdivisions of state land tend to be planned in a grid pattern.[18] In all these examples, settlers appear to take the opportunity of a clientelistic atmosphere to execute larger, more organized land invasions. Preplanned invasions like these are likelier to involve some level of site planning, which would make them take the form of informal subdivisions rather than atomistic settlements. The fact that preplanned invasions are more likely to occur in clientelistic environments and also more likely to be spatially laid out in advance suggests that, even when patrons are not involved in the initial settlement, planned informal subdivisions are more likely to arise in clientelistic environments.

Settlements with strong leadership and more coordination are likelier to be laid out in advance and are also likelier to foster clientelism (neighborhood leadership → informal subdivisions; neighborhood leadership → clientelism). Some accounts of the growth of informal settlements suggest that informal settlements with strong leadership and coordination from the outset are both likelier to be laid out in advance and better able to successfully engage in clientelistic bargaining with politicians.[19] These communities often proactively seek out patrons, but even if they do not, patrons may be attracted to communities that appear able to provide unified political support. This means that even if there were no clientelism at the time of the emergence of the settlement, the existence of a cohesive community under strong leadership could induce clientelism. The fact that such a community is also likelier to be spatially organized is consistent with the finding that informal subdivision and clientelism go together, even if clientelism does not directly cause these types of settlements to form.

Clientelism leads to the "informalization" of subdivisions (clientelism → informal subdivisions). Given that the *Atlas* does not distinguish between settlements on the basis of their legal status but only according to their physical characteristics, some settlements that were settled legally may still be classified as informal subdivisions because they are poorly served by infrastructure. Clientelism may be a factor in this scenario if political patrons are able to prevent infrastructure from being formally provided or maintained, acting as gatekeepers such that access to infrastructure is contingent on political support. The example of the Shivajinagar-Bainganwadi settlement in

Mumbai suggests that such a mechanism is plausible. Here, the local government itself laid out the settlement in a grid pattern and allocated land to households in the 1970s, suggesting that it was originally "formal" in terms of government approval, but antipathy on the part of subsequent political leaders toward its residents caused it to deteriorate into what is now widely considered an "informal settlement."[20]

Informal Subdivisions and Urban Population Growth

It is not immediately clear why, in the first *Atlas* models discussed, clientelism in 1990 only becomes a statistically significant predictor of 1990–2015 urban population growth when controlling for the share of informal subdivisions in 1990, which itself has a strong negative correlation with population growth. Hypothetically, this could be because informal subdivisions stifle future urban population growth. For example, informal subdivisions might restrict future population growth if the informal but relatively secure nature of tenure in such settlements means that these settlements are less likely to be replaced by high-rise buildings. This is plausible, but the share of informal subdivisions in 1990 is also negatively correlated with the 1990–2015 growth in the city's overall built-up area. One would expect that if informal subdivisions restrict population growth within themselves, *more* spatial growth would need to occur in order to compensate.

It is possible that, instead, these negative correlations between informal subdivisions and both population and spatial growth can be attributed to the prevalence of an informal, and therefore inefficient and restricted, land market. Clientelism might help partially overcome the restrictions on population growth caused by an informal land market by accommodating more people in the city as a whole. This might explain why clientelism would be positively correlated with population growth only when controlling for informal subdivisions.

Implications for Planning Research and Practice

This analysis is the first to measure the relationship between urban growth and informal politics empirically across a large number of cities around the world. Using new data, the models find evidence for theoretically plausible relationships between clientelism and changes in population growth, population density, and the share of informal subdivisions in cities. The analysis here supports the argument that informal growth is not associated only with poverty or a lack of planning and enforcement, but also with politics. It also suggests that powerful state actors are as implicated in the creation and perpetuation of informality as the urban poor.

The fact that informal politics appears to help accommodate population growth also implies that it is meeting a need unfilled by formal plans and regulations. This should prompt urban planners and policymakers to examine how formal plans and regulations can be amended to provide some of the same access to land and services that informal political forces do, but in more equitable and transparent ways. For example, although clientelism may interfere with the ability to implement formal spatial plans, some degree of informal planning already appears to take place in clientelistic environments, resulting in informal subdivisions. This suggests that professionally trained planners might find it effective in certain cases to provide their expertise directly to informal settlers, or perhaps even to political patrons and their brokers. Planners may find it beneficial to become involved at the stage of initial formation of informal subdivisions because their specific spatial pattern—that of straight, gridded streets and regularly sized parcels—could be conducive to the upgrading of infrastructure in the future. Chapter 9 develops a version of this recommendation in the context of Ghana.

Analysis at this global scale using standardized data is useful for establishing broad regularities but nonetheless leaves several questions unanswered. How do clientelism and urban growth interact on the ground in a complex urban environment? How do the various other forces specific to a particular context affect this relationship? Where does the formal planning system fit into the picture? These questions are best explored by focusing on case studies, which I do in forthcoming chapters.

CHAPTER 3

Transitioning Away from Clientelism: Global Cases

"All mass democracies in the modern age have passed through (or remain in) highly clientelistic conditions," writes the political theorist Robert Alan Sparling.[1] This statement emphasizes the importance of clientelism in the political history of the world but also might give the impression that clientelism is a passing phase. If countries tend to move inevitably away from clientelism toward programmatic politics as their economies grow and their institutions mature, then perhaps urban planners and policymakers need not worry about how to adapt to clientelism.

Unfortunately, the evidence I examine in the first section of this chapter suggests that urban clientelism is not disappearing on its own. If anything, urban land and services have only become more important as currencies of clientelistic exchange in many developing democracies. Nonetheless, there are historical instances in which clientelism has loosened its grip on the urban poor, whether at the scale of an individual neighborhood or an entire country. In the second section of this chapter, I explore these examples and discuss whether they hold any lessons for planners today.

Will Clientelism Disappear on Its Own?

Political scientists have traditionally assumed that clientelism declines naturally as incomes grow. The assumption is that clientelism becomes less viable as a political strategy as incomes rise, for several reasons. First, the cost of the clientelistic benefits demanded by nonpoor clients becomes prohibitive to patrons. Second, economically secure voters are able to risk voting on the basis of policies and do not have to sell their vote for basic necessities. Third, the growing number of middle-class voters, who are typically not the prime target group of clientelism, punish clientelistic politicians in elections. Fourth, economic growth is associated with urbanization, and the voting behavior of dense urban settlements is harder to monitor.[2]

However, the evidence does not support these assumptions of an inevitable decline in clientelism. The clientelism index, introduced in the previous chapter (and discussed in more detail in the Appendix), allows us to measure changes in clientelism over time. It does show that when countries are aggregated by income, wealthier countries are less clientelistic (i.e., have higher values in the index). It also shows that, on average, each income group improved slightly from 1990 to 2015. Figure 5 shows these changes, with countries grouped according to their 1990 income (i.e., they are not reclassified between 1990 and 2015, in order to depict changes in clientelism within unchanging cohorts of countries).

However, this grouping masks variation within groups. At the level of individual countries, only a moderate correlation exists between GDP per capita and clientelism (correlation coefficients: +0.40 in 1990 and +0.44 in 2015). More important, there appears to be no uniform linear trend away from

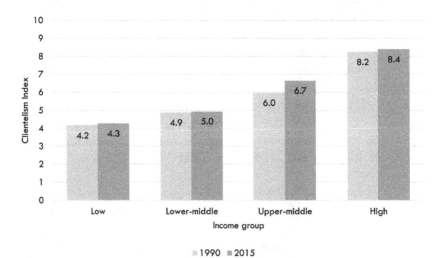

Figure 5. Average clientelism index values in 1990 and 2015 for countries grouped by 1990 income. Source: Author's analysis of clientelism index data (Coppedge et al., "V-Dem Country-Year Dataset 2018") and World Bank country classification by income (World Bank DataBank, http://databank.worldbank.org/data/download /site-content/OGHIST.xls, accessed January 7, 2019).

clientelism over time. No correlation exists between change in GDP per capita and change in clientelism during this period. This is evident in Figure 6 and Figure 7, which depict changes between 1990 and 2015 in GDP per capita and clientelism, respectively. For example, several developing democracies in Asia and Africa, including Bangladesh, Ghana, India, Indonesia, and the Philippines, saw significant economic growth during this period. Yet they remained nearly constant in terms of clientelism, improving or declining by only half a point or less on a 0–10 scale. This suggests that clientelism is a problem that economic growth alone will not cure.

Several factors may explain why the assumed relationship between increasing wealth and declining clientelism appears not to hold true. First, the argument that the cost of patronage becomes prohibitive as an economy grows may not apply when one of the benefits is urban land. As an economy grows, so do voter demands, but so also does the value of urban land. This means that the value of this clientelistic benefit to the client increases as the

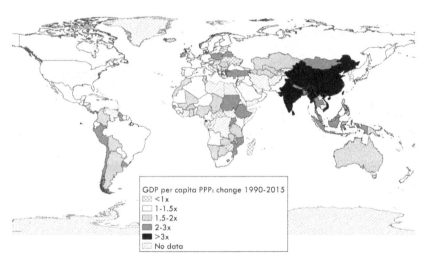

Figure 6. Change in GDP per capita (based on purchasing power parity, or PPP, in constant 2017 international dollars) by country, 1990–2015. Sources: Author, using GDP data from World Bank and Eurostat-OECD (International Comparison Program, World Bank; World Development Indicators database, World Bank; and Eurostat-OECD PPP Programme, https://data.worldbank.org/indicator/NY.GDP .PCAP.PP.KD, accessed April 19, 2021) and country boundaries from UIA World Countries Boundaries (ArcGIS Hub, https://hub.arcgis.com/datasets/UIA::uia -world-countries-boundaries, accessed November 13, 2018).

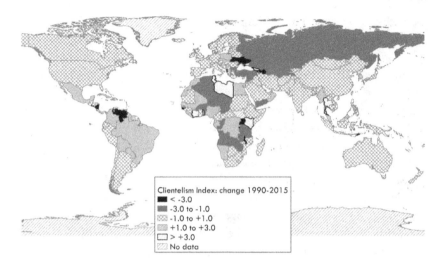

Figure 7. Change in clientelism by country, 1990–2015. Sources: Author, using data from V-Dem (Coppedge et al., "V-Dem Country-Year Dataset 2018") and country boundaries from UIA World Countries Boundaries (ArcGIS Hub, https://hub.arcgis .com/datasets/UIA::uia-world-countries-boundaries, accessed November 13, 2018).

economy grows. The cost to the patron, that of protecting informal developments from regulation, remains largely unchanged.

Second, while it is true that middle-class voters prefer less clientelistic, more programmatic politicians, they often simply disengage from politics rather than trying to discipline candidates through their votes. For example, Noah Nathan finds that, in Ghana, middle-class urban voters, at least those living in areas with basic service provision, do prefer "universalistic" policies to particularistic ones. However, they do not believe that the politicians they are presented with can deliver such policies. As a result, they disengage from politics and abstain from voting altogether.[3] Increasingly, middle-class and wealthy residents pay private suppliers for urban services, particularly for water, security, education, and sanitation. This reduces their reliance on public systems of service delivery, which also reduces their incentive to put pressure on governments to improve these systems.[4] For their part, politicians do not risk promising programmatic policies that are complex and costly. Instead, they ignore middle-class preferences and focus on particularistic exchanges with the poor.[5] This suggests that the growth of the middle class alone may not be enough to conquer clientelism.

The evidence does not support the idea that urbanization thwarts clientelism. As we have seen, clientelism is very much alive in cities. The Asian and African countries listed previously as having nearly stable levels of clientelism in the period 1990–2015 have also experienced rapid urbanization during the same period. A recent study finds that in parts of Indonesia that have relatively undiversified economies, clientelism is actually more prevalent in urban areas than in rural areas.[6]

In fact, the importance of clientelism as a driver of informal urban growth may have increased in many parts of the world since the late twentieth century, owing to a confluence of factors. In several postcolonial democracies (e.g., Ghana, India, Indonesia, Kenya, Mexico, South Africa), political competition between different parties emerged or accelerated in the 1990s, increasing the incentive to engage in clientelism. Around the same time, the contraction of state employment during the era of structural adjustment reduced the availability of government jobs to distribute as patronage, leading politicians to turn to other types of benefits.[7] As these countries were now urbanizing rapidly, urban land and services filled this gap. As a result, clientelism may have grown in importance and shifted toward urban land and services.

A rejection of clientelism on the part of patrons is unlikely because it presents a collective-action problem. As long as clientelism is affordable and popular, no individual political party or candidate has an incentive to drop it as an electoral strategy. For successful reform on the patron side, every candidate would have to agree simultaneously to campaign without resorting to clientelism, trusting that everyone else would stick to that agreement. This is an unlikely scenario. Aspinall and Berenschot demonstrate that, in Indonesia, politicians feel compelled to engage in clientelism even when they would rather not, out of fear of being outbid by rivals and of failing to meet voter expectations of election-time benefits. Politicians who have tried to discard clientelism as a strategy without already having a strong political base have lost elections.[8]

Global Examples of Transitions away from Clientelism in Low-Income Urban Settlements

Even if there is no uniform trend away from clientelism, the grip of clientelism on informal settlements does loosen occasionally. Scholars acknowledge that they have been unable to identify a systematic reason why this happens in some places and not others.[9] Given that existing theory does not reliably point to a way out of clientelism, real-world examples may provide better guidance. The discussion that follows identifies and briefly describes cases in which clientelistic urban service delivery has given way to more programmatic service delivery and examines whether these cases hold any lessons for planning.

Bureaucratic Reform, National Welfare, and Other Changes (United States)

"The man in the slum votes according to his light, and the boss holds the candle," quipped the pioneering photojournalist and social reformer Jacob Riis in 1902, referring to the political "bosses" in the slums of New York City.[10] However, "bossism"—the form that clientelism took in the United States— lost its grip on the urban poor over the first half of the twentieth century. A once-popular explanation for the demise of clientelism in American cities was sheer demographic growth in the number of middle-class voters, who opposed clientelism. However, recent scholarship questions this explanation, pointing out that clientelism persisted long after the establishment of the middle class. In fact, it ended during a period when middle-class residents were fleeing to the suburbs, as a result of which the average urban household was becoming poorer, not wealthier.[11] Scholars also cite restrictions on immigration from the 1920s onward as an explanation for the decline in clientelism, as it reduced the number of vulnerable and factionalized newcomers in American cities. However, scholars now question this explanation too, noting that the political "machines" that were not dependent on immigrant groups also declined at roughly the same time as those that were.

Other plausible explanations for the decline of bossism in the United States involve broader shifts in society and technology. For example, increased access to education provided better opportunities to urban youth for attaining wealth than did patronage jobs. Mass communication technology made it more efficient for politicians to appeal to constituents beyond the neighborhood level.

Some explanations refer to concerted civic reforms originating in the Progressive Era. Civil service reforms dating from the 1890s made it harder to manipulate jobs as patronage. Reforms in municipal accounting made irregular expenditures harder to hide. Business elites and an emerging professional class centralized power in the city. They removed it from ward- and community-level bosses and placed it in the hands of municipal-level technocrats, aided by new "organization technologies" and institutions. Progressive reformers promoted professionalized, technocratic urban planning as a tool to undercut patronage politics. Later, the implementation of national welfare programs, especially the 1930s New Deal and the 1960s Great Society programs, undermined the power of local bosses further.[12] In summary, bureaucratic reform, national welfare programs, and other changes appear to have led to the decline of clientelism in the United States.

Political Crisis and Reform (Naples, Italy)

Naples, Italy, saw clientelism decline in the 1990s as a result of a national political crisis that prompted electoral reform. Corruption scandals destroyed Italy's long-incumbent Christian Democratic Party, and reforms followed. Mayors, who until then had been appointed by elected local councils, were now to be elected directly and required to win an absolute majority of votes. Whereas the previous coalition-based system allowed candidates to get a seat at the table by making deals for only a few thousand votes each, this was no longer possible at the scale made necessary by the new system.[13]

Neighborhood-Scale Crisis as an Inflection Point (Rio de Janeiro, Brazil)

A crisis at a much smaller scale appears to have led one Rio de Janeiro community to reject clientelism in the 1970s and 1980s. Robert Gay describes how a favela called Vidigal originally had the same relationship with politicians as other poor neighborhoods in the city: a local politician served as its patron, giving the settlement the occasional handout, sometimes using public money, in exchange for the residents' electoral support. This changed when the government announced that it planned to demolish the settlement. The government claimed that the decision was prompted by the danger of landslides in the area, but the residents believed that this was just a pretext to clear the site for luxury residences. The government promised to relocate the residents of the favela to an apartment complex in a suburb. However, residents who accepted the offer of relocation found that these apartments were no better than their homes in Vidigal. What was worse, these homes were located more than two hours away from where most of the residents worked. When community leaders sought help from their political patron in fighting the eviction notice, he proved unable or unwilling to intervene on their behalf. The community instead joined with civic groups in protest of the eviction, and together, they managed to fight off the threat. Stung by this incident, community leaders changed their political approach, no longer making deals with politicians in exchange for their endorsement. They explained to residents that infrastructure and services were their right as citizens, and that they did not need to pay for them with votes. Instead, the community took its demands straight to city hall. If politicians showed up in Vidigal, community leaders ensured that they discussed their broad policy platforms rather than simply bringing handouts.

Gay is cautious in his appraisal of this apparent success, partly because the residents of Vidigal did apparently continue to reward parties electorally that had initiated public works in the favela. Gay labels this behavior as "semiclientelism." He observes that even if the public works influenced voting, residents did not vote for candidates as part of a quid pro quo deal or under any coercion or pressure. Rather, they voted independently in response to parties whose actions had benefited them.[14]

The Role of Local Reformers During a Broader Political Transition (Mexico)

Veronica Herrera describes how the actions of local reform coalitions against a backdrop of a national political transition changed water provision from clientelistic to programmatic systems in several cities in Mexico. In the 1980s and 1990s, an opposition party had come to power in some local governments, displacing the more autocratic party that had held power across the country for decades. The opposition party initiated a move toward market-oriented and democratic reforms in these cities.

In the city of León, the local business community became actively involved in the water sector following a severe water shortage. This prompted reform that resulted in the city's water utility becoming effectively independent from political interference, according to Herrera. The reform focused on charging user fees that, at times, appeared to favor the business interests that were represented on the board, which led to protests from poor communities. Still, service delivery improved citywide and became less clientelistic in nature. Similarly, in Irapuato, the same newly incumbent party moved the water utility toward cost recovery as a means of breaking clientelistic ties between the former incumbents and residents. These had involved low negotiated rates between the utility and community leaders in informal settlements.

Two other Mexican cities—Naucalpan and Celaya—were similarly successful in pursuing water utility reforms. Unlike the previous pair of cities, they did so through narrower coalitions of reformers, with mayors rather than broader groups of elites leading reforms in both cities. Nonetheless, as in León and Irapuato, they geared the changes toward collection of user fees, which led to protests that eventually subsided, leaving less-politicized service provision.

Herrera describes four other Mexican cities whose experiences differ from the four just mentioned. In Toluca, Xalapa, Neza, and Veracruz, the newly incumbent parties preferred to retain or even expand the old clientelistic networks of water provision inherited from the former incumbents. Herrera uses these eight cities to argue that the presence of a strong middle-class political base, as well as water-intensive industries, were key factors in initiating and sustaining programmatic reform of water provision.[15]

National Land Titling Programs to Weaken the Power of Local Incumbent Parties (Mexico)

Explanations of the decline of clientelism tend to focus on institutional reform and political shifts. However, a specific government program may also weaken clientelism in informal settlements even in the absence of broader change. An example of such a program is a large, long-term national government program in Mexico referred to as CORETT, after the Committee for the Regularization of Land Ownership (Comité para la Regularización de la Tenencia de la Tierra). The program has provided land titles to residents of informal settlements on communal land in urban areas in Mexico since the 1970s. Many of these settlements were originally formed with encouragement from politicians, who would then condition the community's ability to remain on the land on its demonstration of political support. Incumbent parties at the municipal level benefited from their ability to manipulate these voters, giving them an incumbency advantage.

Recent research demonstrates a correlation between the receipt of titles from the federal CORETT program and reduced vote share for municipal incumbents in future elections. This suggests that the federal titling program helped to weaken the clientelistic advantage of municipal incumbency. This was a successful strategy for the federally incumbent party. Even though the titling program also cost it, too, some ability to engage in clientelistic politics where it was in power locally, voters rewarded the party in national elections.[16]

Similarly, a national land titling program in Kenya may also have been motivated partially by an attempt by national incumbents to weaken the clientelistic networks of their national predecessors and local opposition.[17] Although this program focused on rural land, its existence suggests that Mexico's CORETT program may not be alone in using land titling as a means of weakening clientelism.

Broad Political Reform and Fiscal Crisis (Bogotá, Colombia)

Bogotá, a city with extensive informal settlements, also experienced a shift away from rampant clientelism in the 1990s. According to Eleonora Pasotti, the introduction of direct mayoral elections in 1986 set the conditions for reform. These direct elections replaced the previous, highly centralized system in which the national parliament controlled the nomination of mayors. When a new constitution that favored independent electoral candidates without party affiliations came into effect in 1991, identification with established parties among the electorate declined rapidly. This led to the collapse of the clientelistic political machine in Bogotá. Campaigns now sought to mobilize public opinion instead of buy votes. Bogotá also faced a fiscal crisis in the early 1990s, which led to several reforms that consolidated and strengthened the authority of mayors and also prompted them to move away from clientelistic politics.[18]

The Legacy of a Technocratic Dictatorship (Santiago, Chile)

Alisha Holland describes the transition from politically supported squatting to public housing provision in Santiago, Chile. The early 1970s saw a spike in the formation of informal settlements, with four hundred thousand people participating in land invasions, which the government of the time did not oppose. The military dictatorship that took over in 1974 cracked down on new land invasions and initiated a formal housing subsidy program through a technocratic housing ministry. When Chile redemocratized starting in 1990, the democratic government took advantage of the existence of this technically competent housing ministry. The new government used it to establish a housing program of its own, as a means of demonstrating that democracy could deliver public goods to the poor. In order to prevent squatting from reemerging as a housing option for the poor, which would have undermined the housing program, the new democratic government continued to suppress squatting.[19]

A Move Toward Right-Wing Politics (Istanbul, Turkey)

Holland also discusses the example of Istanbul, which had a history of clientelistic support for informal settlements prior to 2002, when the conservative Justice and Development Party (AKP) came to power. The AKP took advantage of Turkey's declining poverty rate, which meant that the median voter was no longer poor. The party's political base was the majority Sunni population, who were no longer highly represented among urban migrants. This meant that the government was able to associate informality with Kurds, Roma, and other ethnic minorities. The ruling party's political fortunes did not rely on clientelistic ties to the urban poor, and the government proceeded to demolish some informal settlements.[20]

Grassroots Community Organizations (Multiple Countries)

Grassroots NGOs active among the urban poor in Asia and Africa have been partially successful in moving communities away from clientelism. These organizations include Shack/Slum Dwellers International (SDI) and its various affiliates around the world, such as the Society for the Promotion of Area Resource Centres (SPARC) in India, Muungano wa Wanavijiji in Kenya, Ghana Federation of the Urban Poor, and others; Karachi's Orangi Pilot Project (OPP); the Asian Coalition for Housing Rights (ACHR); and others. These self-help organizations tend to rely primarily on community savings to build neighborhood-level infrastructure. The leaders and members of many of these organizations are mostly women, many of whom have never previously been involved in civic or community activities.[21]

These organizations tend to be highly critical of the clientelistic provision of services, understanding it to be insufficient, unreliable, unequal, and divisive.[22] They are determined not to "deliver the poor as a vote bank to any political party or candidate."[23] Still, they typically avoid contesting existing power structures through protest and confrontation. Instead, these organizations engage constructively with whomever is in power and aim to empower themselves and loosen the hold of political patrons through more subtle strategies.

Diana Mitlin highlights three approaches that "encapsulate the essence of the strategy to address clientelism."[24] The first is the prevalence of women-led, alternative forms of organization such as savings groups, which political elites do not see as threats. These groups are highly accountable to residents. Jane Weru of Pamoja Trust, a Kenyan NGO, describes savings groups as the "glue" that holds groups of the urban poor together, as their establishment and management promotes trust and cooperation in communities.[25] Second, community-led mapping and surveying provides grassroots NGOs with information that is useful not only to themselves but to government officials. Third, these organizations form networks of poor communities and other partners, both throughout their city and internationally. This facilitates the sharing of information and practices, and strengthens the collective power of communities to bargain for rights.[26]

These organizations do not claim to be self-sufficient, and they recognize the need for government support in scaling up. However, rather than angling for patronage, they prefer to start with "precedent-setting" projects that demonstrate the kinds of interventions they consider necessary.[27] For example, in Mumbai, community women affiliated with SPARC's women's savings group, Mahila Milan, developed housing prototypes themselves. They then invited senior government officials at the ward, city, and state levels to view and consider implementing them.[28]

The extent to which grassroots organizations like these can eliminate clientelism altogether is debatable. Ayona Datta suggests that the work of Mahila Milan and another NGO in an informal settlement in Delhi, India, did in fact help to "connect working-class women to civil society organizations and subsequently move away from informal structures of patronage, privilege, and customary authority."[29] However, as noted earlier, other authors do not find that mobilization among the poor necessarily helps transition away from clientelism, even if it helps the poor bargain more effectively for clientelistic benefits.[30] Grassroots organizations tend to move opportunistically between various strategies, including openly contentious politics, collaboration with state actors, and subversion of state regulations, which suggests that they may not necessarily reject clientelistic opportunities altogether.[31] As Satterthwaite and Mitlin observe, "It is clearly not possible for a bottom-up process alone to either overcome clientelism or to provide the finance for universal solutions to be implemented."[32]

A Role for Planners?

While each of the aforementioned transitions away from clientelism took place in a specific political and institutional context, it is possible to identify some recurring features. Crises appear to have acted as inflection points in the movement toward change in Rio de Janeiro, León (Mexico), and Bogotá. In the United States, too, the Progressive reform movement that pushed for the advent of professional urban planning and the decline of clientelism was responding to what it perceived as a crisis of corruption and inequality in the country.[33] In Mexico, Colombia, Chile, Turkey, and Italy, the move away from clientelism is inseparable from broader political transitions at the national level, which had impacts beyond informal settlements. The Chilean case involves a military coup, while the Turkish case involves demonization of informal settlers, and neither of these is likely to be in the best interests of the poor. Beyond being opportunistic in capitalizing on broader conditions that support urban planning, lessons for planners are hard to discern from any of these examples.

It is easier to imagine urban planning playing a role in supporting the grassroots organizations and NGOs. Álvarez-Rivadulla notes that when land invasions are organized and planned in advance, squatter organizations often "imitate" formal urban planning. They subdivide the land into streets and parcels and reserve land for public spaces and community facilities, with the expectation that the settlement may eventually be integrated into the formal city.[34] This is a type of informal spatial planning. Urban upgrading by ACHR or the provision of neighborhood-level sanitation by OPP involves organizing the provision of long-term public goods through community participation. This, too, is effectively a form of planning. To the extent that these organizations do help communities move away from clientelism, the fact that they perform planning-like functions indicates a potential role for professional planners in facilitating a transition from clientelism.

The idea that professionally trained urban planners might offer their expertise directly to individual urban communities rather than to city governments has a long history, going back at least to Paul Davidoff's call for "advocacy planning" in the United States in the 1960s.[35] In the context of informal settlements, however, the relationship between professionals and communities is often challenging. Community-based organizations such as SDI are open to professional help but are often careful to ensure that they do not become dominated by outside professionals.[36] SDI uses various strategies to manage the relationship between communities and professionals, including getting involved in the training and recruitment of professionals and maintaining clear boundaries between professionals and communities so that communities can maintain control over projects.[37]

Mitlin discusses some of the challenges with regard to the "coproduction" of solutions between professionals and communities. Professionals are often expected to arrive with solutions prepared, despite a lack of sufficient local knowledge. They are expected to act as intermediaries between communities and the state, a role they may not be equipped to play. Academic researchers and consultants often have their own agendas, such as the preparation of research papers or reports, which differ from those of communities.[38] For all these reasons, even though working with grassroots organizations may offer a way for planners to help communities move away from clientelism, planners have often found it challenging to do so effectively.

Clientelism, which constrains effective urban planning, will not disappear on its own. Historic examples of its decline do not illuminate any straightforward way in which planners can help communities extricate themselves from it. Planners must, therefore, adapt to the realities of clientelism in order to bring about more inclusive and sustainable outcomes. This argument is hard to make in the abstract, however. To ground it in a specific context, the next several chapters develop a case study of Ghana, a middle-income African democracy in which clientelism and related informal political dynamics are the binding constraints to effective urban planning.

PART II

Politics and Planning in Urban Ghana

CHAPTER 4

Urban Informality and Planning
Failure in Ghana

G hana, a West African country of around thirty million people, is among the more economically advanced and politically stable countries in sub-Saharan Africa. It is a middle-income country with one of the most rapidly growing economies in the world. It has had peaceful, democratic transitions of political power for a quarter century and is relatively free of violent crime, terrorism, and sustained armed conflict. It also has regulations and bureaucratic institutions in place to support the preparation and implementation of city plans. In other words, Ghana might seem to have the ideal economic and political conditions for urban planning to serve its growing urban population effectively.

Instead, practically all academic, governmental, nongovernmental, and news publications describe planning in Ghana as ineffective. According to Eric Yeboah and Franklin Obeng-Odoom, "Planning has failed to exert effective influence on the growth of human settlements in Ghana. . . . The district assemblies undertake little forward planning and the few plans that are prepared are rarely implemented."[1] Patrick Brandful Cobbinah and Rhoda Mensah Darkwah concur, writing that "urban planning has failed to create livable and functional cities in Ghana."[2] In the words of Accra's chief planner, it is impossible for planners to "do any real planning."[3]

The extent to which urban growth in Ghana occurs informally, without regard to plans and regulations, lends credence to this narrative of planning failure. Between 65% and 80% of construction across income categories in Greater Accra, the largest urban area in the country, does not comply with building permit regulations.[4] In the country's second largest city, Kumasi, almost all new construction starts without a building permit, and only a small fraction of buildings successfully obtains permits at any stage.[5] An estimated 80% of development in Ghana occurs without land title.[6] Development control through land use and building permits is the means by which spatial plans are implemented. The fact that the need for such permits is ignored supports the notion that planning in Ghana is ineffective. Poor urban infrastructure and service provision is additional evidence of the weak state of planning. For example, in Accra, only half the population has access to an improved toilet facility.[7] Unreliable water supply requires three-quarters of the city's population to purchase drinking water from private providers.[8] Most drainage is uncovered and frequently clogged,[9] resulting in frequent and often fatal floods.

Why is urban planning in Ghana so ineffective? Building on the arguments and findings from previous chapters, in the next few chapters I demonstrate that the primary constraints to planning in Ghana are political in nature. I also explore how planners respond to informal politics. By situating the relationship between clientelism and informal urbanization established in previous chapters in a specific context, this case study aims to provide texture and depth to the picture. I base this case study on interviews and site visits in the field,[10] as well as on analysis of government documents, news stories, quantitative data, satellite imagery, and other academic studies.

Ghana is an ideal case in which to investigate the interactions between clientelism, informality, and urban planning. Countries that lend themselves to an exploration of these issues are urbanizing low- or middle-income countries that have meaningful elections and, therefore, have scope for clientelistic exchanges. Among this group of developing democracies, Ghana can be considered representative in terms of its size, level of urbanization, and wealth.

Ghana is also representative of this group in terms of the relevant political dynamics. In recent years, Ghana has had a medium clientelism index score, fluctuating between 4.1 and 5.5 out of 10 since its democratic transition of the early 1990s. When countries are ranked from least clientelistic (Norway) to most clientelistic (Somalia), based on their 2017 clientelism index scores, Ghana places 103rd out of 178 countries. This suggests that Ghana is far from an extreme case, and that the planning issues arising from clientelism in Ghana are likely to be representative of those in several other countries. These include other urbanizing middle-income democracies such as South Africa (ranked 56th out of 178), Brazil (64th), Bangladesh (65th), Mexico (83rd), India (89th), Kenya (106th), Indonesia (118th), Nigeria (132nd), the Philippines (147th), and Pakistan (155th).[11] These countries, including Ghana, together represent more than a third (36%) of the global urban population and close to half (45%) of recent global urban population growth.[12]

An Introduction to Urban Ghana

National Context

Ghana lies at the center of the standard world map, close to where the prime meridian and equator meet. Most of the West African country's inhabitants trace their heritage to groups that are believed to have migrated to the area within the last 700 to 1,000 years. The inhabitants of the area were influenced by Islamic empires of northern Africa since the fourteenth century and began trade with the Portuguese in the fifteenth century.[13] In subsequent centuries, the United Kingdom, Denmark, Sweden, the Netherlands, and Prussia colonized and exploited the country, first for gold and eventually for enslaved people. It was officially a British colony (the "Gold Coast") from 1901 to 1957, when it achieved independence.

Kwame Nkrumah, a leader of the independence movement, served as the newly established republic's president during its first nine years, before being deposed in a coup in 1966. Political instability marked the next several years. Jerry Rawlings, an air force officer, seized power in another coup in 1982 and presided over a decade-long military junta in the country. The Rawlings government eventually led a transition to multiparty democracy, enacting a new constitution in 1992. Since then, the country has successfully maintained a stable electoral democracy. However, as this case study discusses in detail, democratic competition has at times created perverse incentives with respect to the delivery of long-term public goods. A classification of governing regimes by the Economist Intelligence Unit categorizes contemporary Ghana as a "flawed democracy."[14]

Ghana's economy, based mostly on the export of gold, oil, cocoa, and other natural resources, has achieved strong growth in recent decades. This is true even in per capita terms, despite a more than fourfold increase in population since independence. In 2011, the World Bank reclassified Ghana from being a low-income country to being a lower-middle-income country in GDP per capita terms. As a lower-middle-income country, Ghana belongs to the same group as India, Kenya, Nigeria, the Philippines, Ukraine, and others.

Ghana is officially a secular country, although religion plays a prominent role in daily life. An estimated 60% and 18% of Ghanaians practice Christianity and Islam respectively, with the remainder following traditional and other religious practices.[15] The official state language is English, though Ghanaians speak many ethnic languages, including Twi as a *lingua franca*, and others including Ewe, Ga, and Hausa.

Ghana is one of the most ethnically diverse countries in the world, home to more than a hundred ethnic groups and subgroups. Violent interethnic conflict is rare in Ghana. Instead, interethnic marriage is common, and many people speak multiple ethnic languages.[16] The largest ethnic group is the Akan, which accounts for nearly half of the national population and is subdivided into several subgroups.[17] The Ashanti, an Akan subgroup, established an important kingdom in the seventeenth century with its capital at Kumasi, and the Ashanti king (the "Asantehene") remains the most powerful figure in the Ashanti Region. The indigenous people of Greater Accra are known as the Ga. Although the Ga remain locally influential, today the majority of Greater Accra's population is Akan.[18]

Since its democratic transition in 1992, Ghana has had two major political parties: the New Patriotic Party (NPP) and the National Democratic Congress (NDC). The constitution created high barriers to entry for new political parties; as a result, the two main parties have dominated politics in recent decades and given Ghana one of the most well-institutionalized party systems in Africa.[19] The two parties have fought close elections and have regularly exchanged power since the 1990s. The NDC was in power under presidents John Atta Mills and John Mahama from 2009 to 2017. The NPP then came to power under president Nana Akufo-Addo, who was reelected in 2020.

Urbanization in Ghana

Ghana has experienced steady urbanization in recent decades. Official sources estimate that around 55% of its population lives in urban areas (as of 2017, having increased from 30% in 1975), based on a definition that counts all localities with more than five thousand inhabitants as "urban."[20] Alternatively, the European Commission's Global Human Settlements database classifies

50% of Ghana's population as residing in fifty-one urban centers and an additional 28% as residing in towns and suburbs. The corresponding values in 1975 were 21% in urban centers and 45% in towns and suburbs.[21]

The two largest urban areas in Ghana are Accra and Kumasi. Accra, the political capital and economic hub of Ghana, lies on the country's southern coast. No one local government unit has boundaries coterminous with the urbanized area of Greater Accra. Recent estimates suggest that the population of the Accra urban agglomeration is around 4.5 million, up from 1 to 1.5 million in 1990. According to the *Atlas of Urban Expansion*, the population of the Accra urban area grew at 4% per year from 2000 to 2014. This was a slightly lower growth rate than the average for sub-Saharan African cities in the *Atlas* sample (4.6%). However, it was higher than the average of all cities in its global sample of two hundred cities (2.8%). Accra's built-up area has a relatively low population density: fifty-one people per hectare in 2014. This is lower than both the average for sub-Saharan Africa (seventy-nine) and the world (sixty-seven) in the *Atlas* sample. This relatively low density reflects the fact that residential development in Accra primarily takes the form of low-rise housing.

The Greater Accra Region has the lowest incidence of poverty in the country, with a poverty headcount ratio of 6.6% in 2015. The Accra Metropolitan Assembly (AMA), which covers the center of the metropolitan area, had a poverty headcount ratio of 2.6% that year.[22] Using a measure based on education, English literacy, and formal-sector employment, Nathan estimates that the share of Greater Accra's middle class grew from 7% in 1993 to nearly 25% in 2014.[23] Access to health facilities in the Greater Accra metropolitan area is relatively high (77%). Access to electricity is even higher (93%);[24] however, residents of informal settlements are often unable to acquire electrical connections formally and, therefore, must pay bribes and high prices to intermediaries to access it informally. A study of three informal settlements in Accra found that 75% of residents access electricity "illegally" and that they pay 60% more than other city residents for electricity. The study notes that electricity theft is widespread in formal settlements as well.[25]

Only 50% of Accra residents have adequate access to an improved toilet facility, and only 30% of households have a toilet at home.[26] Thirty percent of AMA residents rely on public toilets, but this proportion varies across the city, increasing to 60% of households in the Ashiedu Keteke area, which includes the indigenous settlement of Ga Mashie.[27] Between half and three-quarters of Greater Accra has access to piped water,[28] but the supply is intermittent, requiring households to fill the gap with water delivery from private tanker trucks.[29] Less than a quarter of Accra's population uses piped water for drinking due to fear of contamination, with the rest buying drinking water packaged in bottles or sachets.[30] The majority of neighborhoods have municipal drainage infrastructure, but most drains are uncovered.[31] Waste management is a major challenge for Accra. Poor waste management causes drains to become clogged by solid waste, which contributes to flooding. This frequently causes loss of life and property and spreads waterborne diseases.[32]

Kumasi, Ghana's second-largest urban area, lies approximately 125 miles (200 kilometers) inland in south-central Ghana and has an estimated population of 2.5 to 3 million. Kumasi has a poverty headcount ratio of 5.3%.[33] Nathan estimates that Kumasi's middle class grew from constituting just 3% of the area's population in 1993 to 20% in 2014.[34] Though 80% of residents have access to piped water,[35] 40% rely on public toilets, most of which were found, in a 2015 study, to be in poor condition.[36]

Local Government in Ghana

Ghana is a unitary (as opposed to federal) republic, with an elected president as head of state, as well as members of Parliament (MPs) elected simultaneously. First-level administrative subdivisions in Ghana are known as regions. There were ten regions in the country until 2019, when the government created six more. Each region comprises local governments classified as metropolitan, municipal, or district assemblies (generically, MMDAs) depending mainly on population size. Chief executives, often referred to as "mayors," lead MMDAs and are appointed by the president rather than being locally elected. In addition to the chief executive, local assemblies consist of locally elected assembly members, MPs from the area, and presidential appointees.

Urban Land in Ghana

One of the primary constraints to state regulation of urban growth in Ghana is the fact that most land in the country is controlled by traditional authorities, or "chiefs." The Ghanaian constitution considers 80% of land in Ghana, including roughly that proportion in both Accra and Kumasi, to be customary land. Customary land controlled by chiefs is known as "stool land" (or "skin land" in the North; both *stool* and *skin* refer to symbols of chieftaincy). It may also be "family land," which is allocated by chiefs to family heads. According to the Ghanaian constitution, traditional authorities hold the land "in trust" for their communities, though as Chapter 6 discusses, chiefs often treat it as their private wealth. Technically, private entities may lease land for fifty or ninety-nine years from customary owners. However, these arrangements typically involve high upfront payments and nominal recurring rents, if any, which makes them more like sales than leases.[37]

Disputes over family land are common. These disputes may be between different branches of a family or between different buyers who have bought the same piece of land as a result of fraudulent duplicate sales. Notices put up throughout urban Ghana, like those in Figure 8, are evidence of these disputes over family land.

Some liken land in Accra to cocaine, presumably alluding not just to its high price and desirability but also to the violence that accompanies its possession and trade.[38] The disputes over land parcels around Accra have prompted many landowners to hire gangs of armed "land guards" to patrol their properties and keep off prospective encroachers, buyers, sellers, private surveyors, and even government officials. Land guards use violence against anyone entering a property, though visitors can sometimes pay land guards to allow them in.[39] Land guards are particularly prevalent on the fringes of Greater Accra, where there is still undeveloped land.[40] Customary authorities, families involved in land disputes, and property developers are the most frequent employers of land guards. However, public institutions have also resorted to using land guards to remove unauthorized structures on their land, while residents of informal settlements, in turn, hire land guards to keep authorities away.[41] Chapter 6 discusses the implications of this privatized violence for planners, some of whom have been violently attacked or threatened by land guards in the course of their work.

Twenty percent of land in Ghana is state land. The government may acquire land from customary owners for a compensation for public purposes. The land acquired is not always used for the intended purposes and is sometimes sold to private interests.[42] For instance, in recent decades, the government has allocated state-owned land in the upscale neighborhoods of Airport Residential,

Figure 8. Signs in Greater Accra indicating land disputes and fraudulent land sales. Source: Photographs by the author.

Cantonments, and Ridge, which it has owned since independence, to private real estate developers.[43]

Planning in Ghana: Past and Present

A Brief History

The Cameroonian planning scholar Ambe Njoh describes planning policies in Africa during the colonial era as "instruments of power, domination and social control" that were more concerned with segregating populations and demonstrating European superiority than with improving the lives of native residents.[44] The colonial planning history of Ghana centers primarily on Accra, where planning efforts were both the most extensive and best documented. In the 1660s, the Danish built Christiansborg Castle on the coast at Osu, now part of Greater Accra. They used it to trade in gold as well as in enslaved human beings, whom they kept in the castle's dungeons before forcing them through the "door of no return" onto ships bound for the Americas. Denmark ended its slave trade in the early nineteenth century and sold the castle to the British in 1850.[45] The British and Dutch had also built smaller forts, Fort James and Fort Crèvecœur (later known as Fort Ussher), respectively, in the seventeenth century. The Ga settlements around these historic forts are still known as James Town and Ussher Town. The earliest Ga settlers of this part of the coast established "quarters" based on family lineage, which evolved into today's indigenous neighborhoods.[46]

Under British colonial rule in Ghana, like elsewhere around the world, public health concerns prompted early attention to the urban built environment. British medical officers blamed the density of housing and lack of free-flowing air for the "deplorable" sanitary conditions and "foul stenches" in mid-nineteenth-century Accra. When the British moved their capital from Cape Coast to Accra in the 1870s, they constructed new buildings and implemented public works in the city related to drainage, sanitation (public latrines), roads, and bridges. Infrastructure during this period was largely oriented toward making trade as efficient as possible. A fire that destroyed much of the indigenous James Town settlement in Accra in 1894 prompted the British government to acquire and replan the affected land, laying out wide roads and drains and specifying plot sizes.

By the end of the nineteenth century, the British had instituted a program of intrusive household sanitary inspections, ostensibly to control the spread of malaria. However, this was not the most practical approach to disease eradication and may have been more a means of imposing control over native neighborhoods than of eradicating malaria. The disease was equally prevalent in European cantonments, but the British claimed that the native population was responsible for the spread of the disease. This claim led to stricter segregation of native and European settlements. The mistaken notion that mosquitoes only bit at night resulted in the imposition of nighttime curfews. The government did not fully enforce either of these measures. However, the 1901 Towns Act increased government control over the built environment and gave the director of public works the power to lay out roads and regulate even the architecture of buildings.

When a plague broke out in Accra in 1908, British medical officers again fixated on the built environment of native residents. They called for a separate European business quarter and wide spacing of buildings in the native settlements. The government created an "Accra improvement committee" in response to the outbreak, which began demolishing houses to widen streets and remodel neighborhoods, and resettling residents to newly built areas. Another outbreak, this time of yellow fever, again led to calls for stricter segregation between Europeans and natives. However, many European merchants continued to live and trade in native quarters like James Town. A new official map was prepared, depicting large swathes of land as "taken for public purposes" and native settlements simply as "congested." In the former zone, the British built several new residential, recreational, and institutional structures.[47]

Public works continued in the first few decades of the twentieth century, with colonial officials laying out streets on the outskirts of Accra in 1910,[48] initiating public water supply in Accra in 1917, building the Ring Road around the city in the 1920s, and laying out planned suburbs in the 1930s with the cooperation of landowners.[49] Several of the annual reports produced by the colonial administration of the Gold Coast in the 1930s repeat a passage explaining that, while there was no "planning" in a strict sense, the government was able to ensure "orderly" urban growth through agreement with traditional authorities and landowners:

> Town-planning, in the strict application of the term, does not
> prevail, although legislation provides for it. . . . A substitute for

town-planning has been found in the provision, as conditions warrant, of lay-outs by agreement with the local chiefs or land-owners. This system has been effective in ensuring correct development of many towns, both large and small. Extensive lay-outs of stool lands adjacent to Accra have recently been effected and in these cases the allocation of any vacant plots remains under the control of the chiefs. In towns where development is anticipated, agreements are made with the local chiefs whereby such development shall proceed only on orderly lines and in accordance with the lay-out as designed. Arrangements are concluded at the same time to enable Government to acquire free of claims for compensation the land required for roads and for such other sites as are required for public purposes. A plan of the lay-out superimposed upon a survey of the town affected is attached to the agreement, which thus defines clearly and finally the position and enables the orderly development of the town to take place without undue expenditure. Repeated requests are received for the lay-out of towns and villages to which no lay-out scheme has yet been applied.[50]

The colony's governor, Gordon Guggisberg, launched a development plan for the colony for the years 1920–30, which the government implemented largely successfully. It emphasized the importance of spatial planning and infrastructural development, but also institutional development, resulting in the construction of roads, schools, hospitals, and housing for the local population. The government transferred Guggisberg, who was popular with the local population, out of the Gold Coast in 1927, a move that some in Ghana speculate may have been a result of his efforts to empower the native population.[51]

In 1945, the government hired the architect Edwin Maxwell Fry to study and propose plans for the major cities of West Africa. His plan for Accra proposed a new "outer ring road" connecting a string of neighborhoods, each of which would have its own shops, community centers, schools, and parks. However, the British never substantially implemented Fry's plan for Accra, partly because it required the demolition of large parts of James Town at a time when the grip of the British on the Gold Coast was starting to weaken.[52]

Also in 1945, the British colonial government in Ghana enacted the Town and Country Planning Ordinance, based largely on British planning regulations.[53] When Ghana became independent in 1957, it retained a version of the

British planning ordinance on the books for another half century. This was not unusual; many postcolonial governments in Africa and elsewhere retained and even further entrenched colonial planning practices rather than reimagining planning after independence,[54] even as changes to the political and institutional environment often made it difficult to enforce them as originally imagined. In 1958, the year after independence, Ghana's first president, Kwame Nkrumah, introduced a detailed new plan for Accra.[55] The plan imagined monumental squares and buildings intended to inspire national sentiment among citizens, but it too was not implemented.[56] The new government formed the Accra Slum Clearance Committee in 1961, which, despite its name, identified James Town and other settlements for upgrading projects rather than clearance.[57]

In 1961, the Greek firm Doxiadis Associates prepared a master plan for the large new industrial port town at Tema on the eastern edge of Accra, which was implemented relatively successfully.[58] Around this time, United Nations consultants and others also drafted the country's first National Physical Development Plan, for the 1963–70 period. However, Nkrumah was deposed in a coup in 1966, and the plan was not implemented; little planning occurred during the political instability of the subsequent two decades.[59] A plan to relocate residents of Nima, the large Muslim-majority migrant settlement, or *zongo*, in Accra, to make room for commercial development, was introduced in the 1970s. However, protests from chiefs, landlords, and university students meant that this plan was never implemented either.[60]

Beginning in 1983, the World Bank and International Monetary Fund (IMF) initiated the Economic Recovery Program (ERP) in Ghana. While the program focused mainly on monetary and macroeconomic policy, it also encouraged decentralization of urban management to the local level. The Accra Planning and Development Programme accompanied the ERP, and it was carried out with assistance from the United Nations Development Programme and UN-Habitat in three phases from 1985 to 1990. It culminated in the completion of a strategic plan for the Greater Accra metropolitan area in 1991, which also included a spatial plan.[61] (The 1991 plan remains the latest city-level spatial plan for Accra, though the AMA has updated smaller local plans since then.[62]) Up to this time, an area had to be officially declared a "planning area" before a plan could be prepared for it, but new regulations in 1993 declared all settlements in Ghana, both urban and rural, to be planning areas.[63]

Regulatory and institutional reforms enacted in 1994 put in place the "development planning system." Development planning, which did not take a spatial approach to planning, dominated over the next decade. The Land Use Planning and Management Project, funded by the government of Ghana and the Nordic Development Fund and implemented between 2007 and 2010, revived spatial planning as a parallel system. These reforms resulted in the enactment of the Land Use and Spatial Planning Act in 2016, which finally replaced the 1940s-era town planning regulations. The Town and Country Planning Department was renamed with the passage of the act as the Land Use and Spatial Planning Authority (LUSPA). The new act also streamlined the planning process by instituting national, regional, and local spatial development frameworks (SDFs). SDFs would now form the basis for structure plans, which addressed zoning, and local plans, which were to be detailed subdivision plans.[64]

A regional SDF for the Greater Accra Region was released in 2017.[65] In 2018, the national government announced that it intended to hire Liu Thai Ker, known as the "master planner" of Singapore in the 1970s and 1980s, to help "transform Accra into a modern city" after Ker met with the Ministry of Finance and investors.[66] However, no progress appears to have been made on this collaboration since this initial announcement.

In 2017, President Akufo-Addo initiated the Marine Drive project. The project, which President Nkrumah had first envisioned around the time of independence, is poised to transform 241 acres (around one square kilometer) of Accra's city center and waterfront with new tourist attractions, residential and commercial developments, and government buildings. The Ministry of Tourism, Arts and Culture leads the project, and the designer is the Ghanaian-British architect David Adjaye.[67]

Planning has been less active in Kumasi. A 1962 land use plan for Kumasi, which led to the construction of a ring road, remained the latest land use plan until 2013. In that year, the Japan International Cooperation Agency prepared the Comprehensive Urban Development Plan for Greater Kumasi. The agency's plan also included a spatial development framework for the Ashanti region.[68] Four years later, in 2017, another SDF was prepared for the region, this time with World Bank funds.

The 2016 act also promoted the decentralization of spatial planning to MMDAs, so that LUSPA at the national and regional levels was under the Ministry of Environment, Science, Technology, and Innovation, but at the local level it was under the Ministry of Local Government and Rural Development.[69] Accordingly, in 2019, 790 officers from the national Civil Service under LUSPA were transferred to the Local Government Service under the Department of Parks and Gardens, as a step toward greater administrative decentralization. This included 110 professional planners, 430 technical officers, and 103 auxiliary staff, to be deployed across regions and MMDAs throughout Ghana.[70]

Planning in Ghana Today

The distinction between development planning and physical planning (also called spatial planning) is an important part of the planning landscape in Ghana today. Development planning, in this context, is the identification and coordination of planned projects of an MMDA's departments and their alignment with the national government's strategic economic, social, and other goals. An MMDA's Planning Coordinating Unit, chaired by the chief executive ("mayor") and with members from the Department of Physical Planning and other departments, is responsible for development planning. The unit prepares a medium-term development plan (MTDP) covering four to five years. For example. the 2018–21 MTDP for the AMA runs more than nine hundred pages, with detailed lists of intended projects from each department for each year within the planning period.[71]

While development planning has a broad remit, physical planning (which this case study focuses on) pertains specifically to the preparation of spatial plans and zoning regulations and the issuance of development and building permits. MMDAs have a Spatial Planning Committee, also chaired by the chief executive, with the director of physical planning as secretary. Other members of the committee include representatives of the Department of Works, Department of Roads, Department of Disaster Prevention, the Lands Commission, and the district's traditional council.[72] Private consultants, overseen by LUSPA, prepare SDFs throughout Ghana, often with donor funding.[73]

Many planners in Ghana are affiliated with the Ghana Institute of Planners (GIP), an autonomous organization unaffiliated with any government body. The GIP sustains itself through membership dues from its approximately seven hundred members, which include both development planners and physical planners in the public and private sectors. While most local government planners are members, not all are. Local government planners, communities, the media, and even politicians call upon the GIP occasionally, seeking technical advice or commentary on planning issues.

Urban Informality in Ghana

The primary evidence for the failure of the formal planning system to regulate and direct urbanization in Ghana is widespread informality. If we take *informality* to refer to activities that violate some regulation, but where regulations are unenforced or enforced irregularly, informality dominates urban Ghana. The informal sector in urban Ghana includes informal settlements and informal economic activity, including informal retail, informal transportation services, and informal waste collection.

The Informal Urban Economy

Informal spatial growth in Ghana must be understood against the broader background of informality in the country and its economy. Scholars typically ascribe the growth of the informal sector of the economy in Ghana to the decline in state employment and the rise in urbanization that followed structural adjustment.[74] Even the World Bank now blames the growth of the informal sector in Ghana on the collapse of industrial establishments that occurred as a result of structural adjustment and globalization.[75] Statistics on formal employment in the 1980s and 1990s support this narrative. The World Bank and IMF initiated structural adjustment in Ghana under their Economic Recovery Program in 1983. Between 1985 and 1991, formal sector employment contracted by an average of nearly 4% each year. From 1987 to 2000, the state sold more than three hundred enterprises, and seventy thousand formal sector employees lost their jobs. Some returned to the formal sector at much lower salaries, and many others entered the informal economy.[76]

Employment in urban Ghana is now overwhelmingly informal. An estimated 89% of employment in the country as a whole, and 83% of employment in urban areas, is informal.[77] Even in the largest cities, most workers are informally employed: 74% of the working population in Accra[78] and 70%

of the population of Greater Kumasi[79] are employed in the private informal sector. Informal vendors operating out of makeshift structures or carts, or simply carrying goods in containers on their heads, are ubiquitous on pedestrian pavements or between vehicles stopped at traffic lights. These informal vendors sell everything (snacks, electronics, framed artwork, and much more) to pedestrians, drivers, and passengers. The vehicles, too, are often part of the informal sector. *Tro-tros*, minivans operated as a form of informal public transportation, account for 60% to 70% of journeys in Greater Accra.[80]

Informal waste collectors collect a quarter of all waste in Accra,[81] and 80% of the recycling of metallic waste is done informally.[82] Ghana imports large amounts of electronic waste and processes nearly all of it informally. The electronic waste processing hub of Agbogbloshie in Accra achieved international notoriety following journalistic articles that described it as the world's largest electronic waste dump and one of the most toxic places on earth (though scholars believe these labels to be exaggerations).[83]

Informal Settlements

Designating a settlement as a "slum" or "informal settlement" is fraught with ambiguity and subjectivity. In Ghanaian cities, settlements that are described as slums or informal settlements because of their high densities, lack of adherence to building standards, or lack of access to services and infrastructure may be one of at least three different types of settlements. First, they may be indigenous settlements, whose right to the land on which they are located is supported by both tradition and the Ghanaian constitution. For example, Ga Mashie in Accra, comprising James Town and Ussher Town, may appear to be a slum by certain criteria, such as the number of inhabitants per room; however, the government considers it to be a legitimate settlement and, in fact, celebrates it as Accra's historic center, channeling development efforts toward its residents.

A second category of low-income settlement occupies land originally acquired from local chiefs. While these settlements, too, may have "slum"-like features, state and customary authorities consider them legitimate by virtue of the nature of their initial settlement. These settlements include *zongos*—communities settled mostly by Muslim migrants from the North on land acquired from local chiefs. For example, a migrant group purchased the land for the neighborhood of Nima, in what is now central Accra, from local chiefs in the early 1930s.

By contrast, the government considers low-income settlements whose residents occupy state land without formal authorization, like Old Fadama in Accra, to be "squatter settlements." Government agencies, as well as indigenous Ga residents, are often hostile to their existence. (I describe how these settlements manage to survive despite this hostility in Chapter 7.)

Estimates of the share of informal settlements in Accra vary widely, because they may or may not include all three categories in their definitions. According to the AMA, there are twenty-nine informal settlement communities in Accra,[84] and 58% of the city's residents live in informal housing.[85] People's Dialogue on Human Settlements, an affiliate of Shack/Slum Dwellers International (SDI), conducted a survey of informal settlements in Accra in 2016. It included *zongos* and squatter settlements, but not indigenous settlements, as informal settlements. The survey identified 265 informal settlements in the AMA area, including 116 "developing/infant" settlements, 73 that are "growing/consolidating," and 76 that have "matured."[86]

The *Atlas of Urban Expansion* makes none of the locally specific distinctions just described but instead categorizes settlements according to a globally standardized typology based on physical characteristics (see Appendix).[87] It estimates that the share of new residential growth between 1990 and 2015 that occurred in the form of atomistic settlements (informal settlements not laid out before occupation) was 48%. This is higher than the average of 43% for the eighteen sub-Saharan African cities and 31% for the two hundred global cities in the sample. The share of new residential growth during this period that occurred in the form of informal subdivisions (informal settlements that show signs of prior spatial planning) was 47%. This is equal to the average for the sub-Saharan African cities but higher than the global sample average of 29%. This means that, in total, informal settlements as defined and measured in the *Atlas* (atomistic settlements plus informal subdivisions) made up 95% of new residential growth in Accra. This is higher than not only the global average (60%) but also the sub-Saharan African average (90%) in the *Atlas* sample. In 2015, 92% of Accra was made up of such settlements, compared to 86% and 52% in the sub-Saharan African cities and global cities, respectively (Figure 9).

Informal subdivisions in particular have been growing in importance in Accra. The 1991–2014 period was the first time since the beginning of the

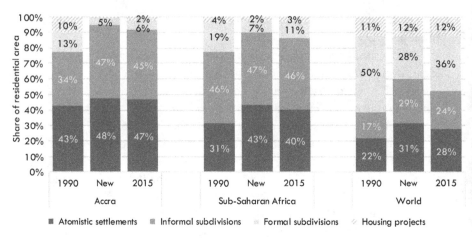

Figure 9. Shares of residential land use by type in 1990, new growth (1990–2015), and 2015 (Accra and averages for sub-Saharan African and world cities in *Atlas* sample). Source: Author, using data from Angel et al., *Atlas of Urban Expansion*, vol. 2, *Blocks and Roads*.

twentieth century that informal subdivisions were the most common form of residential growth in the city (Figure 10).[88] Some areas that are classified as atomistic settlements within Accra's 1990–2015 growth appear to be peripheral villages whose built form may in fact be much older, even if they only merged with the growing city after 1990. Excluding these, a majority of new residential growth in Accra may be informal subdivisions. Chapter 6 discusses the prevalence of this particular type of growth in Accra.

Kumasi is not included in the *Atlas* sample, but other studies suggest that informality also dominates Kumasi's urban fabric, at least in terms of violations of land use and building regulations. A study based on interviews of residents in an informal settlement in Kumasi found a low level of awareness of building and zoning regulations. It also found that nearly two out of three respondents perceived land use laws to be irrelevant to them. More than 90% believed these laws to be too rigid for them to obey and the process of acquiring building permits to be cumbersome and costly. More than 80% believed that the land-use planning authorities could not stop them from building, demolish their structures, or punish them for building without a permit.[89]

Of course, informality cannot be equated only with poverty and the physical characteristics of structures associated with it. In Ghana, as elsewhere in the Global South, middle-class and elite residents engage in informality

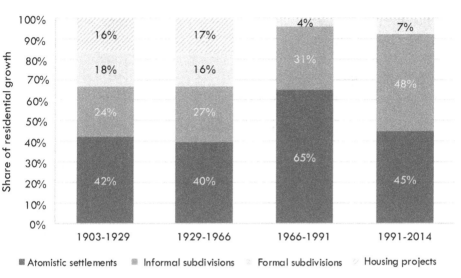

Figure 10. Shares of residential growth in Accra by type, 1903–2014. Source: Author, using data from Angel et al., *Atlas of Urban Expansion*, vol. 2, *Blocks and Roads*.

too. Most new construction in Greater Accra and Kumasi, regardless of income level, proceeds without a formal land title or building permit. A study of urban expansion around Kumasi found that almost all the home builders interviewed had started construction before obtaining a permit from the local government. More than a third had never even attempted to obtain such a permit. Only a fifth had successfully obtained it, albeit after have already started construction without one. (However, every single household surveyed had obtained "allocation papers" from chiefs.)[90]

Informality and the Government: Policies and Actions in Conflict

Although many government agencies and policies profess support for the informal sector, government actions toward informal activity on the ground are often far from supportive.

Government Policies: Rhetoric of Support
for the Informal Sector

At least four national policy documents released since 2012 acknowledge the need to recognize and support the informal sector. In 2012, the Ministry of

Local Government and Rural Development released the National Urban Policy, which lists several actions related to the informal economy as part of its action plan.[91] These include changing the official attitude toward informal enterprises "from neglect to recognition and policy support." It also encourages planning legislation that protects and facilitates informal economic activity and local plans that incorporate the needs of the informal sector.

In 2014, the Ministry of Employment and Labour Relations established a National Employment Policy, taking a similarly positive attitude to the informal economy. The strategies it proposes to address informality include facilitating and supervising the transition from informal to formal economy; maintaining a national database on the informal economy; integrating informal enterprises into urban plans; assisting informal enterprises to grow and employ more people; and providing financial assistance.[92] The National Housing Policy includes upgrading slums and preventing the occurrence of new ones among its main policy objectives.[93] It proposes a National Housing Fund to support slum upgrading, the formulation of a slum infrastructure improvement policy, and the empowerment of slum dwellers to participate in decision-making, among other initiatives. The National Spatial Development Framework also acknowledges the importance of the informal sector, discussing "neighbourhood regeneration or informal settlement upgrading projects" as possibilities for cities.[94]

In addition to these national policies, the Greater Accra Regional Spatial Development Framework lays out the need to "ensure that urban planning provides for the activities of the informal economy." It advocates allotting 500,000 Ghanaian cedis (around US$100,000) for the national government and regional coordinating council to adopt an "informal sector plan" to help convert "informal localised business and micro-survivalist enterprises into formal, small and medium sized mainstream business enterprises."[95]

In its 2018–21 Medium Term Development Plan, the AMA discusses building capacity in the informal economy as an adopted strategy.[96] One of the five "discovery areas" listed in the AMA's Preliminary Resilience Assessment, sponsored by the Rockefeller Foundation as part of its 100 Resilient Cities program, is "recognizing, embracing and supporting the informal sector." It lists in situ upgrading, integrating informal waste collection into formal systems, and the expansion of water infrastructure into informal settlements as example initiatives.[97] The Accra Resilience Strategy, released in 2019, reiterated AMA's support for the informal sector, with one of three pillars aiming to "embrace informality's contributions to resilience building."[98] The Greater Kumasi Spatial Development Framework recognizes the importance of the informal sector as a source of employment but also emphasizes the need to modernize the informal sector by creating "linkages" with the formal sector, including research institutes.[99]

Government Actions: Sporadic but Brutal Antagonism
Toward Informality

The policies expressing support for the informal sector are starkly at odds with the Ghanaian state's reputation for sporadic but brutal antagonism toward the informal sector in practice. Obeng-Odoom describes the state's approach toward residents of informal settlements and informal workers as "aggressive, combative, and impulsive."[100]

Residents of many informal settlements are under constant threat of having their homes demolished by the AMA, often with no compensation or resettlement. In 2016, People's Dialogue estimated that 43 of the 265 settlements within the AMA's boundaries faced the threat of eviction.[101] In August 2018, not long after releasing the Preliminary Resilience Assessment that expressed its support for the informal sector, the AMA announced its intention to demolish a thousand structures along the railway line in Agbogbloshie. An AMA spokesperson stated, "We have given them ample time to ensure that they move their belongings and failure to do so we will be forced to eject them. They are not supposed to be there, and the assembly is not making any arrangement to relocate them to any other place."[102] Across Greater Accra, bulldozers demolish homes, often under the direction of municipal planners and engineers, in the presence of armed police or army personnel, and allegedly without prior warning. For example, in the month of August 2019 alone, at least three local governments in Greater Accra carried out such demolitions.[103]

The AMA has repeatedly announced its intentions to demolish the Old Fadama settlement in Accra, as Chapter 7 explores in detail. The settlement has existed since the 1980s and includes among its eighty thousand inhabitants families who were resettled there by the government itself in the 1990s. When the residents of Old Fadama took the AMA to court following an eviction notice in 2002, a high court judgment ruled that the AMA had no legal obligation to compensate or resettle the residents, and that evicting the "trespassers" from their "illegal occupations" did not in any way infringe on their human rights.[104] The settlement has also faced eviction threats in 2009 and 2012, and the AMA demolished part of the settlement in 2015, amid riots of protest.[105] The timing of another demolition of structures in Old

Fadama in 2020 was particularly callous, as it occurred during the nationwide lockdown in response to the COVID-19 pandemic, leaving more than
a thousand residents homeless during an already desperate time for the
urban poor.[106] In 2021, community leaders in Old Fadama preemptively demolished some structures as a compromise, to avoid the fate of the scrapyards and markets in Agbogbloshie, which had been completely razed by the
government.[107]

In 2014, the AMA demolished Mensah Guinea, a waterfront settlement
of five thousand residents in central Accra, having given them three days' notice to clear out. The AMA told residents that the reason for the demolition
was a cholera outbreak, but residents claim that there had been only ten cases
of cholera and that the patients had been treated in hospital.[108] In any case,
some have pointed out that the appropriate response to an outbreak of a con-
tagious disease would, in fact, have been to contain the patients rather than
to disperse them.[109] Activists and scholars believe that the demolition was
really to clear the area for the Marine Drive project mentioned earlier.[110]

In many cases, however, demolitions of informal settlements are threatened but not carried out at all, or if they are, residents often return immediately. This is usually due to political pressure, often from party leadership, as
discussed in the next chapter.

The AMA is also notorious among street and market vendors for its aggressive "decongestion exercises," in which AMA officials knock over, burn,
or bulldoze stalls and confiscate merchandise belonging to informal street
vendors.[111] Little of the government rhetoric in policy documents about supporting the informal economy has translated into a change in the legal status of informal activities in cities. Vending on public property such as streets
and pavements remains illegal. The 1993 Local Government Act allows cities
to make their own bylaws relevant to local government functions, and the
AMA has made several policies that target street vendors in aid of "decongestion." These include a 1995 bylaw stating that "no person shall offer for sale
or sell any article in a street market other than the space of selling allocated
to him by the AMA."[112] Another AMA bylaw from 2009 established a "special task force" to evict street vendors.[113] The AMA invokes these laws in order to justify its actions.[114]

A 2019 study found that crackdowns on informal vendors in Ghana have
been constant in recent years, regardless of the political party in power. Between 2000 and 2016, thirty-two such crackdowns occurred in Ghana, of

which half were in Accra.[115] In 2007, roadside structures used by vendors both for trade and as accommodation were demolished in preparation for the arrival of international visitors on the occasion of the fifty-year anniversary of Ghana's independence.[116] In preparation for Barack Obama's 2009 visit to Accra, AMA officials set fire to informal vendors' stalls along the US president's route, in order to clear them away to "beautify" the city.[117] In 2011 and 2012, the AMA demolished kiosks and ordered the police to beat or arrest anyone who resisted.[118] Tom Gillespie recounts the story of a street trader who fell into a coma after being hit on the head with a paving stone when he resisted the confiscation of his wares by the AMA in 2011.[119] Street vendors also accuse AMA officials of harassing them for bribes.[120] The violence is not only in one direction, however: vendors are known to push to the ground, throw stones at, or even bite officials as they conduct decongestion exercises.[121] Decongestion exercises are also common in Kumasi. There, too, guards armed with whips and batons drive traders away from their locations; however, traders usually return after bribing the guards with cash, or sometimes even with sexual favors.[122]

Decongestion exercises are generally initiated and carried out by local governments under direction from the chief executive, with national government agencies taking no responsibility for them.[123] Still, national politicians are concerned about the electoral implications of these harsh crackdowns. As with the demolition of informal settlements, national leaders in the ruling party often instruct local officials to halt the eviction of informal vendors, fearful that the actions would cost the party votes in the next election. For example, in 2005, the ruling NPP government instructed the AMA to stop evicting street vendors for fear of losing popularity,[124] and the NDC government did the same in 2009.[125] The local government of Kumasi rarely conducts decongestion exercises during election years, and if a mayor does attempt one, party leaders overturn it. An exception was 2008, an election year in which the city administration did conduct a decongestion exercise, and the incumbent party believes that it cost them the election.[126]

Victims of these demolitions are quick to blame the ruling party and threaten electoral boycott. In turn, political figures deny being behind the actions. For example, when demolitions were carried out in Ga West in 2019, traders called for the president to discipline the chief executive or risk losing their votes in the 2020 general election. The chief executive claimed to not have known about the demolitions before they began. He told the press that he would never carry out a demolition while also running for MP in the area, an admission of how campaign incentives influence the timing of such demolitions.[127]

Martin Oteng-Ababio and Richard Grant describe this disjuncture between progressive policy positions in government documents and actions as a form of "hypocrisy."[128] However, they argue that this "hypocrisy" may not necessarily be bad, as the policy documents may act as a means of formulating and expressing planners' aspirations of the direction in which policy should go, even if they do not reflect present-day reality.

A tentatively positive development in recent years has been the creation of a ministry dedicated to issues of poor urban neighborhoods. The NPP government that took office in 2017 created a new Ministry of Inner-City and Zongo Development (MICZD), with the president pledging the equivalent of US$50 million to the associated Zongo Development Fund.[129] Many perceive the MICZD as a politically motivated initiative to allow the NPP to build bridges with Ghana's Muslims, with which it has had a difficult relationship over many decades.[130] The ministry has started to implement small projects in poor urban settlements, such as organizing waste collection drives and building sports facilities.[131] Whether the new ministry will be effective remains to be seen. Based on interviews conducted in early 2018, a year after the creation of the ministry, Colleen Brady and Michael Hooper found that *zongo* communities felt left out of the planning of the ministry's activities, and also that there was a mismatch between the kinds of interventions *zongo* residents and the ministry had in mind.[132]

In a national address in February 2019, President Akufo-Addo announced plans for the MICZD and the Ministry of Works and Housing to redevelop the low-income, Muslim-majority community of Nima, which he referred to as "Accra's first slum."[133] In May, the minister of works and housing elaborated on these plans. He explained that part of the 1,039-acre (1.6-square-mile, or 4.2-square-kilometer) area of Nima and neighboring Maamobi would be redeveloped into a "glamorous," "world-class residential enclave" for sale. Some of the revenue from the new development would be used to resettle the existing residents and build government offices on the remaining land, at no cost to the existing residents or the state.[134] Though Nima residents were in favor of redevelopment in principle, they were skeptical about whether the government would be able to get the community on board and implement the plans with no cost to the residents.[135] Little progress appears to have been made on the project since the initial announcements in mid-2019.

Other Organizations and Informality

A handful of nongovernmental and membership-based organizations have stepped in to help organize the informal sector and protect it from harassment from officials. Projects funded by international organizations are also active among the urban poor.

Community-Based Organizations

In response to an eviction notice in 2002, residents of Old Fadama sought the help of visiting leaders from the South African branch of Shack/Slum Dwellers International, the global network of community-based organizations active in informal settlements. With SDI's help, the residents of Old Fadama organized themselves into People's Dialogue on Human Settlements, which helped create savings groups and facilitated negotiations between the residents and authorities. In 2004, People's Dialogue helped create the Old Fadama Development Association, which performs tasks similar to that of local government (waste management, regulation of buildings, policing) while in other ways mimicking practices usually associated with traditional authorities, such as collecting discretionary contributions from residents.[136]

People's Dialogue has expanded beyond Old Fadama to form a national network, the Ghana Federation of the Urban Poor (GHAFUP). GHAFUP has worked with SDI on building public bathrooms and a hostel for the homeless, and with UN-Habitat on building a block of cooperative housing units.[137] In 2016, People's Dialogue, Cities Alliance, and the AMA worked together on the mapping exercise mentioned earlier, which mapped 265 slums across Greater Accra, recording numbers of residents, access to services, land tenure security, and other attributes.[138] GHAFUP is also active in Kumasi, Ashaiman, and Takoradi.

Unions and Associations

Informal street vendors in Ghana often belong to local associations, such as the Makola Market Traders Association, Oxford Street Vendors' Association, Circle Traders Association, and others, in Accra. These associations are intended to protect traders' right to space and prevent harassment by authorities.

They are organized under an umbrella organization called the Informal Hawkers and Vendors Association of Ghana.[139] Ghana's informal transportation system also consists of unions and associations, including the Ghana Private Road Transport Union, Progressive Transport Owners Association, and the Ghana Co-operative Transport Association.[140]

International Organizations

Various international organizations have been active in urban upgrading projects in informal settlements in Ghana. For example, the Urban Environmental Sanitation Programme, funded by the French Development Agency, the Nordic Development Fund, and the World Bank, was implemented in five cities in Ghana, including Accra and Kumasi, in the 1990s and 2000s. Its work involved stormwater management, urban sanitation, solid-waste management, community infrastructure development, and institutional strengthening. The United Nations' Slum Upgrading Facility was active in Kumasi from 2005 to 2009.[141] The UN-Habitat Participatory Slum Upgrading Programme conducted collaborative planning exercises and paved alleys in James Town in Accra. It also supported a community-driven housing project in Ashaiman. In 2020, during the COVID-19 pandemic, UN-Habitat provided handwashing facilities in three informal settlements in Greater Accra and employed women to make masks, soap, and hand sanitizer to help prevent the spread of the virus.[142]

Slum upgrading projects in Ghana have had mixed success. In the case of James Town, the AMA's failure to provide the counterpart funding to which it had committed delayed the project's progress.[143] A study of slum upgrading projects in Kumasi, most of which involved international donor funding, noted challenges arising from inadequate involvement of residents, lack of coordination, political interference, and overreliance on donor support.[144]

In 2016, Dutch consultants working for UN-Habitat drafted a "planned city extension" to accommodate 1.5 million people for the district of Ningo-Prampram on the eastern periphery of Greater Accra. This effort aimed to address "explosive unplanned urban sprawl in the Accra region, the need to accommodate flooding during peak rainfall, and the necessity to provide housing for all in Accra." Following a stakeholder consultation process, the district assembly approved the plan in July 2016.[145] However, implementation has apparently ceased since the member of Parliament driving the project lost his seat in the 2016 election.[146] Meanwhile, local residents have complained of people claiming to represent the UN-Habitat project trying to defraud landowners in Ningo-Prampram into selling their land.[147]

The World Bank's Greater Accra Climate Resilient and Integrated Development Project plans to spend US$200 million between 2019 and 2023 on activities mainly related to drainage and solid-waste management. Besides these activities, the project also aims to "increase access to services, infrastructure and housing in most vulnerable informal settlements within Greater Accra Region." One of the components of the project involves "strengthening capacity for planning, coordination, monitoring and evaluation," including "support for climate smart urban development planning, facilitating access to climate risk information . . . and improving planning and coordination between the Metropolitan, Municipal and District Assemblies in Greater Accra, Ministries, Departments and Agencies and other relevant stakeholders."[148] International organizations have implemented various other initiatives that directly or indirectly relate to urban informality and planning, involving financial support in the form of loans or grants amounting to several hundred million US dollars.[149]

The international organization most actively working with informal vendors in Accra is Women in Informal Employment: Globalizing and Organizing (WIEGO). Its activities promote occupational health and safety and strengthen the vendor associations' ability to provide welfare to its members. WIEGO also trains vendors in understanding the workings of government in order to help them engage and negotiate more effectively with the AMA and other municipal and national government bodies.[150] One of the successes of WIEGO's engagement has been the abolition of fees for informal "head porters" (*kayayei*) collected by the AMA task force.[151]

Ghana has a growing economy, a stable political environment, a supportive institutional and legislative framework, and significant infusions of aid money and technical support from international development organizations. Yet, urban planning in Ghana has failed to influence urbanization effectively. Informality is widespread, characterizing every aspect of urban life in Ghana. A range of government policies proclaim support for those working and living in informality, but official government actions toward the informal sector consist instead of neglect alternating with harsh evictions and demolitions. International and community-based organizations are active in Ghana's cities and have improved conditions in certain areas, but have made little impact on informal growth, which continues. Why have none of these efforts helped make planning in Ghana more effective? The following chapters explore this question.

CHAPTER 5

How Clientelism Undermines
Planning in Ghana

The chief planner of a newly created district had not been at her job for long when an application came across her desk. It sought permission for commercial construction on a site that was zoned as a public playground. She rejected the application, even though she knew that the applicant was close with the chief executive of the district. The chief executive had made it clear that he supported the application. When he heard of the planner's decision, he was upset. He had no patience for a planner who prioritized plans and regulations over his important political relationships. He complained to the national head office of the Town and Country Planning Department that he could not work with her, without providing any formal justification. She was removed from her role and reassigned to her previous district. She had no choice but to accept the decision. She knew that it would be useless to try to resist the will of a chief executive who, like all chief executives in Ghana, had been appointed by the president himself.

The incident just described is one of countless similar incidents that planners in Ghana face on a routine basis, in which political leaders interfere in planning decisions with their own short-term political interests in mind rather than the long-term interests of the city. This individual incident is not a particularly dramatic one, and it illustrates how little it takes for informal politics to undermine the effectiveness of planning. Planning agencies in Ghanaian cities do lack adequate funding and staff. However, informal politics, particularly the competitive clientelism that pervades politics at all levels, is the primary constraint to urban planning in Ghana. Politicians have a greater incentive to cultivate personalized relationships with urban

communities through the selective enforcement of regulations and the granting of favors than to implement plans in an objective, coordinated, and im-
partial manner. As a result, politicians frequently put pressure on planners
to support politically motivated decisions, undermining the effectiveness of
planning and of local government in general. This suggests that simply providing more resources and building technical capacity without also adapting planning practice to cope with this political environment would be
ineffective.

Local governments in Ghana have planning departments that are enabled by legislation to plan for and regulate urban growth, but, as I discussed
in the previous chapter, their impact is minimal. In this chapter, I explore
the reasons behind the moribund state of planning in Ghana. I start with
insufficient capacity and unsuitable plans and regulations, before moving
on to the impact of informal politics.

Capacity Constraints to Planning in Ghana

Low Technical and Financial Capacity

Planning authorities in Ghana lack both human and financial capacity.
Trained planners are in short supply in the country. Ghana had only an estimated 150 accredited planners in 2011, which amounted to just 0.6 planners
per 100,000 people. This compares poorly to the 12 accredited planners per
100,000 people in the United States, or the 38 planners per 100,000 in the
United Kingdom. However, Ghana lacks planners even by African standards.
A survey of a dozen African countries found that the average country had
just under 1 planner per 100,000 people. Nigeria had 1.4 planners per 100,000
people, and South Africa had 3.3.[1] Many of the planners I spoke to complained
of this lack of human resources. The planning director for the Ashanti region noted that there were only 20 qualified planners overseeing forty-three
local governments in the region, with some individual planners in charge of
up to five MMDAs.[2]

Local governments in Ghana also lack financial capacity. The gap between
the cost of the projects identified in the Accra Metropolitan Assembly's 2018–
21 Medium Term Development Plan and the funds that were expected to
be available for these projects is astonishing. The total cost of the projects
identified in the plan is over 4 billion Ghanaian cedis (US$700 million). The

expected revenue during this period, combining transfers from the national government, internally generated funds, and donor funds, is less than 300 million cedis (US$50 million), leaving a budgetary gap of 3.8 billion cedis (more than US$650 million) or 93%.[3] This budgetary shortfall is mentioned only briefly in the plan, in a section buried more than three hundred pages into a nine-hundred-page document. Nonetheless, it calls into question the seriousness of the entire development planning exercise and its proposal of hundreds of future projects.

Internally generated revenues from property tax, land rents, fees, licenses, and other sources make up only a small fraction of local government funds in Ghana: 4% by one estimate[4]; 12% by another.[5] This is higher for wealthier local governments. According to the 2018–21 Medium Term Development Plan of the AMA (which covers only a small, central portion of the Greater Accra metropolitan area), 74% of total revenue during the plan period was expected to be internally generated.[6] However, given the total budgetary shortfall, this still means that internally generated funds would cover only 5% of the estimated cost of implementing the plan. In 2011, property tax accounted for 27% of internally generated revenue in the AMA (the equivalent of 1.4% of the cost of the plan), an average of 16% in MMDAs in the Greater Accra Region, and 17% in Kumasi.[7] According to an act passed in 1992 and not revised since, local governments also have very limited borrowing capacity; they can only borrow up to 2,000 cedis (less than US$350 as of 2021).[8]

As a result, local governments in Ghana rely heavily on intergovernmental fiscal transfers from the national government, which make up two-thirds of their revenue.[9] The most important unconditional transfer to local governments is the District Assembly Common Fund (DACF). However, the national government unilaterally deducts large portions of the DACF (e.g., between 66% and 72% each year in 2012, 2013, and 2014) for its own purposes (a problem I discuss further in the next chapter). The disbursement of the remaining funds is irregular.[10] For example, DACF transfers for the second quarter of 2018 reached the AMA only in mid-2019, one full year later, while local government offices, unable to pay electricity bills, struggled to keep the lights on.[11]

Physical planning functions are particularly underfunded. Practically all the local government planners I spoke to listed the lack of financial resources as a major constraint in their work. Planners sometimes have to use their personal computers and cars for official business.[12] International donor organizations often fund the preparation of plans but rarely fund their implementation.[13] Planning authorities do have the power to raise some revenue through fees for permit applications and other activities, but most must deposit it in their city's general operating budget. The planning departments of Accra and Kumasi are the exception, as they can keep up to 15% of internally generated funds. However, this revenue-raising potential is inadequate: for example, in 2009, the AMA's planning authority generated an amount equivalent to only 10% of its annual expenditure.[14]

While lack of capacity may initially seem like a politically neutral issue, I demonstrate later in this chapter that this is not necessarily the case. Clientelistic politics interfere with intergovernmental fiscal transfers, divert resources, and give political leaders little incentive to build planning capacity.

Unsuitable Planning Practices

Physical planning in Ghana takes the form of rigid formal plans that do not suit the reality of informality and mixed land use in the country. In part, this is because planning education in Ghana relies on obsolete and unsuitable ideas from British town and country planning, as promulgated during the colonial era. Only in 2016 did the government replace planning regulations based on the Town and Country Planning Ordinance of 1945, modeled on British town planning law of the time, with the Land Use and Spatial Planning Act.

The public has limited opportunities to participate meaningfully in planning decisions.[15] Public participation occurs only indirectly, through the inclusion of invited representatives of stakeholder groups to meetings of the Spatial Planning Committee. The 2016 act aimed to address this shortcoming by requiring three rounds of consultation in the preparation of spatial development frameworks and local plans, accompanied by publication of plans in various venues. Many are optimistic about the ability of the 2016 act to encourage more bottom-up, participatory, and coordinated planning. Others are skeptical that a change in legislation will be transformative. Since the passage of the 2016 act, participation still occurs mostly through invited representation of stakeholder groups, who tend to accept the alternatives promoted by planners without full comprehension, according to Ransford Acheampong.[16] Even the physical planning director of the AMA does not believe that the new law has brought about much improvement in the situation.[17]

Physical planning authorities are responsible not just for preparing plans but also for enforcing development controls. Studies list several reasons for noncompliance with building regulations in Ghana. These include bureaucratic administrative processes, poor management, and inefficiency (e.g., permits take three to five years to obtain); the high cost of construction permits (up to 5% of the land value); the perception that planning officials are unhelpful and corrupt; restrictive, cumbersome, and outdated planning regulations; and lack of enforcement.[18]

Clearly, lack of planning capacity and unsuitability of plans are real constraints. Whether overcoming these constraints would be sufficient for planning to be effective, and whether it is even possible to overcome them in Ghana's environment of competitive clientelism, are the important questions.

Competitive Clientelism in Ghana

Planning in Ghana is pulled in many directions by political forces of precolonial, colonial, and postcolonial origin. These forces, in turn, are shaped by the country's history in complex ways. For example, traditional authorities are precolonial in origin, but their power was strengthened by colonial regimes that ruled the country indirectly through these authorities. They are also strengthened by the postcolonial constitution, which recognizes the power of traditional authorities over most of the land in the country. Formal town planning is of British colonial origin, but postcolonial governments retained colonial planning regulations well into the twenty-first century. The dominant force that has flourished in the postcolonial era, particularly since the democratic transition of the early 1990s, is the "competitive clientelism" that characterizes modern Ghanaian democracy. It, too, has roots in both traditional norms of customary leadership and patron-client relationships under British rule.[19] For these reasons, it is difficult to identify any present-day institution or practice with a specific era.

Urban planners and policymakers aiming to adapt planning practice to the political realities of a country, particularly one dominated by informality, might find the concept of a country's "political settlement" to be useful in characterizing the balance of powers in that country. (The word *settlement* in *political settlement* is used in the sense of agreement or arrangement rather than inhabitation, as in *informal settlement*.) An increasing number of researchers of the Global South apply the political settlements approach, first developed by institutional economist Mushtaq Khan,[20] to issues around urbanization,[21] land governance,[22] and international development policy.[23]

Ghana's political settlement is one of "competitive clientelism," in which the ruling coalition has weak implementation capabilities and strong competition. Bangladesh, India,[24] Kenya,[25] and Nigeria[26] are other examples of countries that have been characterized as having a competitive clientelistic political settlement. When clientelistic countries have too many factions to be included in a ruling coalition, and no one faction is strong enough to permanently exclude the others through legal or military means, the compromise reached is that of competitive clientelism. This involves sharing power through credible elections. This political settlement is more stable than a conflict situation and more inclusive than authoritarianism. However, it is typically characterized by low enforcement capacity and short time horizons. Although countries with clientelistic political settlements may have formal institutions such as courts, laws, and property rights, these institutions function differently—in a more personalized, informal manner—than they would in what Khan refers to as "advanced" countries.[27]

By contrast, Rwanda is an example of what the political settlements literature refers to as a "potential developmental" state, with strong implementation capabilities and weak competition. The lack of meaningful competition to the ruling party allows it to enforce regulations and make policies with long time horizons without having to appeal to excluded factions.[28] Tanzania is characterized as a "vulnerable authoritarian" political settlement, with high implementation capabilities but also high competition. Regimes in this situation use their power to repress and forcibly exclude opposition. The vulnerability of such regimes results in shorter time horizons.[29] Ethiopia today and India under the Congress Party in the 1950s and 1960s are examples of "weak dominant" political settlements, with weak implementation capabilities but also weak competition. Excluded factions are able to secure some redistribution. The regime's time horizons may be longer, but it does not have sufficient capacity to implement policies.[30]

International organizations such as the World Bank typically group countries by per capita income and geographic region and avoid characterizing countries by the type of political regime under which they operate. Yet a country's political settlement is arguably a more meaningful criterion with which to distinguish planning systems across countries than is geographic region or even income. For example, Vietnam and Indonesia are both lower-middle-income countries and are both in Southeast Asia, and they are grouped together for those reasons. However, the political environment of planning in Vietnam may have more in common with those of other single-party-dominated or otherwise nondemocratic states, such as Rwanda, Singapore, or the United Arab Emirates, than with Indonesia. Indonesia, as a clientelistic democracy, may be better compared to India or Ghana.

Agents of Competitive Clientelism in Ghanaian Cities

The principles of clientelism described in Chapter 1 apply to the delivery of urban land and services in Ghanaian cities today. Political patrons provide neighborhood-scale benefits in the form of infrastructure, services, and informal property rights in exchange for political support, in a manner that circumvents and undermines the formal planning system.

Many services that are demanded by urban voters in Ghana's informal settlements, including both private benefits, such as jobs and loans, and club goods, such as water pipes and schools, are what the political scientist Noah Nathan describes as "fundamentally targetable."[31] In a survey of voter preferences in Greater Accra, Nathan found that 64% of respondents demanded at least one club good (e.g., sanitation, water supply, or schools). This was higher than both the proportion of respondents who demanded at least one universalistic policy (55%) and the proportion that demanded at least one purely private good (53%).[32] Local politicians meet at least some this demand for club goods: Nathan's survey respondents recalled local politicians providing infrastructure such as roads and street lights (48%); sanitation, including drainage (23%); educational facilities (8%); water pipes, tanks, and boreholes (6%); and health facilities (6%).[33]

Several figures act as political patrons in the Ghanaian context, including chief executives of MMDAs (i.e., mayors) who belong to the incumbent political party, and (incumbent or aspiring) members of Parliament and district assemblies.

Political Parties

Both of Ghana's major political parties, the NDC and the NPP, engage in competitive clientelism, narrowly targeting benefits to specific groups in the

interest of winning or maintaining their loyalty. Electoral outcomes probably depend at least as much on clientelism as they do on promises of broader
policies and programs or ethnic loyalties. The NDC describes itself as more
socialist, whereas the NPP describes itself as center-right and probusiness.
However, analysis of their manifestos and policies has revealed them to be
ideologically incoherent or inconsistent. Moreover, 70% to 80% of the content of their election manifestos overlap and focus largely on "valence"
issues—that is, things which are indisputably desirable. In any case, surveys
find that the manifestos lack credibility among the public. This suggests that
the parties are not meaningfully distinguished by their broad programmatic
promises. The parties are not ethnically defined, but broad trends do exist in
the support for the parties among ethnic groups and their corresponding regions of origin. For example, the indigenous Ga of Accra, as well northern
migrants settled in Accra, have mostly supported the NDC, and the NPP has
been more popular among the Ashanti of Kumasi.[34]

Chief Executives

Appointed by the president, the metropolitan, municipal, or district chief executive (MMDCE, sometimes referred to as the mayor) is aligned with the
political party that is in power at the national level. The chief executive, who
chairs the Spatial Planning Committee, exerts heavy influence over planning
decisions. Yeboah and Obeng-Odoom explain that the chief executive is "the
single most powerful political person in the district" and that "his views on
planning issues can override professional planning decisions."[35] New chief
executives also routinely abandon incomplete projects initiated by their
predecessors.[36]

The chief executive is seen as the local representative of the president and
the ruling party, rather than as independently powerful. A former mayor refers to the position as the president's "viceroy in the city."[37] As a result, the
chief executive often faces political pressure from above, making him or
her unaccountable to the local public. A former president of the Ghana Institute of Planners, described chief executives as "toothless" and "powerless,"
"pawns" manipulated by national government officials and their political
agendas.[38]

During its 2016 campaign, the NPP promised a change to a system whereby
mayors would be locally elected rather than nominated by the president.
On winning the election, the NPP government took steps to implement

this change. Lawmakers placed a bill for a constitutional amendment to this effect before Parliament in February 2019. The bill passed, following which the public was to vote on the matter in a referendum in December 2019. The referendum was to pass if 75% of votes cast were in favor of the change, and if the turnout was at least 40% of eligible voters. If passed, the first chief executive elections would have taken place in June 2021.[39] The NDC opposed the change, possibly believing that a victory would boost the NPP's chances of reelection in the following year's general election. The president, apparently fearing the consequences for his reelection bid if the referendum were to fail,[40] abruptly canceled the referendum at the beginning of the month in which it was scheduled to take place.[41]

Many observers, including planners, were optimistic about the potential for this change to make mayors more accountable to the local electorate and allow them to take advice from planners,[42] as well as to make local governments more financially independent.[43] Mayoral candidates were to be allowed to affiliate with political parties, unlike locally elected assembly members. The hope was that the collective strength of opposition-party mayors would help create pressure on the incumbent party to deliver on promises, increasing accountability.[44] However, others cautioned against seeing this change as a magic bullet that would automatically make mayors more locally accountable. They expressed concern about the fiscal consequences of a local government's electing a mayor from a different party from the president's, given that local governments depend so heavily on fiscal transfers from the national government, which can withhold or delay these transfers.[45] An AMA planning officer pointed out that members of Parliament are already locally elected, and yet their behavior is not much different from appointed officials.[46] (I discuss how a move to locally elected mayors might affect clientelism in the next chapter.)

Unless the proposal to change the system is revived, the chief executive remains more of a conduit for patronage from his or her party rather than an independent patron. The exception is when an incumbent chief executive is also campaigning for an elected position in an upcoming election at the end of his or her tenure as chief executive. For example, a recent AMA chief executive campaigned, while in office, to become the member of Parliament for the Ablekuma South constituency in Accra. As a senior planner explained to me, "Eventually, about 60% or 70% of the resources of AMA was [directed] towards Ablekuma South—construction of drains, roads, and everything. And eventually he won, so he is now an MP!"[47]

Members of Parliament and District Assemblies

Members of Parliament in Ghana can be even more powerful than chief executives, but only if they belong to the nationally incumbent party. While MPs are nominally legislators, their power is felt mostly through their informal role as the de facto heads of the local branch of their party. In this role, they campaign on behalf of their party's presidential candidate and influence appointments and resource allocation in local government.[48]

MPs also often have their own "development apparatus" in parallel with the local government structure.[49] They use the MP's share of the DACF to implement small infrastructure projects for their constituents, like the construction of roads. At times, they may consult with local government planners and engineers on the details of these projects. For example, one planner recounted the case of an MP who specified an amount he was willing to spend on roads from his share of the DACF but let planners and engineers select their location.[50] However, MPs also use their influence to allow people to violate land use and building regulations.[51]

Clientelism is an established and seemingly accepted part of parliamentary elections in Ghana. A 2018 survey of three hundred parliamentary candidates found that 83% of them approved of the practice of rewarding loyal voters for their electoral support during a previous election.[52] Various kinds of private and club goods and services are provided through these personalized political channels. For example, during a campaign for MP of Odododiodio—the constituency in Accra that contains Old Fadama, Agbogbloshie, James Town, and other informal and indigenous settlements—a candidate provided private goods to households (jobs, school fees, loans, rice, clothes) and also promised to pave alleyways in the entire community if elected.[53] The setting of water tariffs has also become subject to political interference, with tariffs being set far below levels necessary for operation and maintenance, and increases being blocked during election campaigns.[54]

Mohammed Awal of the Ghana Center for Democratic Development (CDD-Ghana), himself a resident of Nima, the large *zongo* in Accra, explains that MPs and assembly members provide street lights, sanitation, drainage, and paved roads in his community. They often do so with their share of the

DACF, and are able to target such benefits based on close monitoring of the voting behavior of households. The small margins of victory in recent elections in Accra have forced politicians to compete for support from these communities, but this has not yet translated into the communities' organizing to make sustained demands for long-term public goods.[55]

Even if MPs do support long-term plans, the plans are often dropped when a new MP is elected. For example, Dutch consultants working for UN-Habitat drafted a "planned city extension" for the district of Ningo-Prampram on the eastern periphery of Greater Accra, and the district assembly approved the plan. However, implementation ceased once the MP driving the project lost his seat in the 2016 election.[56]

Local assembly members are less powerful than MPs, but they too can affect some local outcomes. This is partly through their use of the Electoral Area Fund set aside from the district budget. They use this for such private or club goods as streetlights and drainage. In his study of clientelism in urban Ghana, political scientist Jeffrey Paller recounts meeting an assembly member in Greater Accra who had purchased a stack of bulbs for street lights with his own money, so that the assembly could use them to replace ones that had gone out.[57] Candidates for local assemblies do not campaign on policies at all, relying entirely on clientelism and constituency service.[58] In interviews, planners explained the various ways that assembly members interfere in planning decisions: they oppose the demolition of buildings constructed in flood-prone areas, support construction without building permits (sometimes allegedly in exchange for bribes rather than just political support), and try to get planners to deny permits to applicants who do not support their party.[59]

Informal politics in Ghana does not consist simply of "vote buying" by politicians in an impersonal, purely instrumental quid pro quo manner before elections. The public views local leaders in Ghana as benefactors. Constituents expect them to channel private and public goods to them. Formal duties of elected officials in Ghana coexist with informal expectations of them. These expectations are often rooted in traditional notions of the leader as the head of family, with a moral responsibility to solve problems.[60] Paller describes these multiple informal leadership roles as "friend, entrepreneur, parent, [and] preacher."[61] These informal expectations create a mechanism of accountability for members of Parliament and district assemblies that is more present on a day-to-day basis than elections are. As Awal and Paller describe it: "Formal mechanisms of democratic accountability are seldom accessible for the poorest. But urban residents have found other ways to hold leaders to account that fit within informal networks and social norms."[62]

Impacts of Competitive Clientelism on Ghanaian Cities

The Impact of Competitive Clientelism on Local Government Capacity

Political leaders in a competitive clientelistic setting have a disincentive to build long-term, formal bureaucratic capacity in order to maintain the informal institutions that support their power.[63] A report commissioned by UK Aid and Cities Alliance argues that the economic impact of competitive clientelism in Ghana has been far-reaching, having "engendered institutions and practices that undermine meritocracy and administrative decentralization."[64] Similarly, Danial Appiah and Abdul-Gafaru Abdulai argue that competitive clientelism in Ghana "is central to understanding the country's limited success in improving the effectiveness of public institutions."[65] Even the AMA's 2018–21 Medium Term Development Plan mentions political interference as one of three key problems that Accra's local government faces in the implementation of projects.[66]

Nathan argues that in the context of Greater Accra, clientelism and low-quality urban governance are mutually reinforcing, acting as a vicious circle or "trap."[67] The state's inability to deliver universal urban services leads voters who prefer programmatic policies, primarily the urban middle class, to disengage from political participation in frustration. (In terms of Albert Hirschman's classic model, they choose "exit" over "voice."[68]) This allows politicians to ignore their preferences at no political cost and focus on those voters who seek particularistic benefits. Narrow interest groups can then capture local governments, allocate limited state resources in an inefficient and unequal manner, and neglect investment in state capacity. This reinforces the belief that politicians are unable to deliver urban programmatic policies, further causing disengagement from voters with programmatic preferences. This is especially the case for those who can afford to pay for private services. For example, many households supplement unreliable piped water supply with drinking water from bottles or sachets, and water for other uses from private tanker trucks.[69] Between a quarter and a third of primary school enrollment in Greater Accra and Kumasi is in private schools.[70] This middle-class "exit" further allows politicians to focus on clientelism. In other words, clientelism not only undermines state capacity in urban Ghana but also removes the electoral incentives to build state capacity.

Competitive clientelism also depletes local governments' fiscal capacity. Political interference in the collection of property tax and other revenues undermines local governments' ability to raise their own funds.[71] This leads them to rely heavily on intergovernmental fiscal transfers from national governments. However, clientelism also complicates these transfers, in the form of another vicious cycle. During election campaigns, the national political parties promise to deliver, as "priority projects," the urban services that local governments have been unable to provide. Once in office, the winning party then takes money out of the DACF to fulfill these promises, which undermines local decision-making and implementation. This makes it all the more difficult for local governments to provide these services, further increasing the need for national parties to step in. In 2012 and 2013, between 65% and 75% of the DACF allocations were withheld by the national government and by MPs to fund their own priority projects.[72] The national government can also withhold or delay the release of the MPs' share of the DACF to MPs who belong to other parties.[73]

This politicization of fiscal transfers leads to the use of the DACF for projects that do not conform to the Medium Term Development Plan, especially in election years.[74] For example, municipalities sometimes give funds from the municipal budget as "donations" to electorally important communities or chiefs during festivals.[75]

Competitive clientelism requires some formal institutions (e.g., elections, political parties, intergovernmental fiscal transfers) to continue to exist as vehicles for patronage. It, therefore, props up these institutions, like a parasite that needs its host to remain alive. At the same time, it could not operate in a fully formal environment, so it also prevents formal institutions that would threaten competitive clientelism from flourishing. It is the coexistence of these formal and informal elements of urban governance that sustains the current equilibrium in Ghana.

The Impact of Competitive Clientelism on Planning

Government officials in Ghana readily acknowledge that politicians resist the strict enforcement of plans among electorally important groups. In my conversations with them, local planners and other government officials at all levels—for example, a former mayor, a senior advisor in the Ministry of Inner-City and Zongo Development, and the director of the Ga Mashie Development Agency—all accepted that this is the case.[76] Politicians in Ghana routinely interfere in planning decisions for short-term electoral gain. Clifford Amoako, a professor of planning at Kwame Nkrumah University of Science and Technology in Kumasi, refers to this phenomenon as a "war against ethical planning" in Ghana.[77]

Nearly all the planners I spoke to readily related examples of political pressure they have faced in their own careers to take actions that they believed to be detrimental to the public interest. These actions tended to involve rezoning or ignoring zoning violations in environmentally or culturally sensitive areas (e.g., waterways, forests, flood-prone areas, cemeteries) or on land reserved for public space (e.g., streets, playgrounds) in order to allow private development of some kind.

Such private development may be in the form of middle-class residential neighborhoods or commercial establishments, which are often as "informal" in terms of the violation of regulations as low-income neighborhoods. One experienced planner in Accra described urban growth as a "free-for-all," explaining that if landowners or developers wish to start a new residential community somewhere beyond the urban fringe, in violation of existing plans, they can do it as long as they have political connections.[78] Traditional authorities often allocate land to middle-class settlers, regardless of whether the traditional authorities legally control that land (see the next chapter). Local governments often paint warning notices on structures that lack permits, prompting the owners to seek the help of politically and socially influential "big men" who intervene to allow the developments to remain.[79] Middle-class settlers may also use their relationships with influential actors to obtain piped water connections from the Ghana Water Company Limited. They then use the provision of such services as evidence that the state considers the settlement legitimate.[80]

However, even if informal politics is not restricted to low-income settlements, such settlements are the ones most likely to be affected by it. They present political patrons with large, dense communities that are vulnerable and have material needs that are easily met. Residents of these communities also vote in larger numbers, because their survival depends on it. In the words of a planner interviewed by Yeboah and Obeng-Odoom: "A nicely planned neighborhood does not vote but people who live in unapproved developments do."[81]

Low-income settlements in urban Ghana may be indigenous neighbor-hoods or migrant settlements built on land purchased from indigenous chiefs. The government views these settlements as legitimate. By contrast, they may be squatter settlements, which neither traditional nor state authorities consider legitimate. Clientelism may operate in any of these types of settlements, at least in theory.[82] Clientelistic provision of land through noneviction is more pertinent to squatter settlements, at least on a large scale. However, even in indigenous settlement or a settlement built on purchased land, politicians may "provide" land by not enforcing land use and building regulations, or by tolerating construction on public or unsafe land. The provision of urban services and infrastructure in any of these types of settlements may also rely on clientelism.

The fact that the demolition of informal settlements appears to occur along party lines demonstrates the importance of clientelism to their survival. For example, in 2009, the AMA announced plans to demolish two informal settlements in Accra. Residents of the first settlement, Old Fadama, primarily supported the incumbent party. They protested and threatened to defect to the opposition. In response, the president called off the demolition, saying, "When we are working to improve the economy, it is not proper for us to treat our people in this manner."[83] Residents of the other settlement, who tended to support the opposition party, also protested and called for the president to intervene. In their case, the demolitions continued as planned.[84] (In Chapter 7, I further explore the role of clientelism in perpetuating the existence, but also the vulnerability, of Old Fadama.)

Chief executives sometimes force planners to change the location of planned facilities based on electoral calculations rather than need. As a planner in the Land Use and Spatial Planning Authority's national headquarters explained:

> When [local planners] want to site a school or a health facility, the district chief executive will say: "No, I do not want it here; I want it located here." So, in the end, where they site it becomes problematic. People are not able to access these facilities, and they become a waste of resources. . . . [T]hey make the plans sometimes ineffective or useless. . . . [Politicians do this] based on where they think they will get their votes, or where most people voted for them. They will prefer to site those things there, even when those locations have an abundance of those facilities. . . . [W]here they go against the plans that have been made, it's mainly for getting more votes.[85]

Why do planners have to go along with these politically motivated decisions? Planners are career civil servants and not officially political appointees, which means that, in theory, they should be insulated from politics. However, politicians at the local level, with the help of their party colleagues at national ministries, can easily derail the careers of planners who do not cooperate with politically motivated decisions. The use of transfers of this sort as a tool for political control over bureaucrats is common in other developing democracies as well (e.g., India[86] and Indonesia[87]). The ever-present threat of a transfer to an undesirable post acts as a mechanism by which politicians discipline planners. "It is very difficult for you to challenge [the chief executive], because if you are not careful, he will change your destiny," said one senior planner.[88] To avoid getting transferred, planners have to "tread carefully" when working with chief executives, another planner explained.[89]

The threat of an undesirable transfer is sometimes made explicit, but it does not have to be. The frequency with which the possibility of such a transfer came up in my conversations with planners suggests that it is a constant concern. Planners were quick to recall instances in which they or others they knew were transferred or threatened with a transfer, such as the one that opens this chapter. Another planner mentioned the story of a municipal engineer who was transferred to the Western Region because he was "becoming too powerful."[90] Another mentioned that a chief executive who had fought with a municipal employee in another department was now threatening him with a transfer to the Northern Region, and that the employee was considering resigning.[91] Yet another planner recalled that the previous chief executive of his district had threatened the former planning director with a transfer because he had resisted approving an application to rezone a portion of a cemetery to allow development.[92]

Such a transfer may not be immediate, and when it comes, the planner is not officially given an explanation. Being branded among the ruling party as a supporter of the opposition, or simply as "difficult to work with" or "no good," damages a planner's professional reputation and has a detrimental effect on the planner's career.[93] Not only do transfers to remote rural districts derail planners' careers, but they also cause disruption for their families.[94]

Ghana's atmosphere of competitive clientelism has undermined its state institutions, including urban planning, such that short-term political interests determine urban decision-making. At times, clientelism has helped some politically important informal settlements to escape demolition. However, it has not delivered long-term benefits and has deepened the dependency of the poor on political patronage. Planners cannot openly defy politically motivated decisions from politicians, out of fear of retaliation that would derail their careers.

The political dynamics outlined in this chapter are not the only ones that affect urban growth and planning. The role of traditional authorities, the subdivision of local government jurisdictions into ever-smaller areas, inefficient decentralization, corruption, and land-based violence all shape Ghana's cities and the ability of planners to influence urban growth. However, all these seemingly disparate factors can be traced back to clientelism, at least partially, as I explain in the next chapter.

CHAPTER 6

Chiefs, Thugs, and Boundaries: Other Political Constraints to Planning in Ghana

*I*t was nighttime in the suburban town on the western fringes of Accra when the town's planner heard something crash into the front door of his house. It sounded like a group of men were trying to break down his door with a cement block. It wasn't the first time this had happened.

The first time, a few months earlier, the intruders had been unable to break through the burglar-proof door. The planner's wife, who spoke the local dialect, had pleaded with the intruders through the door to leave them alone. Finally, they had left with a warning to the planner to "stay away." The planner had moved away with his family to stay with relatives in central Accra for a few months, returning when he felt the danger had passed.

No one had tried to break in again while he had been away. Now that he was back, the intruders were back too. He didn't know exactly who was behind the intrusions, but he had his suspicions. He had been a thorn in the side of powerful local interests who had been building structures in access roads and on sites meant for schools and parks. When he had refused to play along, he knew they would not leave him in peace.

This time, the burglar-proof door didn't seem like it could hold against what sounded like ten men outside. The planner's family hid in a bathroom. The planner phoned his neighbor, a soldier who kept firearms at home. The neighbor fired a gun, and the intruders fled. The planner could not allow his wife and children to be traumatized this way any longer. Local friends had advised him against any attempts to get justice through formal channels. Crooked police officers would thwart the investigation and tip off the people who were behind the intrusions. He had no choice but to leave town and not return. Ever

since then, he has been unable to sleep soundly. "It was my worst nightmare,"
he recalls.

Not all the challenges to planning in Ghana are caused by clientelism. Planners also face several other institutional, administrative, and practical constraints. These are not all directly related to an exchange of benefits for political support, but they are also political in nature. Privately hired thugs use violence to prevent authorities from applying planning regulations, as the incident just described illustrates. Traditional authorities distribute land with no regard for the city's land use plans. The proliferation of new local government units exacerbates the shortage of planning staff and makes metropolitan coordination more difficult. National agencies withhold autonomy from local governments, while simultaneously decentralizing planning staff in a way that makes them vulnerable to local political control. Corruption abounds. While this may seem like a litany of unrelated woes, I try to demonstrate in this chapter that the clientelistic politics of Ghana either partially cause or intensify each of these other challenges.

The Power of Traditional Authorities over Urban Land

Scholars once expected customary practices and indigenous social institutions in Africa to fade with the advent of state institutions, economic modernization, and urbanization. Instead, the customary and the modern now intertwine and coevolve in complex ways across the continent. The institution of traditional chieftaincy in Ghana may be precolonial in origin, but the British reshaped it during the colonial period as a means of supporting indirect rule. The British referred to the Gold Coast, as Ghana was then known, as a "colony," but it was arguably more a protectorate. Not only did the British never settle there in large numbers, they also ruled it through existing local authorities who never gave up their power.[1] Chiefs in Ghana under British rule were able to become less accountable to their communities and more predatory and self-serving than they had been in precolonial times.[2] In countries that were never colonized, such as Ethiopia, customary practices simply became codified into state law. By contrast, in Ghana, colonization permanently enshrined "legal pluralism," with competing factions making claims through different systems.[3] This competition between the

state's authority and traditional sources of authority is one reason it is difficult to understand the political landscape of many African cities through the
lens of urban theory imported from the Global North.[4]

The Ghanaian constitution recognizes the customary authority of traditional chiefs over 80% of land in the country.[5] The customary land controlled
by chiefs is known as *stool land* in most of Ghana and *skin land* in the North.
These terms refer to the ornamental stools and animal skins that are traditional symbols of the authority of chiefs (like *crown land* in the United Kingdom refers to its sovereign's ornamental headdress.) Customary land in
Accra constitutes 78% of land in the city and belongs either to Ga chiefs (stool
land) or to Ga families represented by family heads to whom chiefs have allocated land (family land). Land in and around Kumasi, the capital of the historic Ashanti kingdom and present-day Ashanti Region, belongs to chiefs
who are all subordinate to the Asantehene (Ashanti king). The Asantehene's
land secretariat manages stool lands, which make up 81% of the land around
Kumasi.[6]

Customary land tenure remains a powerful force in shaping urban growth
in urban Ghana. According to the constitution, chiefs hold land in trust for
their people. The land is not meant for sale but rather to be used and passed
down by the community. However, in urban and peri-urban areas with increasing land values, chiefs have commodified customary land. Households
seeking a chief's approval to settle on stool land traditionally pay their re-
spects to the chief in the form of "drink money." In the past, this amount
was equivalent to the price of a "few bottles of imported schnapps," but it is
now effectively the market price of the land.[7] The constitution dictates that
55% of the revenue from stool lands must be given to the local government,
with the rest divided between the chief and the stool elders. However, since
stool-land transactions are not a matter of public record, the amounts actually paid are impossible to determine.[8]

Chiefs often treat this money as private wealth, which means that the stool
land is effectively their private property to sell for personal enrichment. In
some cases, chiefs even go to the extent of officially registering land in their
own name as personal property.[9] Chiefs are also involved in fraudulent land
sales, reselling land that the state has previously acquired. This sometimes
results in the state's having to repurchase land that it has already acquired
once. Chiefs also sell land that plans have set aside for waterways, roads, or
public space.[10] A former Accra Metropolitan Assembly official I spoke to

related the example of an area known as Lavender Hill in Accra, which the state had acquired in 1908. The AMA recently had to pay a local chief again in order to use Lavender Hill for a sewage management project funded by the Danish government.[11]

The nature of interactions between chiefs and planners in the Greater Accra region can vary. Though chiefs are supposed to be on the spatial planning committees of metropolitan, municipal, and district assemblies (MMDAs), they may or may not participate in planning meetings.[12] Planners sometimes have cooperative relationships with chiefs. For example, a few planners told me of instances in which chiefs have invited them to help plan their land.[13] At other times, chiefs have helped communicate information from planners to their communities, including conveying the need for relocation of informal structures.[14]

However, cooperation between chiefs and planners may be the exception rather than the rule. Chiefs often subdivide and allocate stool land without regard for any extant land use plans and without coordination between adjacent subdivisions.[15] They frequently employ unlicensed ("quack") surveyors to prepare subdivision plans. In these subdivision plans, parcels often are smaller than the legal minimum, do not have adequate street access, or are used for purposes not permitted by the local plan.[16] This practice means there is little opportunity for public input into decisions about land use.[17]

Chiefs believe that they alone, rather than planners, have the right to make decisions about the land in their custody.[18] Cobbinah and Darkwah quote a traditional leader as saying, "The land is ours. We are the traditional custodians. . . . Nobody can develop our land without our consent, not even the government. If the planning people want to plan our community or land, they should contact us first and seek our approval."[19] Many believe that land acquired from chiefs is not subject to planning laws at all.[20]

Beyond their role in subdividing and allocating land, chiefs also play a facilitating role in arranging the provision of services to newly subdivided peri-urban stool land. Depending on the needs of a settlement, a chief may persuade the utility companies to extend water and electrical connections to new settlers. They may also negotiate with judges, police officers, and municipal agencies, including the planning agency, to legitimize the new settlement.[21]

Traditional authorities in indigenous settlements, such as Ga Mashie, have an incentive to keep residents' property rights ambiguous in order to benefit personally.[22] They also use their authority to demand public services (public toilets, roads, drainage systems, streetlights, schools, markets) from the state on behalf of residents. Paller describes this as a form of patron-client relationship.[23] However, these public services are usually unequally distributed, disproportionally benefiting a small number of families. As with clientelism in nonindigenous squatter settlements, this informal channel of service delivery undermines formal regulations and institutions, including planning.

The role of traditional authorities in planning in the Ashanti region, including Kumasi, is different from in the rest of the country. There, all chiefs are subordinate to the Asantehene and, for all practical purposes, so is the state. In some ways, this clear hierarchy facilitates cooperation and coordination.[24] Chiefs in Kumasi actively participate in planning meetings and in the preparation of spatial development frameworks, and they sometimes donate the land necessary for the implementation of plans.[25] The Asantehene need not consult planners before making a decision relevant to planning,[26] but once he has made it, planners face little resistance in its implementation.[27] The current Asantehene encourages chiefs to prepare subdivision plans and submit them to the customary land secretariat, which reduces land disputes. He then leases out his own land in accordance with existing plans.[28] He even punishes subordinate chiefs who engage in the kind of duplicate sales of land that are common in the rest of Ghana, sometimes with "destoolment" (removal from their position).[29] Low-income migrant settlements in Kumasi were often formed with permission from the Asantehene and thus are not as contested as squatter settlements in Accra.[30]

Chiefs in Ghana are seen as too powerful to be challenged and reprimanded by state authorities. "If a chief sells the land, nobody can touch the chief," a former AMA official explained to me.[31] This may be partly down to traditional norms of respect, but it also goes back partly to competitive clientelism. Chiefs influence how their communities vote, and political leaders dare not risk antagonizing them for fear of losing votes.[32]

At other times, however, the power of traditional authorities comes into conflict with the force of competitive clientelism. Traditional Ga leaders complain that the continued existence of the Old Fadama informal settlement in Accra has destroyed the natural ecology of the area and is an affront to their customary authority over the land.[33] Yet, as I discuss further in the next chapter, the settlement's strength as a voting bloc means that it is hard to remove. This indicates the limits of traditional authorities' control over land if a population of informal settlers is large enough to reshape political incentives in its favor.

Administrative Fragmentation

In recent years, successive governments in Ghana have carved more than a hundred new MMDAs out of existing ones. This is in keeping with a trend observed in several other African and Asian countries since the 1990s.[34] In Ghana, the proliferation of local government units has accelerated since the mid-2000s. The total number of MMDAs in Ghana increased from 138 in 2004 to 260 in 2019. This means that nearly half the local governments in the country date from that fifteen-year period.

The Greater Accra metropolitan area had just three local governments until 2004, when the government created a fourth. It created four more in 2008, and another four in 2012, increasing the total to twelve.[35] In 2019, the government carved yet more districts out of the already much-diminished AMA jurisdiction. These include areas close to the city center, leading the AMA jurisdiction to shrink from 137 square kilometers to just 23 square kilometers.[36] For example, the economically important commercial area of Osu in the heart of the city is no longer within the AMA but in the newly created Osu-Klottey district. The government has also split up Kumasi, with five out of its former total of nine subdistricts now new MMDAs.[37]

In theory, the need for effective decentralization and proximity to government resources during a period of rapid population growth may justify the creation of so many new local governments. The increase in the number of MMDAs has, in fact, kept pace with the increase in population. The population per local government is not much lower today than it was in 1988 (Table 2). The government has argued that the need "to facilitate development"[38] and "bring development closer to the people" motivates the creation of new districts.[39] It describes the creation of the latest round of new districts in Accra as a way to facilitate better urban management. In 2019, the deputy local government minister argued that the AMA was struggling to cater effectively to its large population with the transfers it received via the District Assembly Common Fund and the revenues it was able to raise locally. The large subdistricts within the AMA, according to the minister, had no ability to raise their own revenues or operate effectively from their "two-

Table 2.   Local governments and population in Ghana

Year	No. of local governments	National population	Population per local government[5]
1988	110[1]	13,854,214[3]	125,947
2004	138[1]	20,986,536[3]	152,076
2008	170[1]	23,298,640[3]	137,051
2012	216[1]	25,733,049[3]	119,134
2019	260[2]	30,280,811[4]	116,465

Sources: (1) Owusu, "Decentralized Development Planning and Fragmentation of Metro-politan Regions," 7; (2) GhanaWeb, "Government to Inaugurate Six New Districts Today"; (3) United Nations World Population Prospects, via World Bank Open Data (data .worldbank.org); (4) Ghana Statistical Service (statsghana.gov.gh); and (5) author's calculations.

roomed" subdistrict offices. Once elevated to municipalities, he explained, they would have "all the powers of a municipal assembly to have their sub-committees, raise revenue, manage and plan development and get the city in a better shape."[40]

However, geographer George Owusu casts doubt on the notion that the creation of new districts in Ghana is simply an objective exercise in keeping up with population growth. He points out that, in 2010, thirty-one districts did not even meet the minimum population requirements for their category of local government (metropolitan, municipal, or district assembly). Instead, Owusu attributes the creation of this large number of new MMDAs to two distinct political motivations.[41] First, creating new MMDAs allows the incum-bent party to engage in gerrymandering by indirectly creating new electoral constituencies. The incumbent political party can benefit from the creation of certain new electoral constituencies, which could increase its number of seats in Parliament. However, while the constitution does not allow a president to create new constituencies (only the Election Commission can), the president can create new MMDAs at any time. Since a parliamentary constituency cannot straddle two MMDAs, the creation of new MMDAs automatically necessitates the creation of new constituencies, which means that the process can be manipulated for electoral gain. Owusu bolsters this argument by pointing out that the recent increase in political competition between the two major parties has coincided with a sharp increase in the creation of new MMDAs. Whenever either the NPP or NDC has created new MMDAs when in power, the opposition party has objected.

The second political motivation for creating new MMDAs, according to Owusu, is to increase the number of chief executive positions to which an incoming president can appoint loyalists in the form of patronage jobs. (This is consistent with a study of Uganda that found that of all the theoretical explanations for the proliferation of new local government units there, the creation of patronage jobs was the most plausible.[42]) In these ways, the proliferation of new local governments is motivated at least in part by Ghana's politics.[43]

The creation of new MMDAs in this manner has debilitating effects on urban planning and management. The government does not consult planners in the creation of new districts, which means that planners cannot take such new districts into account in future planning. A regulation in the original draft bill of the Land Use and Spatial Planning Act of 2016 stated that planners and statisticians had to be consulted before the creation of new districts, but allegedly, Parliament removed this regulation to allow the process to be controlled by political parties.[44] Metropolitan coordination mechanisms are weak, and administrative fragmentation of contiguous urbanized areas makes it even more difficult to plan. The creation of new districts leads to boundary disputes between neighboring jurisdictions, which exacerbates this problem.[45] The dearth of planning staff in Ghana means that the more MMDAs there are in total, the more there are that do not have any trained local planning staff. In interviews, some local planning staff expressed frustration that their teams were being broken up in order to transfer staff to newly created MMDAs. As of mid-2019, only six out of the ten districts that were previously part of AMA had planners on staff.[46] Contrary to government statements, administrative fragmentation of urban areas may make it harder, not easier, for some local governments to be fiscally self-sufficient. This would increase their reliance on transfers from the national government.

For these reasons, like the power of traditional authorities over land, administrative fragmentation initially seems unrelated to politics. However, it too turns out to be supported by political incentives and interferes with planning.

Inefficient Decentralization

Decentralization in Ghana was an extension of the Economic Recovery Program initiated by the World Bank and IMF in 1983. The district assembly system was put in place in 1989, and the 1992 constitution mandated the devolution of power and resources to local governments. Ghana's current level of decentralization interferes with urban planning and management in two ways. The partial nature of decentralization means that national agencies and politicians continue to dominate urban decision-making. Meanwhile, the ways in which the country has decentralized its planning staff has made them more vulnerable to local politics than before.

Lack of Decentralization

The incomplete nature of decentralization in Ghana is evident in many aspects of local governance. Local governments lack own-source revenue and must rely heavily on intergovernmental transfers from the national government. Chief executives, who are appointed by the president, face pressure to enact their national party's political agenda rather than determine local priorities in response to local demands. Fragmentation of metropolitan areas into increasing numbers of MMDAs, driven by national politics, reduces the ability of local governments to plan the delivery of key services that require metropolitan-scale solutions.

The important role played by MPs, as opposed to district assembly members, in everyday problem-solving in Ghana is further evidence of the importance of national-level actors over local ones. In a 2019 survey, more than 60% of respondents in both the low-income Odododiodio and wealthy Ayawaso West constituencies of Accra stated that the first person they would contact about a borehole, school, or road would be their MP, compared to fewer than 20% who said that they would first contact their district assembly member.[47]

Various national agencies also continue to play a major role in urban outcomes. The national utility companies, Ghana Water Company Limited and Electricity Company of Ghana, provide connections to new settlements regardless of whether they conform to a local spatial plan. This is often done under the direction of politicians who use utility connections as a form of patronage, but it is also sometimes simply a way to increase revenue.[48] The Ministry of Inner-City and Zongo Development is another example of a national agency that is directly involved in urban affairs.

The national government also maintains control over certain large contracts for urban services. For example, the Ministry of Local Government and Rural Development awarded a solid-waste management contract to a company named Zoomlion Ghana Limited, through an apparently noncompetitive process. The national government deducts funds for these services, including capital equipment, from local government transfers without sharing any information on the actual costs of the services or equipment.[49] Even the AMA's 2018–21 Medium Term Development Plan alleges that "a large chunk of the Assembly's internally generated revenues which should have been used to implement other projects was used to pay its waste management contractors."[50] This lack of competition and transparency seems designed to enable corruption (and, in fact, the World Bank has previously debarred Zoomlion Ghana Limited for engaging in bribery in Liberia[51]). From a decentralization point of view, this desire to maintain control over lucrative contracts reduces the ability of local governments to make their own decisions.

Similarly, the Ministry of Tourism, Arts and Culture, and not the local or regional planning authority, leads the large Marine Drive project mentioned in Chapter 4. Neither the AMA's nine-hundred-page Medium Term Development Plan for 2018–21 nor the Greater Accra Regional Spatial Development Framework even mentions this transformative project once, despite the project's scale and prominence as well as the involvement of the AMA's physical planning department in the project. This is evidence of the disjuncture between national and local planning processes.[52] These examples suggest that national agencies and officials have not relinquished substantial decision-making power to local governments and in various ways continue to undermine the control of local planners over their jurisdictions.

Decentralization of Planning Staff

Local planners express frustration at the decentralization of their positions. In 2019, the government transferred physical planners who were working in local governments from the national Civil Service to the Local Government Service, with their positions being placed under the Department of Parks and Gardens. (The transfer to the Department of Parks and Gardens appears to be only be notional for now. One planner remarked that the director of parks and gardens did not even know where the physical planning department's office was located.)

Decentralization has reduced some of the oversight that the national and regional branches of the Land Use and Spatial Planning Authority formerly had over local planning. For example, plans at the local government level no longer have to be submitted to these bodies. However, the more significant impact is on the employment status of planners. In the past, they were able to appeal to LUSPA's regional or national bodies on matters relating to their employment. However, the change has orphaned them in terms of human resources, giving local leaders more control over employment decisions. Before this change, planners tended to move back and forth between local, regional, and national posts within the LUSPA system. Now that planners in local government belong to the Local Government Service, they can no longer move to higher levels. Most alarmingly for planners, they expect to have to reapply for their jobs in local government following this change.

Several of the planners I spoke to expressed concerns that, in an environment where planners are already subject to pressure and interference from local politicians, the increased control of local authorities over the employment of planners will result in the further politicization of planning. Local politicians will now be able to install loyalists in planning positions and retaliate with impunity against planners who resist political decisions. Physical planners noted that departments that have always been decentralized, such as development planning or public works, are much more politicized than physical planning has been in the past. One planner believed that the change was a deliberate attempt to reduce the power of technocrats.

Corruption

Unsurprisingly, urban planning and service delivery are undermined not only for political gain but also for financial gain. Corruption is not perceived to be as rampant in Ghana as in many other countries in the Global South. Transparency International's Corruption Perceptions Index 2020 ranks Ghana 75th out of 180 countries around the world (with the least corrupt country ranked first and the most corrupt ranked 180th). This suggests that it is perceived as being less corrupt than, for example, Brazil, China, India, Indonesia, Kenya, Mexico, Nigeria, and other countries.[53] Nonetheless, corruption is a feature of many facets of urban life in Ghana. There are indications of corrupt practices in the award of service contracts, such as for waste management (as previously discussed) and water.[54] Most contracts for the operation of fee-charging public toilets are in the hands of assembly members or front companies controlled by them.[55] It is common for applicants to pay bribes to Lands Commission officials handling land permits to "speed up" the process on their behalf.[56] Land acquired by the state supposedly for

public use is sometimes leased to developers for high-end private developments instead.[57]

As an example of how corruption affects planning, planners I spoke with
related a 2012 incident in the city of Takoradi. Developers wanted to build
commercial establishments on land that was zoned for open space.[58] The chief
executive and ministers from a national ministry had allegedly been promised some of the land in exchange for their assistance in getting the necessary approvals. These figures put pressure on the local planner, who had no
choice but to rezone the area to allow the development.

Gillespie quotes an officer in the Lands Commission, who explains: "The
public lands in Ghana are controlled by the politicians. That is a fact I am
telling you. If you want a government land and you don't know any politicians in Ghana or you are not linked to the ruling party, forget it, you will
never get it. . . . Most of these lands are owned by the politicians and their
friends, and they use their companies to take the lands."[59]

Corruption among politicians and other public officials may at first glance
seem distinct from clientelism. However, Ghana's competitive clientelistic
politics support and perpetuate corruption, in two ways. First, lucrative public contracts for services and public positions in which an official can manipulate procurement have become a form of patronage with which local and
national politicians can reward loyalists. The president alone can directly appoint four thousand individuals in the country, including chief executives
and heads of various state agencies.[60] As a result, when a new party takes over
after winning an election, the incoming party replaces personnel at all levels
with loyalists. This includes a range of appointees, from the board and senior management of the Ghana Water Company Limited to the operators of
public toilets in informal settlements.[61] Allowing these posts to be used as venues for personal enrichment adds to their value as a currency of patronage.

Second, corruption is a way to offset the expense of elections, including
the costs associated with providing patronage. Elections in Ghana are increasingly expensive, with a 90% increase in average expenditure per candidate in parliamentary campaigns between the 2012 and 2016 elections alone.
Adding the cost of party primaries, the average expenditure per candidate is
equivalent to two years of an MP's salary.[62] Candidates get limited financial
support from their parties and mostly have to spend their own money to provide the kinds of clientelistic benefits that are expected of them. These include not just the public services already described but also private ones, such
as school fees, donations to religious organizations, and funds for commu-

nity events. Candidates can only provide these services if the office comes with opportunities to recoup some of the expense.[63]

Some allege that while planners may portray themselves as manipulated or pressured by politicians, the planners themselves may be complicit in corruption. Corruption among planners is beyond the scope of this study, but they do sometimes accept bribes from developers, landowners, and traditional authorities to modify plans.[64] In addition, intentional ambiguity in application fees for planning permits enables corruption in planning. Planning departments are allowed to recover some of their operating expenses through application fees. However, in the absence of a specified fee schedule, an applicant is never sure what part of the payment demanded goes toward operating expenses of the planning office and how much officials pocket for themselves. Planning officers allegedly expect applicants to arrange for their transportation to sites under consideration and to pay for refreshments for planning meetings at which applications are evaluated. Planners may even refuse to process an application without further monetary inducements.[65]

Violence and Intimidation Around Land

Chapter 4 introduced "land guards," armed gangs hired by those who own or control land to ward off prospective encroachers, prospective buyers and sellers, private surveyors, and even government officials through violence and intimidation. Land guards are typically hired by chiefs or families involved in land disputes, but at times state institutions hire them too. Land guards are particularly prevalent on the fringes of cities, where land is valuable but not yet developed.

In interviews, several planners raised the presence of land guards as a challenge. The anecdote that opens this chapter is a particularly egregious example of a planner being threatened with violence. Two other planners told me that land guards had prevented them from inspecting a site in order to evaluate a permit application. One of them recalled visiting a site where construction was occurring on a road reservation and being told by the land guards to leave if she valued her life. Planners also related a recent case in which land guards physically assaulted a planner. Land guards sometimes leave if a planner arrives on site with a police officer, but police officers may themselves be corrupt or have personal associations with landowners and so cannot always be relied on to provide protection from land guards.[66]

Though the various political constraints to planning that I have cata-
logued here may initially seem like distinct issues, this discussion reveals
many of them to be related to competitive clientelism in some way. Traditional authorities are able to subdivide and sell peri-urban land informally
without punishment because of the votes they control as political brokers.
Political party competition and the desire to create patronage jobs motivates
administrative fragmentation. Party leaders distribute jobs with opportunities for rent-seeking as a form of patronage, and elected officials engage in
corruption in order to recoup the expenses associated with providing patronage. Planning staff have been decentralized in a way that allows local politicians to more easily coerce them into supporting their clientelistic decisions.
While violence and intimidation around land and planning are not related
solely to competitive clientelism, this too can be understood as at least partly
the product of an environment in which power and security do not derive
from formal laws but through personalized relationships.

Explaining the Relationship Between Clientelism
and Informal Subdivisions in Accra

Nearly all the growth in Accra in recent decades has been informal, and half
or more of all growth has been in the form of "informal subdivisions" (see
Chapter 4). How does this relate to the finding in Chapter 2 that cities in more
clientelistic countries are likely to see a higher share of informal subdivisions
than cities in countries with less clientelism? Having now examined the complex political landscape of urban Ghana, we can consider what might be
behind the relationship between clientelism and informal subdivisions in
Accra.

It is probably not a coincidence that the increase in the share of informal
subdivisions in Accra's growth coincides with the beginning of Ghana's current democratic era in the early 1990s, when the competitive clientelism that
dominates Ghana took its present form (see Figure 10). However, of the mechanisms by which clientelism and informal subdivisions are linked that were
proposed in Chapter 2, the first one, according to which patrons directly
provide land to their clients, may not be the most relevant. The high proportion of informal subdivisions is related to the use of quack surveyors by traditional authorities to subdivide land in ways that do not conform to planning
standards, as described previously. Although chiefs do act as patrons to

their communities in indigenous settlements, the relationship between chiefs and the buyers of their undeveloped peri-urban land, who are not always from their own community, is not necessarily clientelistic.

Instead, the growth of informal subdivisions in Accra may be better described by the second possible mechanism, in which clientelism encourages the growth and persistence of new informal subdivisions through *postsettlement* protection and regularization. Chiefs are able to subdivide and sell large areas of land at once, rather than small parcels on an uncoordinated, ad hoc basis. This suggests an expectation on the part of chiefs and buyers that authorities will not punish or evict them for their lack of formal planning permissions. This expectation most likely derives from the clientelistic relationships they have with authorities, including chief executives and MPs. Politicians are reluctant to penalize chiefs, as this would anger their community members, who are voters.

A version of the third proposed mechanism applies as well. In this mechanism, strong neighborhood leadership leads to new informal settlements being spatially coordinated and also fosters clientelism in parallel. In Accra, chiefs provide this kind of leadership. They plan out new settlements with the help of unlicensed surveyors while also brokering the relationships with politicians that allow the settlements to remain. In these ways, the relationship between clientelism and the growth of informal subdivisions in Ghana is consistent with the analysis in Chapter 2. However, it also sheds light on a specific variant of this relationship, one that may be relevant to many countries in which traditional authorities have customary land rights.

Cobbinah and Darkwah write that, in Ghana, "traditional and modern political systems have rendered the position of urban planning agencies untenable, and the role of urban residents in planning unimportant."[67] The evidence discussed in this and the previous chapter suggests that clientelism affects nearly every aspect of urban development and service delivery in Ghana's cities. It supports the argument that competitive clientelism in Ghana has "engendered institutions and practices that undermine meritocracy and administrative decentralization."[68] The next chapter illustrates these challenges through the example of Accra's infamous Old Fadama informal settlement, also known as "Sodom and Gomorrah."

CHAPTER 7

How Sodom and Gomorrah Survive: The Case of "Ghana's Biggest Slum"

I n the heart of Accra lies the densely populated settlement of Old Fadama, which journalists invariably refer to as "Ghana's biggest slum." It may be more widely known by its unofficial name: Sodom and Gomorrah. The biblical connotations of this name, as a place of sin that deserves only to be destroyed, are not lost in Ghana. After all, this is a country where even small roadside shops are given names like "Blood of Jesus" and "God is Present."[1] The origins, growth, attempted demolitions, and survival of Accra's Old Fadama informal settlement illustrate the interplay between the various forces shaping urbanization in Ghana.

Old Fadama occupies seventy-seven acres (thirty-one hectares) of land along the Odaw River and Korle Lagoon in central Accra (Figure 11).[2] It is adjacent to Agbogbloshie, which until 2021 was home to vegetable markets and a notoriously toxic electronic-waste processing scrapyard.

Old Fadama is home to at least 80,000 inhabitants. This gives it a population density of more than 1,000 inhabitants per acre (2,500 inhabitants per hectare). A 2010 survey found that two-thirds of residents were from Ghana's Northern Region. Though these households had originally come to Accra from the North to escape conflict, they remain mainly for employment. A very high proportion of the surveyed population, 96%, was employed in some way, and 91% said that their main reason for not returning to their hometowns was a lack of jobs there. Many women work as *kayayei*, or head porters (women who transport loads on their heads for a fee), often living in dormitory-style structures with rooms holding up to twenty women each. The survey found that only one in three children under the age of eighteen was in school, and nearly half of the residents had had no

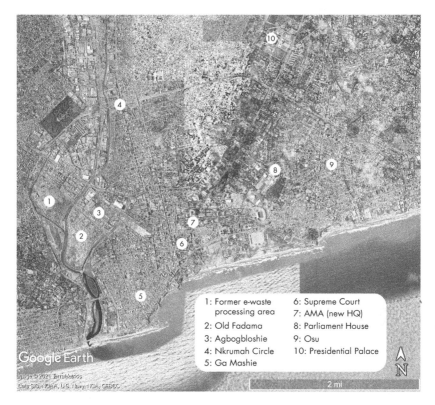

Figure 11. Old Fadama in the context of central Accra. Source: Google Earth (Image © 2021 TerraMetrics; data: SIO, NOAA, US Navy, NGA, GEBCO), with annotations by the author.

education.[3] Some allege that the settlement is home to criminal organizations involved in the illegal trade of guns, human organs, and even babies for use in rituals.[4]

Until 2021, large quantities of electronic waste produced in Europe and the Americas ended up at the waste processing scrapyard at Old Fadama's neighbor, Agbogbloshie. Thousands of workers relied on the waste processing industry for their livelihoods.[5] Workers recycled the waste, burning hazardous materials in open fires with little or no protection, suffering burns, injuries, and respiratory illnesses.[6] Studies found toxins, including heavy metals and flame-retardant chemicals, in the blood of waste workers and nearby residents, and even in the breast milk of mothers living in the area.[7] In 2021, the government demolished the scrapyard with little warning, as part of a "decongestion" exercise led by the Greater Accra Regional Minister Henry Quartey. Some scrapyard workers relocated to a site outside Accra, whereas others continued recycling at a smaller scale in residential areas in Old Fadama. The government announced plans for a hospital to be built on the site of the former scrapyard, with no discussion of how the toxic chemical pollution in the soil would be remediated.[8]

Becoming "Sodom and Gomorrah": A History of Old Fadama

The indigenous Ga ethnic group considers the Korle Lagoon and the land on which Old Fadama sits to be sacred, a part of their customary inheritance. The name Fadama, however, comes from a word in Hausa (the language spoken by Muslim migrants from northern Ghana) that means "marshy, uninhabitable area."[9] In the early twentieth century, commercial interests planned to build first a railway station and then a harbor on the site. The local Ga community opposed these plans, and as a result they were not implemented. In the 1950s, before independence, the colonial government planned to build low-income housing at Agbogbloshie, but the Ga opposed this plan as well.

In the early 1960s, the government of President Nkrumah managed to acquire the land from Ga chiefs, in exchange for monetary compensation, with plans to establish manufacturing and light industry on the site. The government relocated the few inhabitants to an area that was named New Fadama. However, in 1970, a plan determined the area to be too flood-prone for industrial or residential use. Instead, it designated the site for the construction of a retention pond and extensive public recreation facilities.[10] Figure 12 shows the original 1970 plan for the area. Its legend, visible at the bottom left of the plan and reproduced here, lists elaborate facilities:

A. Public garden sector
   1. Offices, caretaker's house with tools room and store
   2. Greyhound races—stadium, restaurant, cafeteria, offices, clubrooms, paddock, kennels
   3. Boating and yacht club, boat hiring
   4. Birds' aviary

5. Public swimming pool with restaurant and tennis courts
6. Public tennis courts
7. Bamboo bush hut with canteen
8. Dance circle
9. Children's playgrounds and cafeteria

B. Gardens and public green sector along the ring road

10. Mosque
11. Ramadan Square, as the extension of the mosque precinct
12. Small residential area
13. Church
14. Open-air cinema and cafeteria
15. Hotel, restaurant, and cafeteria
16. Botanical garden, sightseeing terraces, walkway through green leading to nodal points for relaxation
17. Motel and restaurant
18. Petrol station
19. Small shopping center
20. Cafeteria
21. Bush hut
22. Paddleboat hiring
23. Sewerage pumping station "D" with reserve for future extension

C. Sports sector

24. Stadium with athletic oval and football pitch
25. Sport hall for indoor games with restaurant, changing rooms, clubrooms and stores
26. Sector offices and caretaker's room
27. Football pitch for training
28. Badminton courts
29. Volleyball pitch
30. Cricket oval
31. Tennis courts
32. Netball courts
33. Basketball pitch
34. Hockey pitch
35. Boating and yacht club
36. Nightclub, restaurant, swimming pool, playgrounds
37. Changing rooms with toilets and showers

D. Walkway through green from the site of James Town
  38. Gbotsui Ashifo Shrine
E. Lagoon
  39. Boat racing track

Despite these grand plans, the site remained largely vacant, apart from small settlements, fisheries, and a garbage dump. Squatters started to settle

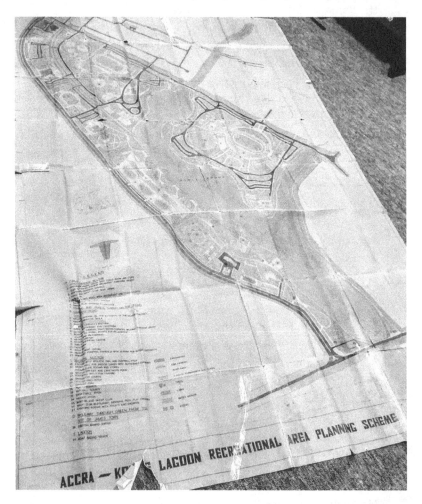

Figure 12. The 1970 plan for the Korle Lagoon Recreational Area, Accra (photograph of original). Source: Photograph by the author of the plan produced by the Town Planning Division.

on the site in the 1980s, building structures from wooden boards and car-
tons on wood-chip floors.[11] Many of the early settlers were Ghanaians who
had been deported from Nigeria during a period of anti-immigrant sentiment
in Nigeria at the time.[12] In the early days of the settlement, some Ga families
informally "sold" land to squatters, despite the fact that the state had acquired
the land from them in the 1960s.[13] In 1991, city authorities removed street vendors from other areas in the city in preparation for a conference of the Non-
Aligned Movement and relocated them to Old Fadama, in what was an
implicit endorsement of the settlement.[14] When a fire in 1993 burned down
the city's largest market at Makola, a replacement market was built at Agbogbloshie to relieve pressure on the original, contributing to the growth of
neighboring Old Fadama. Settlers who were displaced for the construction
of the new market simply moved further into Old Fadama, creating new land
by filling the swamp with sawdust.

In 1994, an MP from Ghana's Northern Region asked the chief executive
of Accra at the time, Nat Nunoo Amarteifio, to allow people who were fleeing
a violent conflict in the North to camp at Old Fadama for a month or two.[15]
At the time, Accra's planners advised politicians against this. They feared
that the settlement would become permanent and grow as more migrants
came south to join their relatives who had settled there. As a former AMA
planning director recalled: "The entire planning department advised them:
'No, if we do that, there will be a multiplier effect because [once someone]
has got the place, he will go and call the brother, the sister, the aunt, and the
rest. "Oh! There's a place here!" If we are not careful, within some small time
the whole place will be inundated with squatters.' They ignored it. They're
politicians. They said, 'No, we need to settle them right now. Go away.' And
then? They settled their people there, and they started multiplying, multiplying, multiplying. . . . It has become a political issue now."[16]

For years, settlers built structures in Old Fadama from temporary materials. This norm was instituted and monitored by community leaders and
People's Dialogue on Human Settlements, the community-based organization that rose to prominence in the area in the 2000s and established
close ties to senior government officials.[17] The residents intended the use of
temporary materials as a signal to authorities that they sought relocation and
did not intend to settle there permanently. However, the outbreak of a fire in
2009 marked a turning point. Following the fire, People's Dialogue and the
affiliated Old Fadama Development Association began encouraging the use
of concrete blocks for reconstruction. They also began to enforce informal

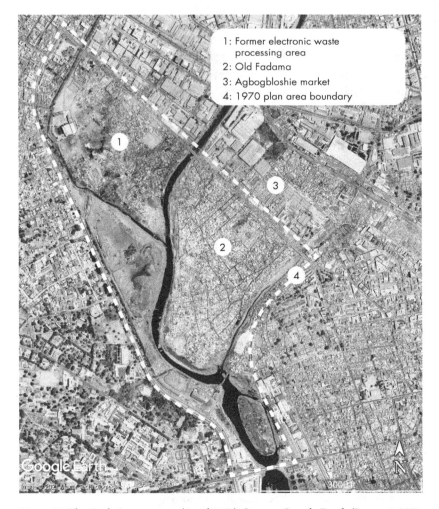

1: Former electronic waste
   processing area
2: Old Fadama
3: Agbogbloshie market
4: 1970 plan area boundary

Figure 13. The Korle Lagoon area (April 2021). Source: Google Earth (Image © 2021 Maxar Technologies), with annotations by the author.

building codes, widen streets, and tax residents.[18] Figure 13 shows the area as it appeared in early 2021.

Today, Old Fadama is stuck in a three-way stalemate, between the state, which owns the land on paper; the Ga leaders, who claim traditional rights to the land; and the settlers who occupy it, partly because they were placed there by the state. The state officially considers residents of Old Fadama to be illegal squatters on state land, as it had acquired the land from Ga authorities in the 1960s. Although in the early days of the settlement, some Ga families had informally "sold" land to squatters, Ga traditional authorities now also strongly oppose the existence of the settlement. However, the Ga also dispute the state's claim to the land. They take the position that the government acquisition is no longer valid, as it did not use the land to provide local development as promised.[19] The settlers claim that, as the settlement was created partly by the government itself, it is legitimate.[20]

The name Sodom and Gomorrah was originally applied only to the newer section of the settlement that was built on flood-prone land in the early 1990s. Various stories circulate regarding the origin of this name. According to one account, a Ga leader gave this rear section of the settlement the name to distinguish it from the earlier-established sections that had been bought from the Ga. The name was popularized when a radio reporter overheard it and used it on the air. Another account ascribes the name to an AMA spokesperson who stated that the people of the neighborhood would be destroyed like the inhabitants of Sodom and Gomorrah in the Bible.[21] Yet another version of events states that a doctor who kept horses in the area warned the earliest settlers that the structures that they built on the swampland would be swept away like the biblical cities of those names.[22] Whatever its origins, eventually the name was applied to all of Old Fadama. Today, the name Sodom and Gomorrah is used as widely as the name Old Fadama, and has even made its way into official government documents.[23] As Paller notes, "Over time, the name shaped the broader public opinion of the neighbourhood, and the perception of the residents as squatters did not change. The settlement was transformed from a temporary place of refuge into an evil problem that needed to be exterminated."[24]

Fire and Brimstone: Attempts at Demolishing "Sodom and Gomorrah"

Over the years the AMA, under both of Ghana's major political parties, has threatened or carried out partial evictions and demolitions of structures at Old Fadama. Yet the settlement has managed to survive, in large part because of its importance in elections. Old Fadama's electoral importance comes not only from the fact that it is home to eighty thousand or more residents, but also because political parties believe that the political views of these residents strongly influence the votes of their relatives in the North. As a former AMA official told me, "Each individual in Sodom and Gomorrah represents a household at Sodom and Gomorrah and also has a link to the Northern part of this country. . . . So no government, no politician takes that place for granted."[25] The constituency in which it lies, Odododiodio, has been important since the country's early years, with Kwame Nkrumah himself having represented it as an MP. Its residents claim that, "If you win Odododiodio Constituency, you win Ghana."[26] Moreover, Old Fadama is also a valuable source of labor for political party business, as it is home to a large population of underemployed youths who can be used as party foot soldiers.[27]

The events surrounding attempts at removing the settlement underscore how its political importance has helped it to remain in place, despite hostility from the AMA and the surrounding Ga population. In 2002, the government served an eviction notice to the residents of Old Fadama, to make room for the Korle Lagoon Ecological Restoration Project. The Centre for Public Interest Law, a Ghanaian NGO, fought this eviction notice in court but lost. However, by now the settlement had become electorally important, and with the launch of campaigns for the 2004 election, the government put aside its plans for demolition. Voters in Old Fadama were seen as being instrumental in the victory of the NDC candidate for MP in that election, providing some respite for its residents.

Although Old Fadama was largely aligned with the NDC, the NDC chief executive appointed in 2008 had close ties to Ga leaders who were hostile to the existence of the settlement.[28] In 2009, the AMA again earmarked Old Fadama for demolition as part of an "urban renewal" program. However, when the residents threatened to defect from the ruling NDC to the opposition NPP, the president quickly and publicly called for the demolition to be stopped. Meanwhile, demolitions in other areas perceived as NPP strongholds proceeded as planned.[29]

A fire in 2012 provided the opportunity for leaders from the NPP to consolidate their organizing machinery in the settlement. They promised disaster relief to their supporters, with the aspiring NPP candidate for MP asking them to "coordinate within their groups and to write down what they needed."[30]

Then, in June 2015, came the "twin disaster" of flood and fire, described in the opening section of this book. Old Fadama was blamed for the disaster, and government bulldozers descended on the settlement. Analysis of satellite imagery reveals that the government removed structures occupying approximately thirteen hectares, making up more than 40% of the settlement (see Figure 14, left and middle). This suggests that the demolitions may have destroyed the houses of around 30,000 to 35,000 residents (a figure in line with the previously estimated "more than 25,000"[31]). The government offered the affected residents small sums of money to "go back where they came from," an offer the residents found insulting.[32] Residents protested, and national NDC leaders called the chief executive and planning director to Parliament to address the situation. The planning director used the 1970 plan, with its gardens, yachting facilities, and sports fields, as justification for the demolitions. However, party leaders admonished the chief executive for his actions, reminding him that the residents of the settlement were key NDC supporters. As the planning director later recalled: "They asked our mayor a question: Where does he get his powers from? You see? They were from the same party. Doesn't he know that what he is doing is going to affect his source of power?"[33]

The AMA called off the demolition. Most of the residents from the demolished structures returned and rebuilt their homes along the waterway (Figure 14, right). Still, observers believe that the attempted demolition hurt the NDC's performance in the 2016 election, which it lost.[34]

NPP leaders saw an opportunity to take advantage of the NDC's loosened grip over the residents of the settlement, with an eye toward the 2020 elections. The vice president of Ghana under the subsequent NPP administration made a high-profile visit to Old Fadama and Agbogbloshie in 2019. He was accompanied by the Ministers of Inner-City and Zongo Development, the Interior, Defense, Water and Sanitation, and Local Government and Rural Development, as well as the new AMA chief executive and other NPP leaders. The vice president acknowledged the mistrust between the residents and successive governments due to neglect and threats of eviction. He promised to improve living conditions in the area through the provision of amenities. These included "four eight-unit places of convenience, 20 four-unit bathrooms, street lights, water, a kindergarten, as well as laying of pavement blocks at the Agbogbloshie Market."[35] Two weeks later, the vice president met with traditional authorities and other community leaders from Old Fadama and Agbogbloshie at Jubilee House, the presidential palace. He announced via Twitter that the government had already provided streetlights throughout the community, and he added to his list of promises a community center, a police station, and waste facilities. "Agbogbloshie and Old Fadama

Figure 14. Satellite images of Old Fadama in 2014 (left), in 2015 after the AMA undertook demolitions along the lagoon (middle), and in 2018, showing reconstruction in the previously demolished areas (right). Source: Google Earth (Image © 2021 Maxar Technologies).

though slums, equally deserve to be served just like any other community in the country," the vice president wrote on Twitter.[36]

If developments in 2019 gave residents of Old Fadama the impression that the government was starting to accept their existence, subsequent events disabused them of that notion. At the end of March 2020, the president of Ghana announced a three-week, nationwide lockdown to curb the spread of COVID-19 during the pandemic. The threat of contagion and the accompanying restrictions were particularly hard for the residents of Old Fadama to cope with, as they were for the urban poor worldwide. With large numbers of people sharing rooms, "social distancing" was impossible. The lack of reliable access to clean water made frequent handwashing difficult. Residents' reliance on daily income made the sudden cessation of economic activity a crisis. In the middle of this particularly desperate time, AMA bulldozers rolled up again. They demolished a part of the settlement to pave way for dredging of the lagoon, leaving a thousand people homeless. The contrast between the vice president's promises and the government's actions was not lost on the residents. "Where is the development the Vice President promised us?" asked a newly homeless resident.[37]

In 2021, after directing the demolition of scrapyards and markets at Agbogbloshie as mentioned earlier, Regional Minister Henry Quartey turned his attention to Old Fadama. Having seen the brute force with which Agbogbloshie had been razed to the ground, Old Fadama's residents had to take the threats seriously. This time, the chief executive of Accra, perhaps having learned from the troubles of his predecessor in 2015, intervened on behalf of Old Fadama. He negotiated a compromise whereby only structures within twenty meters of Korle Lagoon would be demolished. Concerned that government bulldozers would not stop at twenty meters, community leaders took it on themselves to demolish these structures.[38] The events of 2021 reminded the residents of Old Fadama once again of both their precariousness and their reliance on the favor of politicians for survival.

The "Albatross" Around the Necks of Authorities in Accra

The events of 2009, 2015, and 2021, and similar incidents in previous years, have led many scholars[39] and local experts[40] to believe that Old Fadama's electoral importance makes it practically invulnerable to complete removal. The former planning director of AMA described Old Fadama, with its eighty thousand inhabitants in violation of official plans, as an "albatross" around the necks of planners in Accra.[41]

While in Ghana, I had the opportunity to speak to Nat Nunoo Amarteifio, who was mayor of Accra in the mid-1990s. It was he who had allowed the northern migrants to settle at Old Fadama at the time. An architectural historian rather than a politician by profession, he agreed that the residents were able to remain in the settlement because of politics: "The city makes noises about clearing them, but it's not possible to do so, for many reasons. And this is where we come to your thesis. They are now a political fact. Eighty or ninety or a hundred thousand residents—even though they may not be registered to vote in Accra but are registered to vote in other parts of the country—are still assets that a political party does not throw away easily. So, any attempt to dislodge them quickly runs into heavy political headwinds. And that's a fact. Politicians will always seize the opportunity to cultivate a constituency."[42]

Despite frequent floods, fires, and hostility from authorities, Accra's "Sodom and Gomorrah" survives because of its electoral importance. Ghana's clientelistic democracy has saved it from the complete destruction that befell its biblical namesakes. Other informal settlements across Greater Accra are routinely removed. This means that the persistence of certain settlements, not only the large and high-profile Old Fadama but also other, smaller settlements and structures, cannot be put down simply to general neglect or weakness on the part of local governments. The survival of these settlements can only be understood in light of their political importance.

This kind of clientelistic support for informal settlements is a mixed blessing. While it has allowed Old Fadama and others to escape complete demolition, it has not led to substantial improvements either. The residents of such settlements still lack long-term tenure security and access to basic infrastructure and services. Arguably, people in power are incentivized to keep these residents in a state of dependency. The political parties have no incentive to provide long-term solutions when it is the very vulnerability of these communities that makes them useful as client populations.

If, as the vice president claimed, the residents of Old Fadama "deserve to be served just like any other community in the country," the provision of basic services to Old Fadama should be unremarkable. It should be carried out routinely by local government, rather than in the form of a high-profile, media-friendly gift from the vice president and several national ministers. Moreover, it is notable that for all this promised support, the government has not provided secure land tenure or ceased its occasional partial demolitions.

The history of Old Fadama illustrates the complex relationships between planning, informal politics, and informal urban growth. Politically influential traditional authorities acted as land brokers, helping to create the settlement by informally subdividing land. A settlement that was partly formal in origin (as a camp for internally displaced people, in this case) became "informalized" due to political antipathy on the part of political leaders. The informal settlement remained in place and grew due to its clientelistic political ties, despite violating plans and regulations. An ambitious formal plan proved impossible to implement because of informality and politics. Politicians provide its residents with benefits and reprieves from removal in exchange for their political support, but they have not permanently freed them from dependence and precariousness by providing formal tenure rights.

PART III

Politically Adaptive Planning

CHAPTER 8

Seeking a Way Forward for Planning

The previous chapters make clear that informal politics prevents effective planning in Ghana and around the world. The next few chapters seek a way forward. I start in this chapter by making the case that the most binding constraints on effective planning in Ghana are political in nature. Neither government policies in Ghana nor studies of urban planning by academic researchers and international organizations have sufficiently addressed the problem of political impediments to planning, which are unlikely to disappear soon.

A Thought Experiment

A way forward for planning in Ghana, and countries like it, must involve contending with the influence of politics. Earlier, I considered two nonpolitical constraints to effective planning in Ghana: low fiscal and human capacity for planning, and inappropriate planning regulations and processes. Clearly, these nonpolitical constraints are real concerns. However, among the three categories of constraints—which one might term "planning capacity," "planning quality," and "politics"—the last is the most critical.

One way to compare the relative effect of these constraints is to conduct a thought experiment that involves imagining what happens if two of these three types of constraints disappear, leaving only one. How different would the outcomes be in each case from the present situation? First, what would the outcome be if political support for the preparation and implementation of plans existed, and planning capacity were high, but plans remained of low quality? In other words, what would happen if the constraints of planning capacity and politics disappeared, leaving only planning quality? Most probably, this would result in bad plans being implemented. The outcomes would be unsatisfactory in various ways and perhaps even socially, economically, or environmentally damaging. However, this is clearly a different outcome from the status quo, in which plans are largely ignored. The solution in such a scenario might involve better training for planners, perhaps with support from donor organizations or universities.

What if, instead, constraints related to planning quality and politics disappeared, leaving only planning capacity constraints? In other words, what would happen if political support for the preparation and implementation of plans existed, and plans were appropriately flexible and inclusive, but fiscal and human capacity to prepare plans and process applications remained low? In this scenario, perhaps people would be unable to develop new land because their permit applications would languish in underfunded and understaffed planning departments. This would slow down new construction, which would not necessarily be a positive outcome. However, this, too, would be a different outcome from the current situation, in which cities are seeing rapid informal growth. In a scenario in which planning is a political priority, the capacity problem might even resolve itself, as decision-makers would quickly devote the necessary resources to meet planning needs. This, too, would be a situation well-suited to the involvement of donor organizations, who could bring in training and capacity building to local planners.

The final scenario is one in which high planning capacity exists, and the plans prepared are also well-developed and context appropriate, but there is no change to the political context. In this scenario, political leaders remain able to make decisions based on short-term clientelistic imperatives and ignore the advice of planners. Most likely, plans would be of high quality, and planning departments would have high capacity to perform their development control tasks, but they would remain thwarted by political leaders and, therefore, unable to prepare or implement plans effectively. This is clearly the scenario of "least change" from the status quo. It is also the only scenario for which there is no ready solution, as no amount of training or capacity building would change the underlying political challenge.

None of these schematic hypotheticals is necessarily intended to be realistic, but rather the goal is to emphasize the fact that political constraints are the binding constraints to planning to Ghana. As long as political constraints remain and planning is not significantly reconceived in light of these constraints, addressing the other constraints is unlikely to significantly change the status quo.

Past Recommendations for Planning in Ghana

Neither theoretical assumptions nor historical examples of the decline of clientelism point out a clear way forward for planning in the face of clientelism (see Chapter 3). Do policies or studies in the specific context of Ghana provide any actionable recommendations that might be more useful?

Government Policies and Plans

Ghana has many national, regional, and local policy documents that aim to support urban informality in Ghana, but the reality on the ground, in which informal settlers and vendors are the target of harsh antagonism by the state, contradicts these documents (see Chapter 4). Recent planning legislation supports the preparation and implementation of plans, but the results have not been transformative. This suggests that neither broad policy directives nor legislative changes alone are likely to allow planners to work more effectively or the urban poor in informal settlements to prosper.

Spatial plans mention in passing the difficulties that local governments in Ghana have had in implementing previous plans. However, addressing the political concerns that are the main constraints to the implementation of plans in the country is beyond their remit. The government usually outsources the preparation of these documents to consulting firms. These firms have no incentive to stray from the scope of traditional spatial plans in order to take on the broader sociopolitical challenges to planning, even if they are well aware of such challenges and the fact that their spatial plans are unlikely to be implemented.

Perhaps the well-established narrative of "planning failure" in Ghana means that planners never feel much responsibility to make plans that are actually implementable. When plans are unlikely to be implemented because of political factors beyond any planner's control, a plan might as well be ambitious and idealized. An impressive plan on paper reflects well on a planner, even if the most impressive elements also make the plan less likely to be implemented.

International Development Organizations

International development organizations, with their broad expertise and developmental remit, may be expected to take a more holistic perspective in their reports on urban development than spatial plans do. However, while their reports on urban Ghana sometimes do mention political issues in passing, they typically shy away from addressing them in depth. Like many such reports, they often mention the need for "political will," a concept that Edgar Pieterse of the African Centre for Cities describes as being "overused and underspecified."[1]

For example, a World Bank study of urbanization in Ghana mentions "undue political interference" as one of the factors responsible for "unplanned" spatial expansion and mentions that the success of new planning regulations requires "strong political support."[2] However, it does not expand on what this means. Its recommendations concern reforming land regulations, strengthening municipal finance, building transportation infrastructure, institutional coordination, and decentralization, without much discussion of the political environment. Another World Bank study, on urban resilience in Greater Accra, frequently mentions lack of planning and implementation capacity, poor planning methods, lack of enforcement of plans, poor coordination, and insufficient participation. However, it mentions politics only twice: it notes that "insufficient local political will" is a challenge for urban finance,[3] and that sanitation policies remain powerless because political and traditional leaders "plead" on behalf of constituents who do not comply, in order to protect them from punishment.[4] Similarly, a UN-Habitat profile of Accra mentions lack of political will once and political interference three times but does not explore these issues beyond brief mentions.[5] The Accra Resilience Strategy prepared by AMA with support from 100 Resilient Cities mentions politics only very indirectly.[6]

Many of the staff and consultants who lead the preparation of these reports are based abroad or are based in the country only temporarily, and it is possible that they do not have enough of a grasp of informal political dynamics to incorporate them into their analyses. However, even if they are aware of the effects of politics, they might believe that it would be inappropriate for international organizations to get involved in or even comment on local politics. Given the sensitivity around these issues, they may prefer to restrict discussions to technical, financial, and regulatory issues. Besides, pointed political critiques may hit uncomfortably close to home for government officials with whom these organizations must maintain positive relationships.[7] International organizations are right to be cautious about commenting on local politics. However, one cannot disentangle political issues from any of the other issues surrounding urban planning and informality in Ghana. These reports either misunderstand or misrepresent their subject matter by avoiding politics.

The apolitical tendencies of international development institutions have been well-documented. According to Thomas Carothers and Diane de Gramont, "international development assistance has had an uncertain and uncomfortable relationship with politics." Since their early years, aid organizations have "held fast to what can be called 'the temptation of the technical,' the belief that they could help economically transform poor countries by providing timely doses of capital and technical knowledge while maintaining a comfortably clinical distance from these countries' internal political life," write Carothers and de Gramont.[8]

In "The Anti-Politics Machine," James Ferguson describes how a World Bank project in Lesotho focused on technical concerns and ignored entrenched political interests, eventually finding itself ill-equipped to play the political game in which it suddenly found itself.[9] In a study of housing in Ghana, Kwadwo Ohene Sarfoh argues that development theories and prescriptions originating in international agencies suffer by not acknowledging the ways in which they are "inscribed into local structures" or "indigenized" through the influence of politics.[10] Pieterse argues that the achievement of urban development targets put forward by international development organizations is thwarted in part by their own depoliticization of urban development discourse.[11]

The following passage, though written about Indonesia, applies well enough to Ghana, and likely to many other clientelistic democracies, that it is worth quoting at length:

> Policies and development interventions are destined to fail if they
> operate on the assumption that Indonesia's state is a rule-bound,
> Weberian institution only occasionally waylaid by deviant behavior.
> Clientelistic exchange relations pervade state institutions and affect

their basic functioning. Any policy intervention or development
initiative should start by recognizing this reality, rather than
wishing it away. . . .

In our experience, policy makers as well as development
organizations struggle to incorporate this political dimension into
their work. This is understandable: it is much easier and less risky
for them to work on training in technical skills or the preparation
of guidelines and operating procedures than to deal with politics
head-on. Compared to technical fixes, political approaches are
messy and controversial since they involve, in one way or another,
addressing power inequalities. Consequently, much policy making
and development cooperation still proceeds on the assumption (or
hope) that the provision of knowledge and skills, the training of a
few bureaucrats or judges, or the adoption of a particular policy will
fix a problem. This logic gives rise to a never-ending seminar circuit
in Jakarta's upmarket hotels, where new skills and policies are
eagerly discussed, whether the topic at hand is legal development,
the environment, urban planning, or bureaucratic reform. We have
often participated in such seminars; it is very common that someone in the course of the discussions will observe that even if the
policy or law being suggested is adopted, it will have little effect,
because Indonesia's major problems relate to implementation rather
than policy design. Often everyone agrees—but the conversation
typically then resumes its course. The elephant in these hotel rooms,
in other words, is informal politics.[12]

The World Bank itself made a similar argument in its annual *World Development Report* for 2004: "If organizational failures are the result of deeper
weaknesses in institutional arrangements (weak political commitment, unclear objectives, no enforceability), direct attacks on the proximate determi-
nants (more money, better training, more internal information) will fail."[13]

A notable exception to this trend of international agencies avoiding Ghanaian politics is a report on urban governance and services in Ghana prepared
by ICF Consulting Services for UK Aid and Cities Alliance (a publication
that I have cited frequently in this book).[14] Unlike the other reports on urban
Ghana, this report uses competitive clientelism as its framing concept. This
results in an unusually clear-eyed and sophisticated reading of the political
nature of urban issues relating to planning, land, finances, and service delivery

in the country. Still, the recommendations for planning in this report, too, are somewhat conventional and vague, focusing on institutional capacity building and on technical changes that do not follow from the preceding diagnosis.

Academic Publications

Many academic studies feature insightful diagnoses of the problems, including the political problems, that afflict urban planning in Ghana. However, they often follow them up with recommendations that are either nonspecific or unrealistic in the prevailing political environment. The recommendations for planning in Ghana provided by previous academic studies include:

- the creation of secondary and tertiary cities, implementation of participatory slum upgrading programs, and building of institutional capacity and collaboration;[15]
- "having effective land management and land use planning systems in place;"[16]
- making the Town and Country Planning Department (now LUSPA) "an independent entity, devoid of undue political interference and control but work[ing] collaboratively with both urban residents and political elites;"[17]
- "rethinking the overall urban planning and development processes, urban land management and participatory urban governance and the right to urban citizenship;"[18]
- "rethink[ing] the essence of decentralised local government by building stakeholder capacity for effective participation in decision-making as well as delinking overly parochial political interests of individuals and groups from those of societal interests to allow development programmes to progress uninhibited;"[19]
- "introducing and adhering to the philosophy of sustainable urban development in the urban development process;"[20] and
- "political will at all levels of government."[21]

My intention in quoting these studies is not to denigrate the work of these scholars, many of whose other insights I have found very valuable in developing the argument presented in previous chapters. I only point to these examples to identify a gap in the literature around clientelism and planning in

Ghana. Many of these recommendations have a tautological quality: the solution to a lack of public participation is to ensure more public participation; to address the lack of enforcement of plans, plans must be better enforced, and so on. In other words, the solution to the problem is for the problem to be solved.

Possible Futures

Planning in Ghana is at an impasse, unable to guide urban growth effectively. Neither global examples nor studies of planning and urbanization in Ghana indicate a reliable path forward for planners. Yet allowing the status quo to remain in place is a dangerous option. Under present conditions, Ghana's urbanization will continue to occur informally, precluding the possibility for government interventions or regulations to bring about more sustainable or inclusive outcomes. In a future in which business continues as usual, Ghana will not automatically move toward increasing formality or state capacity, despite economic growth and the continued existence of some formal elements of democracy. Urban growth will continue to ignore plans and regulations. Informal settlements will continue to form and grow, benefiting to some extent from clientelistic protection and service provision. However, they will remain without reliable service provision and vulnerable to periodic evictions and demolitions. Plans, policies, studies, and reports may continue to decry the state of planning in Ghana. Some capacity-building efforts might result in marginal improvements in outcomes, but no opportunities for substantial change will come, at least not until Ghana's urbanization process concludes decades in the future.[22] Even then, the physical form of cities will not be easily changed. Future generations will have to pay the environmental and economic costs of Ghana's current mode of urbanization, particularly as environmental disasters become more intense and frequent as a result of climate change.

A change in the social, economic, or political environment may prevent this future, though not necessarily for the better. How likely is it that planning and urbanization in Ghana will change course as a result of such broader changes?

Reform Driven by a Growing Middle Class

Will clientelism eventually fade away as Ghana's economy prospers and its middle class grows? Conventional notions of developing democracies assume that middle classes prefer "universalistic" policies (i.e., those benefiting all citizens) over narrowly targeted clientelism, and as a result, the rise of the middle class in a democracy will bring about a shift away from "particularistic" policies (i.e., those aimed at benefiting small groups of supporters) toward universalistic ones.[23] In theory, this would lead to more support for coordinated urban planning and the provision of long-term public goods.

Part of this proposition is true in the case of Ghana. The growing Ghanaian urban middle class does prefer more universalistic policies. This is potentially significant, because at least in Greater Accra, the middle class is already large enough (25% of the population) to sway elections away from clientelism. However, this has not happened. As Noah Nathan argues (see Chapter 5), politicians do not have the capacity to deliver on universalistic policy promises. Instead, they ignore middle-class voters and focus on the poor, who have needs that can be met more easily with particularistic expenditures. Frustrated middle-class voters with universalistic preferences give up on voting. This, in turn, allows politicians to continue ignoring their preferences and to stick to clientelism without being punished at the ballot box. Middle-class and wealthy residents instead pay private suppliers for urban services such as water, security, education, and sanitation, reducing their reliance on public systems of service delivery and increasing their ability to opt out of local politics.[24] In local assembly elections in particular, turnout in middle-class neighborhoods can be as low as 5%, compared to up to 60% in poor neighborhoods. As a result, politicians can win these elections with a relatively small number of votes, making narrow targeting of benefits a viable strategy. This leads Nathan to believe that "demand-side" pressures arising from urbanization and economic growth are unlikely to yield significant political transformation.[25]

However, the preferences of the nonpoor need not express themselves only through votes. They could also take the form of reform movements. One of the explanations for the decline of machine politics in the United States in the early twentieth century is the efforts of a coalition of reformers from professional and business elites (see Chapter 3). These groups sought to take power away from ward-level "bosses" with strong ties to local communities and put it in the hands of municipal technocrats. The growth of "centralizing institutions" (public administration agencies, specialized professions, large retail establishments) and "organizational technologies" (the telephone, rapid transit, large office buildings) created connections among people of similar class interests across the city. This weakened the importance of neighborhood-level ties and catalyzed this process.[26] Some equivalent to this activity exists among Ghanaian urban elites, who in recent years have been engaging in non-partisan, reform-oriented campaigns and have founded citizen watchdog groups such as Occupy Ghana.[27] The internet, which acts both as an organizational technology and a nonlocal centralizing institution, has enabled these activities.

Still, urban politics in early twenty-first-century Ghana differs from that of early twentieth-century America. Local political "machines" in the United States were typically the result of the complete dominance of one political party, sometimes a single politician.[28] This is a different state of affairs from the highly competitive clientelism of Ghana. The United States was much wealthier and had higher state capacity, even during its days of clientelism a century ago, than Ghana today. Low state capacity means that civil service reforms are less effective in the Ghanaian context than they were in the United States.[29]

Another important difference is the prevalence in Ghana of informal settlements. These differ in their legal status from low-income neighborhoods in urban America during the days of political machines. Nonpoor reformers in the United States could bring about the decline of clientelism in poor communities without directly threatening the physical existence of those communities. Though many American cities did demolish many "slums" because of perceptions of "blight" or crime, these settlements were not necessarily violating the law simply by situating themselves where they were. In Ghana, clientelism is responsible for the very existence of many informal settlements on the land they occupy. This means that insistence on rule of law by nonpoor reformers could easily involve a call for the demolition of informal settlements. This would be a version of what happened in Turkey. When the country's political base shifted away from the migrant poor toward the middle class, a right-wing government was able to abandon clientelism and demolish informal settlements (see Chapter 3). For now, all of this is speculation. It remains to be seen whether nonpoor reform movements are likely to influence urban politics in Ghana significantly, and whether such reform would have a positive or negative effect on the poor.

Elected Mayors

The Ghanaian government scheduled a referendum to be held in 2019, in which the public was to vote on whether to make mayors locally elected instead of appointed by the president. However, the government canceled the referendum shortly before it was to be held (see Chapter 5). It is unclear whether the government will revive the proposal, but as it was the subject of publicity and debate in the Ghanaian media in the months leading to the canceled referendum, the proposal has entered the public consciousness and may resurface sooner or later.

There are mixed opinions about the possible impacts of such a change among planners in Ghana. Some argue that this change would increase local accountability in ways that would encourage mayors to support broad-based planning efforts. A change in Colombia by which mayors were no longer nominated from above but elected locally was one of the changes that did create conditions for increased accountability and the decline of clientelism in that country.[30] Others in Ghana are skeptical. They note that MMDAs depend heavily on intergovernmental fiscal transfers from the national government, and that, as the national government can manipulate these transfers, local governments with opposition-party mayors would be starved of funds under the proposed system.

Additionally, mayors would not necessarily be less motivated by clientelism under the proposed system as long as they still rely on votes to attain or remain in power. If anything, political decentralization of this sort, coupled with the administrative decentralization already partially implemented in Ghana, may enhance both the ability and the incentive for mayors and their parties to engage in competitive clientelism. For example, in Mexico, local governments are "in a particularly good position to exploit the dependency of squatters upon the government" due to their close proximity to squatter communities.[31] Similarly, decentralization in Indonesia simply multiplied the sites of informal dealmaking rather than diminishing it.[32]

For now, Ghanaian politicians cannot act alone and are dependent on party support. Even when an individual constituency has universalistic preferences, politicians cannot easily tailor their behavior to suit these preferences. This suggests that if mayors are to be elected locally and are given enough autonomy to set and implement their own policies, they may pursue differentiated approaches. Mayors of middle-class MMDAs would provide more universalistic benefits, whereas clientelism would be reinforced in MMDAs with larger poor populations. Such "dual appeals" are made in Chile, where spatial segregation has allowed the conservative Independent Democratic Union (UDI) party to combine policy-based appeals to middle-class and wealthy voters and clientelistic appeals to the poor.[33]

However, one potential outcome of such a change could have an anticlientelistic effect. In federal countries, such as Mexico and Brazil, parties in power in national and state governments sometimes establish programs to distribute irrevocable, nonclientelistic benefits—for example, land titles in the Mexican CORETT program (described in Chapter 3) or cash transfers and water infrastructure in Brazil. These programs undermine the ability of mayors from other parties to benefit from clientelism at the municipal level.[34] This recalls the role that federal welfare programs in the United States played in undermining the power of local political bosses. This behavior has not been relevant in Ghana so far because of Ghana's unitary structure, in which chief executives are necessarily aligned with the national government. However, it may become a factor in a system with locally elected mayors who may be from opposition parties. A scenario is possible in which, for example, the incumbent party at the national level, threatened by opposition mayors' clientelistic cultivation of votes from informal settlements, implements a universal (nonclientelistic) land titling or upgrading program across urban areas in order to weaken incumbent mayors' advantage. This would also have a long-term effect of weakening clientelism overall, and thus would be a potential positive outcome of a switch to elected mayors.

Authoritarianism

Although Ghana's political settlement seems stable for now, an unforeseeable economic or environmental shock could create the conditions for some form of authoritarianism to take over. Voters may become frustrated enough to democratically elect a strongman-type populist leader, who would have free reign to target informality. An authoritarian or populist regime might exploit frustration with urban disorder or nativist resentment of migrants. Accordingly, it might consolidate its support by demolishing informal settlements under the banner of rule of law and technocratic efficiency. Such a regime would boost the power of planners to shape the city, but it would do so in a way that would harm the poor.

The search for a way forward for planning to work more effectively in clientelistic environments such as Ghana's has not yet illuminated a clear path. Chapter 3 showed that, internationally, clientelism tends to decline as a result of broad political changes rather than anything within the control of planners. Existing research on Ghana has not wrestled sufficiently with the problem of how planning can operate more effectively in the face of clientelism and political interference. Broad changes to the overall political environment may cause a disruption in the status quo in Ghana, for better or worse. For now, none of the changes discussed appears imminent.

One other potential path remains to be explored, one that is more obscure, in the sense that it is not well theorized or documented. It can be glimpsed in the subtle strategies employed by planners who are forced to find ways to contend with informal politics in their day-to-day working lives. I explore these strategies, and how planning might build on them, in the next chapter.

CHAPTER 9

A Politically Adaptive Approach to Planning

*T*he pressure on planners was becoming intense, and yet they could not bring themselves to rezone the urban forest in Accra for commercial use. Some planners had received anonymous phone calls, offering bribes if they played along and threatening transfers if they did not. The planners knew that these offers and threats were credible. The people behind the project were not just private developers but figures in the national government. The Forestry Commission of Ghana had announced a public-private partnership for an "ecotourism" project in the forest. The minister of lands and natural resources had offered his "personal commitment" to the project's success in a bid to attract international investment.

Planners worried that the "eco" elements of the project would fall away once the land use change was approved. The land in question was the only protected forest in Accra and one of the metropolitan area's few green spaces of any kind. The planners were aware of its ecological role in protecting biodiversity and retaining rainwater, and believed that the proposed development would result in severe floods. Besides wanting to protect the lives and property of nearby residents, the planners were also concerned with protecting their own careers and reputations. Future administrations, looking for scapegoats for floods, might place the blame on them for having signed off on the project. They knew that if they simply voted against the approval in an assembly meeting, they would lose the vote. This also might invite retaliation from political leaders. A young planner who had received threatening phone calls was on the verge of quitting her job under the stress of the situation.

Desperate, the planners tried everything they could to push back. First, they agreed to approve the change, in principle, but included a stipulation for a public consultation before the change could be finalized. They knew that *this condition would deter the politicians from pursuing it. "The public would bash them. They couldn't go for that consultation," recalls a planner involved.*[1] *Meanwhile, the local planners sought help from the regional and national leadership of the Land Use and Spatial Planning Authority (LUSPA) and the Ghana Institute of Planners (GIP). The GIP discussed its concerns about the project with the media. One of the local government planners also noticed a section of the new Land Use and Spatial Planning Act of 2016 that no one had used before. It stated that a "change of use or re-zoning of a public space shall be subjected to approval by Parliament."*[2] *When notified, Parliament officially referred the issue to the LUSPA board, which advised against the rezoning. Faced with a potential scandal, the officials who had pushed the project were forced to let it drop.*

The next election brought the opposition party to power. The new incumbents showed little interest in implementing the project that their rivals had initiated. The new minister of environment, science, technology and innovation, soon after a meeting with planners at LUSPA, announced to the press that he believed that the forest should remain undeveloped.

There is no established guidance for how planners can resist political interference. However, episodes like the one just related reveal that planners are often forced to improvise strategies that allow them to resist political pressures without provoking retaliation, and that these strategies are sometimes successful. These strategies are rarely studied, but they can be instructive. They may help point to a way forward for planning in clientelistic environments. In this chapter, I use examples of such strategies, as well as observations of how clientelism and other relationships operate in Ghana, as the basis for recommendations for a "politically adaptive" planning approach.

Documenting Local Hidden Successes Before Applying
Global Best Practices

International organizations working on urban development routinely collect and disseminate "best practices" on urban planning or governance. For example, the Best Practices Database assembled by UN-Habitat, the United Nations agency that deals with urban development, features "approximately 4,000 proven solutions to the common social, economic and environmental problems."[3] The Asian Development Bank's Urban Innovations series of publications "shares best practices and lessons learned in urban infrastructure, transport, sanitation, as well as urban planning, policies, and urban development financing."[4] The publications and events of global city networks including C40, the International Council for Local Environmental Initiatives, United Cities and Local Governments, and the Global Platform for Sustainable Cities are devoted to sharing case studies from cities around the world that others can emulate or adapt. International organizations see these knowledge-sharing activities as their comparative advantage. They may not know more about any given city than that city's own planners and policymakers, but at least they can bring in case studies and best practices from elsewhere that the locals in that city would not otherwise be aware of. However, the challenges associated with urban planning and governance in a country emerge from its specific political settlement and social, cultural, and institutional environment. This means that international case studies are not always relevant, especially if presented as technical and apolitical in nature, as they often are.

The Ghanaian government recently invited one of the planners responsible for overseeing the growth of Singapore in the 1970s and 1980s to "transform Accra into a modern city."[5] This is in keeping with a growing trend of what Vanessa Watson refers to as "African urban fantasies" of emulating Singapore, Dubai, and Shanghai. (In fact, these fantasies are not restricted to Africa but are common across the Global South.) Such visions tend to override existing plans and planning processes, ignore public participation, and threaten to exclude the majority of urban residents from access to urban space.[6] No doubt Singapore is an expertly planned city, but it is unlikely that the best person to prepare a plan for Accra, given its political complexities and challenges, is someone whose planning experience is in a city-state under a benevolent dictatorship.

An alternative approach is to build recommendations on what Bish Sanyal calls "hidden successes"—that is, practices that have not been documented previously but have been relatively successful within their context.[7] Planning in Ghana is overwhelmingly viewed as a failure, and it is true that it is nearly impossible to identify examples of any unambiguous planning successes. Still, some efforts have paid off, even if only partially, occasionally, or temporarily thus far. International organizations and researchers working in a specific context might do well to identify these kinds of efforts from within that same context and find ways to support them.

How Local Planners in Ghana Respond
to Political Interference

Spatial planners in Ghana feel powerless. Their work is subject to interference from politicians engaging in short-term competitive clientelism. This forces planners to choose between long-term urban development objectives and their own careers, over which politicians have increasing power. If planners oppose any of the actions of the government in power too openly, politicians brand them as being "difficult" or politically aligned with the opposition and transfer them somewhere where they cannot make trouble. Both customary landholding authorities and the general public ignore plans and regulations, often with the tacit support of these politicians. Chief executives of local governments, appointed by the president, face political pressure from above and are not locally accountable. Planners lack financial and human resources to prepare and implement plans, and politics interferes in their ability to access the resources necessary to build capacity. The politically motivated fragmentation of local government jurisdictions exacerbates this situation and makes coordination across a metropolitan area difficult. Corruption, itself often an outcome of competitive clientelism, further undermines planning.

According to the planning theorist John Forester: "That planners can be powerless in a given setting is a thesis, or a plaintive cry, as old as the profession. Taken by itself, the thesis is likely to evoke a response like, 'So what else is new?' The research problem here is to explore just how, in previously unexamined ways, social relations of power (influence? authority?) and powerlessness work to provide whatever 'power' planners might have in particular settings."[8]

This is a research problem worth taking on. How do planners come to have whatever power they do have in the particular setting of Ghanaian cities, despite the pressures and constraints they face? In interviews, planners told me about the subtle strategies that they sometimes employ to contend with political interference and avoid outcomes they consider unacceptable, without risking their jobs by openly antagonizing political leaders.

Calling for Professional Backup

Planners in Ghana often face political pressure to go along with decisions that they disagree with on technical grounds, that they feel compromise their professional integrity, or that might expose them to disciplinary actions by future political leaders. In these situations, planners sometimes call for support from a professional organization or higher-level planning authority, specifically the Ghana Institute of Planners (GIP) or the Land Use and Spatial Planning Authority (LUSPA). Doing so adds weight to their technical opinion. However, under the guise of seeking technical advice, it also exposes a potentially controversial issue to a slightly wider audience. This prompts caution on the part of the politician who is in favor of it.

The GIP is an autonomous organization unaffiliated with any government body. Local government planners, communities, the media, and even politicians request the GIP to provide technical advice or comment on planning issues. GIP officials describe the role of the organization as that of a mediator rather than a regulator. Political figures tend to heed the advice of the GIP, knowing that the body can publicize a controversial issue in the media if its advice is ignored. The GIP may also submit a report on a case to the Ministry of Environment, Science, Technology, and Innovation, as in a recent instance in which a chief executive had allowed the construction of a petrol station where there had previously been a pond.[9]

At present, planners call upon the GIP for advice only occasionally, around five times a year by one estimate.[10] These requests usually come from planners in or near Greater Accra, where the GIP is headquartered.[11] Even within Greater Accra, planners I spoke to varied in their opinion of the GIP's effectiveness and independence. At least one planner felt that she could not appeal to the GIP without the chief executive viewing it as a "betrayal." Still, in at least a handful of cases, the involvement of the GIP has prevented politically motivated decisions that planners disagreed with from being forced through.

Embattled planners have also sometimes appealed to LUSPA, which, unlike the GIP, is a government body. In these situations, LUSPA may send planners from another jurisdiction to provide a second opinion. One planner gave me the example of a developer who was attempting to site a petrol station in a location that would have obstructed traffic. The chief executive was initially in favor of the application. This is possibly because, as the planner eventually learned, the developer had supported the chief executive in a political campaign by distributing T-shirts bearing his image. The local planning officer, concerned about the potential negative impacts of the proposed development, enlisted the support of representatives of LUSPA, the GIP, and other government agencies in opposing the decision. Faced with this unified opposition from planners even beyond his own district, the chief executive backed down. Despite this success, the planner in question also noted the risk he incurred of being punished with a transfer for doing so, particularly during an election year when politicians are especially sensitive to their public image. Indeed, the planner believes that this incident may have contributed to an unfavorable transfer two years later.

Planners in local governments have used their affiliation with LUSPA to insulate them from political pressure in the past. However, planners now worry that the recent moves toward decentralization of planning staff, discussed in the previous chapter, may have cut off this channel of support.

Planners may also conspire with other local government officials. Each local government has a Spatial Planning Committee (SPC), which deliberates over planning decisions. The SPC is chaired by the chief executive, has the physical planning department as the secretariat, and also includes members from other government agencies. Some of these agencies, including the Environmental Protection Agency and fire department, are centralized at the national level. This means that their local representatives are relatively insulated from local politics and have less to fear from opposing a chief executive in committee meetings. For this reason, planners have sometimes found it useful to discuss their dissenting views with these other officials individually, without the knowledge of the chief executive, to try to get them to vote against the chief executive's decision in committee meetings. Planners in Greater Accra mentioned having used this tactic successfully on at least two or three occasions. Local assembly members are also represented on the SPC, and planners have sometimes appealed to assembly members they consider "reasonable." These assembly members may then take it on themselves to convince others of the planner's position. One planner who had used this approach stressed the importance of maintaining a reputation for integrity in order to be able to enlist the support of these other committee members in this manner.[12]

Strategic Use of Public Participation

Another strategy that planners use to push back subtly against political decisions is to include public participation in the planning process, knowing that politicians would prefer not to expose some of these decisions to public scrutiny. The current and former directors of physical planning at AMA both described instances from the last five or ten years when they have used this approach in Accra or elsewhere. In one instance, a chief executive was receiving pressure from national party leaders before an election to approve developments that had been built within the right-of-way of a railway line. The planning director at the time was against this, as it meant that the AMA would have to pay compensation if they had to remove any of these structures in the future. He agreed to review the matter but said he would do so in a participatory manner, allowing the entire surrounding community to weigh in on whether the structures should be approved. In part, this was a stalling technique. He guessed, correctly as it turned out, that the incumbent party would lose the election. The chief executive lost his position when his party lost, and the matter was dropped.[13]

While that example involved planners trying to combat informal growth, others involved partially supporting it. One of the planners I spoke to recounted a land use planning and management project on which he had worked. Political leaders had insisted that an informal settlement be demolished as part of this project. The local planners felt that, as the community was well established and was "living in harmony," it would have been unnecessarily disruptive to demolish the settlement. They preferred to review structures on a case-by-case basis and to remove only those that blocked access for emergency vehicles and utilities. The planners engaged in a sustained outreach effort, meeting with resident associations, church members, elected assembly members, and representatives of other government agencies. They involved traditional chiefs, who recruited elders and other community members to participate in focus groups. The planners even hosted a weekly local radio show in which they discussed planning issues with the public (aired just before coverage of the soccer World Cup to ensure a high listenership). The planners were able to generate support for their approach from a wide array of stakeholders, which ultimately caused the political leaders to accept their position.[14]

Planning discourse often treats public participation as a mechanism through which a powerful institution, state planning, empowers and legitimizes a less powerful group, the public, by giving it a voice. Here, in Ghana's atmosphere of competitive clientelism, the tables are turned. It is planning that is the powerless force seeking to use public participation to borrow power and legitimacy from more powerful groups—namely, the voting public and, in the last example, traditional authorities as well. In some cases, no actual public consultation is even conducted; it is simply the threat of public exposure, disguised by planners in nonconfrontational techno-democratic terms as "public consultation," which causes the politicians to back down from potentially scandalous decisions. In my interviews with them, planners framed public consultation (or the threat of it) not as an opportunity for planners and politicians to get input from the public, but as a way for planners to lend weight to their preexisting opposition to decisions by politicians that the planners perceived as being based on short-term political calculation and potentially damaging to the long-term public interest.

Media Involvement

Ghana has relatively independent media, with the world's 30th freest press among 180 countries, according to Reporters Without Borders' 2020 World Press Freedom Index. This ranking puts Ghana higher than the United States, United Kingdom, and several western European countries.[15] In recent years, it has ranked as high as 22nd in the world.[16]

Television and radio stations carry stories and host debates on urban development issues regularly, and news outlets usually cover the demolition of informal settlements. The involvement of the media has caused politicians to back down from decisions that planners have opposed. One such case involved development on protected wetlands. The planning director of the local government in question secretly contacted the media about the issue, prompting a member of the public to take the government to court, which stopped the development. Another instance centered on the narrowing of a road in order to allow private development along it, a move opposed by the planner but supported by the chief executive. In this instance, it was the residents of the area who alerted the media, not the planner, but again the controversy forced the chief executive to back down.

The case of the thwarted attempt by senior government officials to rezone forest land for commercial use, related at the beginning of this chapter, illustrates both the political pressures that planners face (though in this case, not specifically from clientelism) and their use of various strategies in concert to try to resist such pressure. In this case, an entire suite of strategies worked in the planners' favor. Planners threatened public consultation, sought support from professional planning bodies, alerted the media, and also made use of a previously ignored provision in planning legislation.

Recommendations: Politically Adaptive Planning in Ghana

Rather than basing recommendations for planning in Ghana on supposed "best practices" from elsewhere or on abstract notions of how an ideal planning system should function, in this section I try to build recommendations on observations of what is already working—even if only partially, occasionally, or temporarily—for both planners and urban residents. The recommendations aim to satisfy two broad needs that sometimes pull in opposite directions. One is the need to free planning from political interference in order to facilitate the implementation of plans. The other is the need to support the rights of the urban poor living in informal settlements, in an environment in which the only reason they are able to remain where they are may be political interference itself. Any recommendations must balance these partially contradictory needs.

A Planning Watchdog: Insulating Planning from Political Interference Through an Independent Urban Planning Oversight Organization

The strategies of appealing to bodies such as the GIP and LUSPA and informing the public and the media of unsound political decisions have only been partially successful so far. Planners have had to use them cautiously. At times, their fear of provoking hostility and retaliation from political leaders has prevented them from taking these steps at all. The GIP and LUSPA have played a "watchdog" or oversight role at times, coming to the aid of local planners facing political pressures. However, this is not their primarily role, and they do not have the resources to devote staff to this task full-time. As a government agency, LUSPA is also not completely independent.

This suggests that an independent urban planning oversight organization might play a potentially useful role. Such an organization could be created with the involvement of Ghanaian civil society organizations and media outlets, and perhaps funded with support from international donors. The organization could either be independent from or affiliated with the GIP. It could reduce political interference in planning in several ways. It could respond to calls for support from planners facing political pressures, much like the GIP and LUSPA have sometimes done in the past. It could independently keep track of planning-related decisions, including new building permits issued as well as transfers of planning staff, and investigate those that appear politically motivated, even when local planners are unable to initiate such investigations. It could also alert the public and media to political interference in planning decisions, through the publication of reports and press releases.

An organization of this kind would have to balance the empowerment of planners with the need for accountability and transparency. It would need to prevent planners from abusing their newfound independence and indiscriminately demolishing informal settlements that may have been protected through clientelism previously. To do this, the organization might also ensure that any demolition of informal settlements is strictly justified on safety or environmental grounds, and that any demolition is accompanied by sufficient compensation and resettlement in a suitable location in accordance with international standards. Such an organization could require an independent arm within it dedicated to investigating violations of planning ethics.

As the examples in this chapter have shown, fear of political backlash has at times caused politicians to back down from self-serving decisions. If the work of an oversight organization were to systematically turn planning issues into campaign issues by giving them greater publicity, politics would work in favor of planning.

Planned Patronage: Facilitating the Provision of Coordinated, Long-Term Benefits in Low-Income Settlements

If *informal* means having social or political legitimacy but lacking official or legal legitimacy, then planning in Ghana is an example of the inverse of informality. It has only official or legal legitimacy, without any social or political legitimacy. Planning does not have inherent power of its own and is incapable of reshaping dominant power relations or the political settlement by itself. Planning tends to be taken seriously only when it aligns itself with the institutions that are already powerful within a given political settlement. Ideally, progressive planners can then push these institutions from within to act more sustainably and inclusively. The dominant political settlement in Ghana is competitive clientelism, and this is the powerful institution to which planning must adapt in order to wield any power. This echoes arguments made by other authors that policy should "work with the grain" of politics.[17] This means seeking opportunities for incremental reform that are compatible with the incentives of influential actors and preexisting social relations, even if the long-term aim of this reform is to change these incentives and social relations.[18]

Planners in clientelistic environments can seek ways to utilize the resources and channels that clientelism provides, while simultaneously moving the clientelistic provision of benefits toward more coordinated, long-term goods. This could mean working with poor urban communities and traditional authorities to prepare a coordinated wish list of community needs, with associated costs. Political patrons could then choose from this wish list, similar to how wedding guests select gifts from a registry established by the recipients. This has some similarities to the practice of participatory planning and budgeting, but it would apply not just to formal municipal service provision but also to patronage.

Such an approach could be potentially useful to planners, political patrons, and low-income communities alike. Planners could use their technical knowledge to help communities identify what benefits would be most useful, and include these on such a wish list. Planners could also coordinate the needs of adjacent communities and align them with larger spatial plans. Patrons could publicly sponsor certain benefits on the list, such as land titles, better drainage, paved roads, cement for the construction of public toilets, bulbs for streetlights, and so on, particularly in the run-up to elections. Providing benefits from the established list would then allow them to take credit more easily. The political parties might eventually find it useful to consolidate such lists across different settlements and pay for items or materials in bulk, rather than leaving it to individual candidates to determine and pay for the needs of their constituencies in isolation. The resulting economies of scale would result in greater provision of benefits than what is provided through the current, uncoordinated system.

In this scenario, client communities would be better equipped to hold patrons accountable if they did not deliver. In the competitive politics of Ghana, some communities would see bidding wars, and competing candidates would aim to outdo each other by providing the bigger or higher-priority item on the list, or by providing benefits in nonelection years in order to stand out. Other communities would, at first, be less favored than others. However, because the patronage benefits being received by other communities would be publicly known, these communities would become more aware of their neglect and better able to demonstrate it and demand more attention. In a competitive political climate, politicians would be eager to respond to those demands, especially if they could officially claim credit.

Ideally, local government planners would participate actively in such an exercise, coordinating among different communities and between community-level and city-level spatial plans. International development organizations, planning departments at universities, or others could perform some planning and coordinating functions in this regard, especially if local government planners were unable or unwilling to get involved. Community-based organizations active in informal settlements, such as the various grass-roots organizations affiliated with Shack/Slum Dwellers International, the Asian Coalition for Housing Rights, and others, could also play an important role in identifying community priorities and working with planners to refine and coordinate these priorities. As discussed in Chapter 3, these organizations have often been highly effective in identifying priorities, mobilizing community resources, gathering data, and using a range of strategies to work with, against, or around authorities as needed. However, these organizations have sometimes struggled to find effective modes of collaboration with professional planners.[19] A process such as this might be an opportunity to collaborate on a more level footing, if planners were willing to act as facilitators. Community-based organizations could also track the fulfillment of these needs and push patrons to spread their patronage more equitably across or within communities.

The notion of a "market" for political benefits of this sort may make some uncomfortable. However, a market for political favors already exists in informal settlements. The approach I propose does not create such a market but instead disciplines the existing one, by making it more transparent, inclusive, and demand driven. With the help of planners, communities can ensure that a wish list or "registry" results in the provision of not just the private favors and short-term, uncoordinated, supply-driven club goods that the political "market" currently provides, but also spatially coordinated, long-term public goods based on the needs that communities themselves express.

Chapter 5 mentioned the MP who worked with planners to site the roads he was paying for through his share of the Common Fund. Chapter 7 also described the aspiring MP who, following a fire, asked his supporters in Old Fadama to prepare a coordinated list of their needs. These incidents may be insignificant in isolation; however, they hint at a willingness on the part of political patrons to seek guidance from both planners and residents of informal settlements in determining the exact nature and location of discretionary benefits provided.

This intervention goes with, rather than against, a dominant political institution, in this case competitive clientelism. This may seem to contradict the argument I made in Chapter 1—that planning and clientelism are at odds—but the fact that the two cannot coexist indefinitely is part of the motivation for bringing them together. Just as clientelism has undermined a politically naïve form of planning in Ghana, the more politically astute form of planning I advocate here has the potential to undermine clientelism. A system of "planned patronage" can insidiously weaken clientelism from within, by pushing demands toward more long-term public goods. Such demands would include formal land titles and durable infrastructure in the case of informal settlements, which would eventually release communities from the need to depend on clientelism. This approach is, therefore, incremental at first but potentially transformative over time.

Guided Informal Growth

The prevalence of informal subdivisions globally points to new ways for state planners to engage with urban growth. Informal subdivisions in Accra make up half of new urban expansion and grow mainly through the actions of traditional authorities. As we have seen, these authorities hire unlicensed surveyors to subdivide customary landholdings for sale. Chiefs may prefer to avoid the effort and cost associated with formal subdivision, but the fact that they nonetheless pay for their landholdings to be spatially organized and subdivided before sale, rather than simply creating new plots on an ad hoc basis, suggests that demand exists for some form of spatial planning.

In response to this demand, local government planners could guide urban growth more effectively by developing recommended, but not legally binding, spatial layouts to chiefs who hold vacant land in rapidly urbanizing areas. These recommended layouts and subdivision guidelines could be devised with future infrastructure upgrading in mind. Prospective land buyers would likely demand subdivisions laid out according to these guidelines if this would make it easier for the government to provide infrastructure to them later. The state could also provide a special category of licenses to previously unlicensed surveyors, contingent on following certain minimal guidelines in their subdivisions.

The prospect of formalization of their practice, and the associated increase in demand and fees, would incentivize surveyors to comply.

This approach would follow historical precedent first established by British colonial administrators in Accra in the 1930s. Government reports at the time noted that while there was no formal planning, the government's extensive provision of layouts "by agreement with" the local chiefs or landowners had been effective in "ensuring correct development" of stool lands adjacent to Accra, and that chiefs and landowners actively requested such layouts (see Chapter 4). Even today, chiefs do sometimes seek the cooperation of government spatial planners, which means that the workability of this approach is plausible.

Generalizability of the Recommendations for Ghana to Other Countries

These three specific recommendations have been developed with urban Ghana in mind and may or may not be directly applicable to other contexts. Countries that share the following features with Ghana are likelier to find the recommendations useful:

Primarily political barriers to planning. All three recommendations take as a starting point the fact that the main barriers to the implementation of plans in Ghana are political. Ghana already has relatively supportive legislation in place, especially since 2016. It has at least some trained urban planners available in the public and private sectors, even if this number is relatively low. Funding is available for plans to be drafted, even if this funding is from external sources. The recommendations are likelier to translate to countries where this basic planning capacity exists, which may include several other middle-income democracies.

Competitive clientelism. The recommendations are more likely to be translatable to countries in which the dominant political settlement is competitive clientelism. A watchdog organization like the one described in the first recommendation is likelier to survive in a country where political power changes hands frequently. This would ensure that the incumbent party can foresee a time when it is in the opposition and may need to check abuses of power by its rivals. Close elections also give parties an incentive to compete vigorously in order to respond to lists of demands from an existing or potential client community, as described in the second recommendation.

Well-established and stable political parties. For the same reasons outlined in the previous point, the recommendations are also more likely to work in countries with a small number of relatively strongly institutionalized political parties rather than many independent, fly-by-night candidates who do not seek to build long-term reputations.

Civic activism and independent media. A nascent tradition of civil society activism and an independent media, both of which exist in Ghana, would aid a country in the institution of an oversight organization.

Prevalence of informal subdivisions. The provision of spatial layouts for subdivisions, as discussed in the third recommendation, is likely to be most effective in contexts where informal subdivisions are an established mode of urban growth—in other words, where large swathes of land are laid out prior to settlement. This shows that a demand exists for spatial planning. It is less relevant in places where atomistic settlements are the main form of informal urban growth. Many rapidly urbanizing democracies have significant proportions of new growth in the form of informal subdivisions. For example, on average, half of all the 1990–2015 growth that occurred in the Indian cities included in the *Atlas of Urban Expansion* was in the form of informal subdivisions. The equivalent share for Brazil, Mexico, the Philippines, and South Africa is roughly a third in each case.[20]

Politically Adaptive Planning: A General Framework

Guidelines

The recommendations in the previous section take a politically adaptive approach to planning in Ghana. This approach can be generalized into a set of guidelines that may be useful more broadly, especially in highly informal contexts.

Identify and build on what is already working. New political regimes, newly incumbent political parties or politicians, and donor agencies alike often feel the need to discard past practices or systems that appear to have failed. However, although there is rhetorical power in making a clean break from the past, it is rarely the most practical course of action. It loses the "tacit knowledge" and strategies developed over time by actors who understand the current system and replaces it with an untested system, which may well prove to be impractical in the given political context. A politically adaptive approach would be to identify previously undocumented practices that are already working in that context, both for planners and the public, and find ways to make more room for those practices to succeed more substantially.

For example, in Ghana, planners already use various strategies to circumvent political interference, including appealing to professional organizations, the media, and the public. Other studies and policies have not recognized these strategies or incorporated them into their recommendations for planning. The politically adaptive approach recommended here involves identifying and building on these strategies. Similarly, though the patron-client relationships between politicians and informal settlers have not resulted in long-term land-tenure security or adequate access to urban services, informal settlements have occasionally used these relationships to avoid demolition and receive services. The "planned patronage" approach builds on the positive aspects of these informal political relationships. The specific institutions and practices that are relevant in other contexts will be different from these, but planners can nonetheless apply the principle of recognizing and building on what is working.

Find approaches that "go with the grain" of existing political incentives while still aiming for long-term reform. Planning initiatives usually begin by identifying those who currently have unmet needs, who are the intended beneficiaries of the initiative. However, planners rarely identify in a systematic manner parties who may have a vested interest in maintaining the current situation and how they may use their power to block change. An important guiding question to ask when proposing any planning initiative is: *Why would someone in a position of power who benefits from the status quo support the proposed change?* If the only reason is that it is "the right thing to do" in an abstract sense, the proposal is unlikely to gain purchase.

The means by which these interests may hinder plans, projects, or policies may be overt, such as through public opposition, bribery, or intimidation. However, they may be more subtle, such as through professing support publicly but not providing the required resources to ensure success, or diverting the resources received to other uses. This is particularly relevant when initiatives are funded by international donors. Politicians have an incentive to be seen publicly with foreign officials and receive funds under the banner of a specific donor-funded project, but they may have little incentive to use the funds for the intended purposes. (The staff of donor organizations may also have an incentive to ignore irregularities, in the interest of making the project appear successful.)

For example, in Ghana, political patrons rely on clientelism for political support and thus have little incentive to support broad planning efforts. This leads many to lament the lack of "political will" on the part of politicians, as though it simply amounts to a lack of moral fiber. A politically adaptive approach takes the existing incentive structure seriously and works with, rather than against, the desire of politicians to provide benefits to informal settlements. Similarly, traditional authorities resist planning regulations that interfere with their ability to distribute or sell land. A politically adaptive approach acknowledges this and provides professional planning guidance to traditional authorities when they subdivide land.

Planners may assume that the intended beneficiaries of an initiative are in favor of it. However, intended beneficiaries may trust the established status quo, suboptimal though it may be, more than a proposed change. This is particularly likely in contexts where intended beneficiaries have been antagonized by planning efforts in the past. Communities may have invested their limited social and political capital in establishing the existing relationships and channels of access, and will be unlikely to give them up easily. In many cases, a failed or only partially successful planning initiative may do more harm than good, disrupting existing practices and networks without adequately compensating for them. Communities that oppose planning efforts intended to benefit them may be judiciously defending what little they have and showing understandable caution about the transformative potential of planning. A politically adaptive approach acknowledges this lack of trust and might use established relationships as channels of service delivery.

Recognize the social or cultural roots of existing practices. What appears to be political behavior may instead be a social or cultural behavior manifested through political institutions. The role of politicians in Ghana as patrons is an example of this. While it may appear to be a simple exchange of benefits for votes emerging from the demands of modern electoral politics, it is, in fact, rooted partly in traditional expectations of leaders as benefactors and family heads. As a result, rather than being destroyed by regulatory or institutional changes, clientelism may reemerge in a different form in the new environment. A politically adaptive approach recognizes the social and cultural roots of existing practices and finds paths to reform that maintain the positive aspects of these practices.

What all these points have in common is that they require planners to have a deep understanding of local conditions, including the political relationships and social norms that may not be immediately apparent to outsiders. This is particularly relevant for international organizations involved in urban development. A politically adaptive approach rules out the use of standardized project designs replicated from other contexts.

The Ethics of Politically Adaptive Planning

Politically adaptive planning is not about simply finding ways to implement plans by any means necessary, even if it involves "going with the grain" of an oppressive or otherwise harmful political regime. Planners have long been criticized for hiding behind the veneer of technocratic rationality to implement racist, anti-poor, or environmentally destructive agendas. To take an extreme example, Watson describes how planners in apartheid-era South Africa presented their profession as technically and politically neutral, but in doing so, in fact, became deeply implicated in enforcing the brutal, racist regime.[21] Political adaptation does not imply oblivious complicity, and it cannot justify an abdication of ethical responsibility. The goal of politically adaptive planning is to identify how the most effective ways to plan—that is, the most effective ways to provide long-term urban public goods in an inclusive and transparent manner—may differ based on local political realities. This does not obviate the equity and sustainability concerns that should be at the ethical center of planning.

Nonetheless, ethical questions in planning are rarely simple. Political adaptation may bring an additional layer of complexity that bromides such as "equity" and "sustainability" do little to resolve. What if an adaptive system such as "planned patronage" benefits the poor while simultaneously benefiting the popularity of an exclusionary or corrupt politician who has deep pockets for patronage? What if "guided informal growth" entails working with traditional authorities who are reaping personal financial rewards from the sale of land that is intended to belong to their community as a whole? When does a government's autocratic behavior go beyond the point that adapting one's planning approach to the prevailing regime, even if to do pro-poor work, becomes indefensible? I cannot attempt to answer these questions here. I can only suggest that planners who do attempt to adapt their approaches to prevailing politics prepare to reflect on the ethics of their actions along the way more carefully than they otherwise might.

Recognizing the Play Being Staged

"This sort of academic theorizing may be an amusing occupation for close friends chattering among themselves. But in a king's council chamber, where important matters are debated by important people, there's no time for such matters."

"But," said Raphael, "that's exactly my point. Kings have no time for philosophy."

"Yes they do," I replied, "but not for this ivory-tower theorizing, which makes no allowances for time and place. There's another philosophy, better suited to politics, which recognizes the play that's being staged, adapts itself to playing a part in it, revises what it has to say as the drama unfolds, and speaks appropriately for the time and place. That's the philosophy you should adopt. . . . You will have made a complete mess of the play that's being performed when you mixed it up with another, even if your speeches come from a better play than the one on stage."

—Thomas More, *Utopia* (1516)

T his exchange, written centuries ago, suggests that people have been debating whether policymakers ought to adapt policy to the political realities of their day for a long time. The fictional country from which the book *Utopia* takes its name has become a byword for an unrealistically idealized vision of society. This is ironic, because in the quoted passage, More argues for pragmatism, and against, in modern terms, the adoption of "best practices" that are in use in more successful systems ("speeches [that] come from a better play than the one on stage.") In this study, I have aimed to help planners and policymakers "recognize the play that's being staged." I have tried to make the case that urban growth in developing democracies cannot be fully understood, or guided to be more equitable or sustainable, without knowledge of the informal politics that drive it. The main arguments of the book have been the following:

Informal politics conflicts with urban planning. Politicians whose political power relies on narrowly targeted, short-term clientelism have a disincentive against supporting widely accessible, long-term formal planning, which would undermine the basis of their power. This makes it vital for urban planners in the Global South, along with policymakers and international organizations who aim to support them, to understand these informal political dynamics and to learn how to contend with them.

Informal politics shapes urban growth. New sources of global data allow us for the first time to measure the ways in which urban growth is related to informal political dynamics. They demonstrate relationships between urban spatial growth, which is the traditional concern of urban planners, and informal politics, which planners are not usually trained to recognize or adapt to. These findings reinforce the argument that planners need to understand and adapt to informal politics.

Building on existing local practices may be the most realistic means by which planners can operate more effectively in environments dominated by informal politics. Planning theories, government policies, reports by international organizations, and academic studies have not provided a practical way forward for planners struggling to cope with informal politics. Instead, planners improvise coping strategies that suit their specific contexts. Meanwhile, urban residents, particularly residents of informal settlements, use their limited political capital to get the support of politicians in accessing urban land and services. A politically adaptive approach to planning could recognize and build on these existing practices.

Directions for Future Research

I have aimed my recommendations in this book more at practitioners than at researchers. Nonetheless, the approach I have taken—as well as the important gaps that this book leaves unfilled—might suggest directions for future research as well.

Using New Sources of Quantitative Data for Mixed Methods Research

Most research on informal politics in low-income urban settlements has been qualitative and has focused on single settlements or cities. The analysis in Chapter 2 demonstrates that new sources of global data on land use patterns and political behavior can be combined to generate insights on the spatial impacts of urban politics. These data allow researchers to examine phenomena at spatial and temporal scales that are beyond the scope of a qualitative case study. Research has barely begun to exploit the full combined potential of data sets such as the Varieties of Democracy database, the *Atlas of Urban Expansion*, the Global Human Settlements database, and others. Many more such global data sets are likely to become available in coming years, taking advantage of machine learning, the increasing availability of satellite imagery, and other technological advances. The availability of data alone should not drive the research agenda, but it does promise possibilities for mixed methods research. For example, relationships observed in ethnographic data collection or interviews can be tested empirically across a large number of cities. Conversely, trends first observed in statistical models could be better understood through qualitative fieldwork.

Understanding Informal Subdivisions

Informal subdivisions are an increasingly important form of global urban growth, one that deserves more comparative investigation. According to data in the *Atlas of Urban Expansion*, the mean share of residential area in the *Atlas* sample of two hundred cities that took the form of informal subdivisions before 1990 was 17%, whereas the share in areas that grew between 1990 and 2015 was 29%. In cities in low- and lower-middle-income countries, which are expected to see the greatest amounts of urban growth in coming decades, the 1990–2015 share of informal subdivisions was higher still, at 35% (up from 21% in pre-1990 areas).[1]

While Chapter 2 discusses the broad correlation between informal settlements and clientelism globally, the exact role of informal politics in this type of urban growth is likely to vary based on different mechanisms of formation. The discussion in Chapter 6 suggested that the informal subdivisions in Ghana are often the result of customary land rights accorded to traditional authorities, who hire unlicensed surveyors to subdivide peri-urban land in ways that do not conform to planning regulations. This mechanism for the formation of informal subdivisions may be common in several African countries. It has also been documented in places as diverse as Mexico and the Pacific Islands, where some form of traditional land rights exist.[2] Other studies have described the formation of informal subdivisions through organized invasions of land,[3] the unauthorized subdivision of legally purchased land,[4] or the "informalization" of legal subdivisions over time.[5] These variations in the relationship between clientelism and informal subdivisions, and their implications for planning, warrant further study.

Comparing the Impacts of Informal Politics on Planning Across Sectors

This study has focused largely on the relationship between informal politics and land use. Several studies have examined the politics surrounding other informal urban sectors, including informal transportation,[6] informal retail,[7] or informal waste management.[8] Future research that compares the impact of politics on these other sectors with its impact on informal land use may be instructive to planners and policymakers. For example, is it easier for planners to work with informal transportation operators, because they are organized into route associations and unions, than it is to work with residents of informal settlements? If so, are there equivalent bodies in the case of informal settlements, or could such bodies be created? Do successful attempts at formalization of informal markets have any lessons for informal settlements in a similar political environment? Conversely, are "informal" settlements and other "informal" sectors so fundamentally different that they should not be grouped together as part of the same phenomenon ("urban informality") at all? This kind of comparative political analysis of urban informality across sectors has been rare, suggesting a gap in the literature.

Exploring Gender Dimensions of Clientelism and Planning

Future research should build on the small amount of literature that already exists on how the experiences of patrons, brokers, clients, and planners vary by gender. Studies of India and Argentina suggest that female politicians and brokers have fewer opportunities to engage in clientelistic behavior than their male counterparts.[9] A study in Benin found women voters to be more receptive than men to political platforms based on public policy, as opposed to clientelistic handouts.[10] Many of the grassroots organizations in informal settlements that push back on clientelism are led by women. Whether this means that an increase in the share of female politicians and voters would diminish clientelism deserves further investigation.

Among planners in Ghana, the threat of being transferred to remote locations is particularly potent due to its effect on families: for example, a planner's children or elderly parents may have to relocate with the planner to an inconvenient location to avoid separation. These threats may be more significant to female planners, as women are typically expected to bear a disproportionate burden of caregiving toward children and parents. This suggests that politicians may be particularly able to manipulate female planners. Although roughly half the planners I interviewed for this study were women, I did not focus on the gender dimensions of relationships between politicians and planners, which future studies may be able to illuminate.

Understanding Informality Beyond the Poor

In this book, I have focused on informality among the urban poor and politicians who interact with the urban poor. This is appropriate in the context of an investigation of clientelism, which is particularly relevant to poor communities. However, my intention in doing so is not to reinforce the mistaken notion that only the poor engage in informality or that only low-income settlements are "informal." Middle-class and wealthy residents of many cities in the Global South acquire land, build property, obtain urban services, and interact with the state in ways that might violate regulations just as much as residents of low-income settlements do, even if their dwellings are not called "informal." In addition, corruption has important impacts on how urban land and property markets function and on the ability of urban planning to produce inclusive and sustainable outcomes. While the poor can engage in clientelism because of their large numbers, it is the wealthy who engage in corruption, because they can best afford it. "Elite informality" is increasingly acknowledged among urban scholars,[11] and recent studies examine the phenomenon in individual cities.[12] Urban scholarship would benefit from more such studies that examine informality in a holistic manner, incorporating informality among the poor and nonpoor and the interactions between the two.

Looking Beyond Transnational Forces

The most influential scholarship on urbanization in low- and middle-income countries during recent decades has focused on the ways in which global forces, primarily neoliberalism and globalization, have pushed the poor into informality.[13] Scholars who drew attention to these forces, including Mike Davis, David Harvey, Saskia Sassen, and others, offered valuable insights and critiques. Both the Right and the Left in the Global North have attacked globalization in recent years, but transnational capital remains important, even if much more of it now comes from China, the Middle East, and other countries beyond the United States and Europe. This global capital drives up land and property prices and distorts the incentives of local governments, who feel the need to compete for such investment, often at the expense of the local poor.

However, the tendency to fit all discussions of urban informality anywhere in the world into narratives of neoliberalism and globalization has homogenized urban scholarship. New research can advance scholarship by filling in the local side of the story, which is at least as important but is often messier and more heterogeneous across countries, and more difficult to grasp. This would involve devoting more attention to the ways in which locally specific political factors interact with urban informality, regardless of whether or not they conform to dominant global narratives.

In invoking transnational forces to explain dispossession, displacement, and segregation in cities in the Global South, Davis, Harvey, Sassen, and others take as their conceptual starting point forces emanating from the United States and Europe. They appear to approach the cities of Asia, Africa, and Latin America mainly to collect evidence of the harm these forces do to the world's most vulnerable people, meanwhile paying little attention to the specific institutional structures or political dynamics at work in these cities. Even if this perspective is critical of the role of the Global North, it nonetheless place the Global North at the center of the story. Garth Myers observes that African cities in particular escape the attention of widely cited scholars such as Harvey and Sassen. He notes that despite their many important insights about transnational forces, these authors are "continually missing opportunities for seeing African cities as important loci of global processes or generators of urban stories worth telling and worth learning from."[14]

The dominance of narratives based on transnational forces may partly be a result of the fact that authors, editors, and readers in the United States and Europe, who remain influential in global discourse, relate more easily to narratives in which they see themselves, whether as hero or villain. It may also be that they feel comfortable focusing their critical attention on organizations they perceive as extremely powerful and important, such as international financial institutions or multinational corporations based in "Northern" capitals. They may not feel as comfortable with critiques of players they perceive as relatively powerless, or at least do not know as well, like minor local politicians and political brokers in low-income settlements who never make global headlines. Besides, as South African–origin scholars Susan Parnell and Jennifer Robinson observe, "academic-institution demands for high-impact scholarly publications in 'international' journals are biased against work that is not embedded in dominant theoretical frameworks."[15] An academic article about informality in any given city is probably more likely to be cited internationally if it focuses on the role of neoliberal capitalism than if it focuses on the low-level politician who is unknown outside his or her district.

Parnell and Robinson call for a "post-neoliberal" perspective on urbanization in the Global South. They argue that while critiques of neoliberalism are legitimate, these critiques "have come to dominate theoretical and political reflection in contemporary urban studies, and offer a ready-made interpretive framework for understanding the particular dynamics of urban policy formation in particular cities." This framework overlooks the fact that, in cities of the Global South, "traditional authority, religion, and informality are as central to legitimate urban narratives as the vacillations in modern urban capitalist public policy."[16]

Studies with a more "Southern" perspective, including this one, are much more acutely aware of locally specific economic, social, and political dynamics. Crucially, they also differ in their perception of who holds power on the ground. Studies with this perspective are likelier to perceive local politicians as manipulating international aid organizations to suit their own purposes than as passive, gullible victims of schemes hatched in Washington, London, or elsewhere. Scholars who take this perspective often base their understanding on extensive fieldwork in cities in the developing world. For example,

Durba Chattaraj, Kushanava Choudhury, and Moulshri Joshi, in their study on informal settlements in New Delhi, argue that the Western theories that are often used to explain what is happening in Indian cities, including Harvey's "dispossession by capitalist accumulation," are largely irrelevant to New Delhi. Instead, their discussion centers on the opposite phenomenon—namely, "regularization" of informal settlements by authorities—and on local political factors, including corruption and clientelism, as explanations.[17]

The urban sociologist Liza Weinstein calls into question the narrative of slum residents as hapless, undifferentiated victims of rapacious global forces. She notes that the communities she studied during ethnographic fieldwork in Dharavi, the large informal settlement in Mumbai, "did not resemble the 'surplus humanity' depicted in these writings: excluded, exploited, and expendable. . . . From this vantage point, Dharavi, and the experiences of at least some of its residents, seemed to complicate the typical accounts of the slum."[18] She takes issue with Harvey's characterization of a proposed redevelopment project in Dharavi as simply exemplifying the "obliterating character" of global capital on urban space. She notes that "local political factors shaped these conditions as much as globalization did."[19] The ability of the residents of Dharavi to remain in place suggests that something more complex than obliteration is taking place, she argues. Those who opposed the redevelopment were not innocent victims but often powerful and politically savvy actors with agendas of their own. This leads Weinstein to observe that this was "not a simple David-and-Goliath story of the innocent grassroots struggling against malevolent globality."[20] According to her, "while these authors [Davis, Harvey, and others] associate slum clearance and residential displacements with globalization and the workings of capitalism under conditions of neoliberalism, most scholars of urban India tend to ground their explanations of these processes in local politics."[21]

In 2008, Harvey wrote: "I wager that within fifteen years, if present trends continue, all those hillsides in Rio now occupied by favelas will be covered by high-rise condominiums with fabulous views over the idyllic bay, while the erstwhile favela dwellers will have been filtered off into some remote periphery."[22] The threat of eviction that Harvey alerts us to is certainly real. Some favelas have been demolished, and no doubt condominium developers have their designs ready to replace the rest of them if given the chance. Yet, the favelas mostly endure. Why has Harvey got this wrong? It may be because, in his attempt to use Rio de Janeiro only as an example of the effect of abstract global forces, Harvey fails to consider the agency of specific local actors in combatting these threats. A scholar with a perspective rooted in Rio, regardless of ideological leanings, might not have made the same prediction, because such a scholar might understand the local side of the story better.

Final Thoughts: Living with the Moral Ambiguity of Planning the Informal City

The moral world of informal politics and planning is confoundingly gray. Any honest exploration of it defies attempts to place actors and actions in simple moral categories. Understanding the role of informal politics and planning in the lives of the urban poor requires living with political and moral ambiguity, as I have tried to do in writing this book. Ideally, the accompanying discomfort and confusion can be a productive part of the research and policymaking process.

For example, I found the uncertainty about how exactly to interpret and portray the moral valence of planners in the Ghanaian case study to be a challenge. The case study was motivated in part by a desire to produce knowledge that would help planners to work more effectively in clientelistic conditions in which they typically have little independent power. I relied on information from local government planners in my fieldwork, and I present many issues and events from their perspective. Many planners I met are trying to do their best under extremely challenging circumstances, and it is not surprising that the most capable among them are perpetually on the verge of quitting their jobs. Planners are better equipped to implement participatory, inclusive, and sustainable plans if they are more empowered. However, it is also true that many of them are unsympathetic toward informal settlers. They participate in evictions and demolitions, sometimes accompanied by armed police officers, and might call for more demolitions if they had the power to do so. Empowering planners to do good might also empower them to harm the most vulnerable. In making recommendations for planning, I had to try to balance these conflicting considerations.

Similarly, a study like this one takes a risk in drawing attention to the involvement of the urban poor in patron-client relationships. Suggesting that the poor are "in cahoots with" politicians risks diminishing readers' sympathy for the poor. It might make some readers perceive them less like the helpless oppressed, deserving of aid, and more as opportunists living off the fat of a corrupt system and perpetuating it in the process. *If the settlements that avoid demolition over time are those that have powerful political patrons,* readers might think, *then surely residents of these surviving settlements are not that badly off after all. Why waste resources trying to help them?* To those who want to avoid lending credence to this point of view, it is easier to focus on confrontations between the poor and the powerful, discussing only demolitions and evictions and not informal dealmaking. Such an approach would certainly lend itself more easily to activism on behalf of these vulnerable communities. "It's complicated" does not make a stirring slogan.

However, focusing just on dramatic confrontations presents a misleading picture of the relationship between the poor and the powerful in cities of the Global South. Most residents of informal settlements (and most people anywhere) are not constantly engaged in a heroic struggle against oppression, but instead make a series of unheroic compromises with oppression so that they can go about earning livelihoods, raising families, and achieving modest personal ambitions. Clientelism is one such compromise. The fact that relationships between the poor and powerful politicians are often nonconfrontational and even mutually beneficial does not mean that they are ideal for the poor in the long run. A refrain throughout this study has been that clientelism undermines the provision of long-term public goods and tenure security, which would be better for the poor than short-term, narrowly targeted patronage. It would be misguided to think that residents of informal settlements who are engaged in clientelistic dealmaking do not face deprivation as a result of social, economic, and political inequality.

Finally, drawing attention to the ways in which the urban poor participate in informal politics also forces us to recognize that the poor have agency in their lives. Portraying the urban poor as helpless victims who are incapable of using their wits to maneuver for whatever benefits they can to make the best of a bad situation does a disservice to their dignity. If urban planners, policymakers, and international development organizations acknowledge the agency that the poor already have, they are more likely to include them as agents of change in planned reforms and interventions. This would make these efforts more likely to succeed.

APPENDIX

This appendix provides details on the data used in the analysis described in Chapter 2.

Data on Urbanization

Globally Consistent Urban Growth Metrics

The analysis in Chapter 2 uses two sources of data on global urban growth, the Global Human Settlements (GHS) database and the *Atlas of Urban Expansion*. The European Commission's GHS database maps and measures all human settlements across the world for the years 1975, 1990, 2000, and 2015.[1] It divides the earth's surface into one-square-kilometer grid cells on a map, estimates the population and built-up area in each cell using census data and satellite imagery, and then classifies each one as belonging to one of several types of settlement area. These include the following:

- *Urban center:* a cluster of contiguous grid cells, each of which has a density of at least 1,500 inhabitants per square kilometer or is at least 50% built-up, with a minimum total cluster population of 50,000.
- *Town:* a cluster of contiguous grid cells, each of which has a density of at least 300 inhabitants per square kilometer, with a total cluster population of between 5,000 and 50,000, which is not adjacent to an urban center.
- *Suburb:* cells that have a density of at least 300 inhabitants per square kilometer that are adjacent to an urban center or to a town with density greater than 1,500 inhabitants per square kilometer.

The remaining classifications, not used here, are *villages, dispersed rural areas,* and *mostly uninhabited areas.*

The GHS provides tabulated data on towns, suburbs, and the rural categories only as national aggregates. However, in its Urban Centre Database (GHS-UCDB), it also provides detailed tabulated data on all individual "urban centers," numbering several thousand in total. The GHS-UCDB defines an urban center based on its 2015 boundaries and then measures the population and built-up area in 1975, 1990, 2000, and 2015 within those boundaries.[2]

I used 7,536 GHS urban centers in the models described in Chapter 2. Of the original 13,135 urban centers in the GHS-GHS-UCDB, I dropped 2,832 for not passing the GHS's own quality controls because of false or uncertain positives. Varieties of Democracy (V-Dem) did not have corresponding national clientelism data for 1990 for a further 64 urban centers, and the World Bank's World Development Indicators data lacked corresponding 1990 national GDP data for another 450. Of the remaining urban centers, I dropped 2,253 for having built-up areas of less than one square kilometer or populations of less than 1,000 inhabitants in 1990.

The other source of data on urban growth comes from the *Atlas of Urban Expansion*, released in 2016 by New York University, the Lincoln Institute of Land Policy, and UN-Habitat. The data set presents a range of metrics on a globally representative sample of two hundred cities that had populations of 100,000 people or more as of 2010.[3] The sample is globally representative in two ways. First, the share of cities per region of the world in the sample is similar to the share of cities by region globally. Second, cities in the sample have a similar distribution in terms of the urbanization level of the countries that they are in (measured here as the total number of cities in the country) as the equivalent distribution for all cities in the world. It is not perfectly representative in terms of size, as it intentionally includes a disproportionate number of larger cities. Its urban definition is based on built-up extents. The *Atlas* team used semiautomated analysis of satellite imagery to delineate contiguous built-up areas to define the extents and used detailed population data from censuses and other sources to estimate the populations accommodated by those built-up areas for each city in the sample for the years 1990, 2000, and 2015.[4]

A Global Typology of Formal and Informal Residential Areas

In addition to the overall urban growth metrics, the *Atlas* also provides more detailed data on the built form of urban areas. For each of their two hundred cities, the *Atlas* team digitized and analyzed a random sample of ten-hectare "locales" within areas that existed before 1990 and areas that grew between 1990 and 2015, using high-resolution satellite imagery. They used this analysis to estimate, within both the pre-1990 areas and the 1990–2015 areas, the shares of each of four residential categories: *atomistic settlements, informal subdivisions, formal subdivisions*, and *housing projects*. Examples of the four categories of residential land use are depicted in Figure 3 in Chapter 2.

Atomistic settlements are settlements "with irregular layouts that were clearly not subdivided or laid out before residential construction took place. This category includes squatter settlements that grew incrementally without an overall plan, homes built on irregular parcels of land, or homes built on rural plots that were not regularly subdivided before their conversion to urban use." The other type of informal growth is informal land subdivisions (or simply informal subdivisions). The *Atlas* defines informal subdivisions as residential areas that appear to have been subdivided for urban use, with structures that are "typically laid out along straight or almost-straight roads, with regular intersections and standardized widths" and blocks that are "regular or semi-regular in size and shape, when topography permits," but are nonetheless "informal" as they "lack visible evidence of conformity to land subdivision regulations such as regular plot dimensions, paved roads, street lights, or sidewalks."[5]

The other categories of residential land use in the *Atlas* are formal land subdivisions (or simply formal subdivisions) and housing projects. Formal subdivisions "exhibit a higher level of regularity, a higher level of provision of infrastructure [fully paved roads, sidewalks, streetlights], and better connections to existing roads." Housing projects "range from large apartment tower projects to suburban tract housing" and are characterized by homogeneity of design, suggesting that they were "built by a single developer using variations on the same plan."[6]

Data on Clientelism

V-Dem, which is headquartered at the University of Gothenburg, Sweden, uses thousands of country experts around the world to produce metrics on political practices in 201 countries from the year 1789 onward. It describes itself as "one of the largest-ever social science data collection efforts."[7] The 2018 version of their data set included a clientelism index among its variables for the first time.

The clientelism index is intended to represent an answer to the question, "To what extent are politics based on clientelistic relationships?" Such relationships include "the targeted, contingent distribution of resources (goods, services, jobs, money, etc.) in exchange for political support."[8] V-Dem researchers construct the index from three indicators. The first is for the prevalence of vote buying. To construct this indicator, country experts were asked, "In this national election, was there evidence of vote and/or turnout buying?" Here, *vote and/or turnout buying* refers to "the distribution of money or gifts to individuals, families, or small groups in order to influence their decision to vote/not vote or whom to vote for. It does not include legislation targeted at specific constituencies, i.e., 'porkbarrel' legislation."[9] The second indicator is for the prevalence of particularistic versus public goods. Country experts were asked the extent to which most social and infrastructural spending in the national budget was either "particularistic" or in the form of "public goods." The questionnaire explains: "Particularistic spending is narrowly targeted on a specific corporation, sector, social group, region, party, or set of constituents. Such spending may be referred to as 'pork,' 'clientelistic,' or 'private goods.' Public-goods spending is intended to benefit all communities within a society, though it may be means-tested so as to target poor, needy, or otherwise underprivileged constituents. The key point is that all who satisfy the means-test are allowed to receive the benefit."[10]

The final indicator that is used to calculate the clientelism index relates to the most common form of "linkage" between parties and constituents. This refers to "the sort of 'good' that the party offers in exchange for political support and participation in party activities." Possible responses range from clientelistic goods to "local collective goods" to "policy/programmatic" goods.[11]

The quoted definition of particularistic goods is relatively broad, but this is understandable given the difficulty of distinguishing purely clientelistic spending from closely related categories. The fact that the indicator for party linkages considers local collective goods to score in between clientelistic and programmatic goods is not ideal for the purposes of this study. As I am particularly interested in local collective goods, this study might have been better served by an indicator that focused specifically on the existence of this type of good, rather than treating it as being in between two other types. However, overall, these three indicators combined are a good reflection of the concept of clientelism as used in this book, making the clientelism index a reasonable metric to use in analysis of this kind.

The original clientelism index is on a scale of 0 to 1, but in my models, I rescale it to a 0-to-10 scale to facilitate interpretation. It is calculated for each year. The version of the index I use here was designed so that higher values correspond to less clientelism. For example, the index values in 2015 for France, Sweden, and Norway—the least clientelistic countries in that year—were between 9.7 and 9.8 on a scale of 0 to 10, whereas the most clientelistic countries—

Papua New Guinea and Chad—both had index values of around 1.1. (Confusingly, more recent releases of the V-Dem data set, not used here, reverse the scale, so that more clientelistic
countries have higher index values.)

Limitations and Precautions

Using the GHS-UCDB has certain limitations related to how urban centers are defined.[12]
First, because urban centers are based on density thresholds, among other criteria, they can
exclude low-density suburban growth. However, this may not be a serious issue. Comparing
the urban footprints without suburbs (just the urban centers, as used in this analysis) with the
combined footprints of urban centers and suburbs suggests that using the urban centers alone
is the better option. In most cases, the two are very similar because the suburban fringe is so
small. Conversely, in other cases, the suburban area is so large that it extends far beyond what
one would consider to be the extents of a city. For example, nearly all of Bangladesh, most of
northern Vietnam, and a vast area of eastern China are classified as suburban, even though
satellite imagery shows that these areas are, in fact, densely populated rural areas. The urban
centers capture urban footprints more effectively.

Second, the GHS-UCDB defines an urban center on the basis of its 2015 boundaries and
then measures the population and built-up area in 1975, 1990, 2000, and 2015 within those
boundaries. This could exaggerate the appearance of population growth and densification
in urban centers over time, because cities that lost population, or parts of cities that reduced
in density before 2015 such that their populations or densities fell below the defining thresholds, were excluded, resulting in a selection bias. However, this is unlikely to have affected the
relationships between clientelism and population or density observed in the analysis in
Chapter 2, since there is no reason to expect that this bias varies systematically with clientelism across cities in the database.

Another reason for caution in interpreting results is that, in the absence of city-level data
for clientelism and GDP, national-level data have to be applied uniformly across all cities in a
country. This is unavoidable, even though the levels of clientelism and wealth probably vary
between cities in a country.

Finally, one needs to be cautious about identifying informal settlements on the basis of
standardized, purely visual characteristics, as the *Atlas* data set does. Informality is a complex and multifaceted phenomenon, one that varies widely between contexts. Many scholars
argue that informality is not simply a physical fact but rather a designation resulting from the
perceptions and prejudices of authorities.[13] Settlements perceived as informal may or may not
be illegal in their origins, and properties that are considered formal may violate as many
regulations as those that appear informal. Satellite imagery alone reveals little about the
political circumstances or intentions surrounding the growth of a settlement. Recent
scholarship also argues against what it sees as a reductive and constrictive formal-informal
duality, which implicitly "others" the informal.[14] By using *informal subdivisions* as a globally consistent category, as discerned from satellite imagery, I risk further reinforcing this
formal-informal duality, flattening the cross-context variation in modes of informality and
associating informality primarily with visual characteristics of the built environment. If so, I
do this in service of my larger goal of showing how these seemingly superficial characteristics
are, in fact, linked to informal behavior on the part of powerful actors in the supposedly formal political system.

NOTES

Introduction

1. According to the World Bank's World Development Indicators, the urban population of the world in 2014 was 3.88 billion, and 29.8% of the world's urban population lived in slums that year. These figures are based on the United Nations definition of slum households as those lacking one or more of the following conditions: access to improved water, access to improved sanitation, sufficient living area, housing durability, and security of tenure (World Bank, "Population Living in Slums"). Some scholars are critical of the use of the term *slum* (Mayne, *Slums*) and the statistics on slums used by the United Nations (Myers, *African Cities*).

2. United Nations, "New Urban Agenda."

3. Participatory Slum Upgrading Programme, "Slum Almanac 2015/2016."

4. Klopp, "Towards a Political Economy of Transportation Policy and Practice in Nairobi."

5. Björkman, "Becoming a Slum," 37.

6. Satterthwaite and Mitlin, *Reducing Urban Poverty in the Global South*, 61.

7. Aspinall and Berenschot, *Democracy for Sale*.

8. Nelson, *Access to Power*; Flyvbjerg, *Rationality and Power*; Bayat, *Life as Politics*.

9. Davidoff, "Advocacy and Pluralism in Planning"; Forester, *Planning in the Face of Power*; Flyvbjerg, *Rationality and Power*; Tait and Campbell, "Politics of Communication Between Planning Officers and Politicians"; Roy, "Urban Informality: Toward an Epistemology of Planning"; and Njoh, "Urban Planning as a Tool of Power and Social Control in Colonial Africa," among others.

10. Brooks, *Planning Theory for Practitioners*.

11. Watson, "Seeing from the South."

12. McDonnell, *Patchwork Leviathan*.

13. Zoomers et al., "Rush for Land in an Urbanizing World"; Steel, Van Noorloos, and Otsuki, "Urban Land Grabs in Africa?"; Côté-Roy and Moser, "Does Africa Not Deserve Shiny New Cities?"; and Moser, Côté-Roy, and Korah, "Uncharted Foreign Actors, Investments, and Urban Models in African New City Building."

14. Ghertner, *Rule by Aesthetics*; Roy and Ong, *Worlding Cities*.

15. Parnell and Robinson, "(Re)Theorizing Cities from the Global South"; Chattaraj, Choudhury, and Joshi, "Tenth Delhi"; Weinstein, *Durable Slum*; Pieterse, *City Futures*; and Levenson, "Becoming a Population."

16. Pieterse, *City Futures*.

17. Myers, *African Cities*.

18. Roy, "Why India Cannot Plan Its Cities"; Harvey, "Right to the City."

19. Watson, "African Urban Fantasies"; Graphic Online, "Govt Engages Singaporean Planner to Redevelop Accra into Modern City."

20. UN-Habitat, UN-Habitat Best Practices Database: Award Winners; Asian Development Bank, "Urban Innovations Series."

21. Watson, "Planned City Sweeps the Poor Away," 186.

22. Sanyal, "Hidden Success."

23. Forester, "Exploring Urban Practice in a Democratising Society."

Chapter 1

1. Gay, *Popular Organization and Democracy in Rio de Janeiro*; Gay, "Even More Difficult Transition from Clientelism to Citizenship."

2. Aspinall and Berenschot, *Democracy for Sale*.

3. Some authors, such as Kitschelt and Wilkinson ("Citizen-Politician Linkages"), use the terms *clientelism* and *patronage* interchangeably, a convention that this study largely follows. Piliavsky (*Patronage as Politics in South Asia*) suggests that anthropologists use the term *patronage*, whereas political scientists prefer the term *clientelism*. Other scholars distinguish between these two terms in different ways. Sparling (*Political Corruption*, 106) explains that some political scientists use *patronage* to refer to a highly personalized relationship, as distinct from *clientelism*, which they associate with "mass-based politics and the party machine." Others (Grindle, *Jobs for the Boys*; Herrera, *Water and Politics*) use *patronage* to mean the particularistic distribution of public sector jobs specifically. Yet others use the term *patronage* to refer specifically to the goods and benefits distributed through clientelistic exchange, rather than to the practice as a whole (Aspinall and Berenschot, *Democracy for Sale*, 25).

4. Coppedge et al., "V-Dem Country-Year Dataset 2018."

5. World Bank, *Helping Countries Combat Corruption*.

6. Zinnbauer, "Urban Land"; Zinnbauer, "Leveraging the Role of the Urban Planning Profession for One of the Central Policy Challenges of Our Times"; and Doshi and Ranganathan, "Contesting the Unethical City."

7. Aspinall and Berenschot, *Democracy for Sale*; Ayee and Crook, "Toilet Wars"; ICF Consulting Services, *Urban Governance and Services in Ghana*; and Westminster Foundation for Democracy and CDD-Ghana, *Cost of Politics in Ghana*.

8. Studies of urban clientelism include several in South Asia (e.g. Auerbach, "Clients and Communities"; Banks, "Livelihoods Limitations"; Benjamin, "Touts, Pirates and Ghosts"; Björkman, "You Can't Buy a Vote"; Chidambaram, "Welfare, Patronage, and the Rise of Hindu Nationalism in India's Urban Slums"; de Wit, *Urban Poverty, Local Governance and Everyday Politics in Mumbai*; Hackenbroch and Hossain, "Organised Encroachment of the Powerful"; Inskeep, *Instant City*; Jha, Rao, and Woolcock, "Governance in the Gullies"; Nahiduzzaman, "Housing the Urban Poor"; Roy, *City Requiem, Calcutta*), in Southeast Asia (Hutchison, "'Disallowed' Political Participation of Manila's Urban Poor"; Tomsa and Ufen, *Party Politics in Southeast Asia*), in sub-Saharan Africa (e.g. Adam, "Perceptions of Slum Dwellers and Municipal Officials on Factors Impacting the Provision of Basic Slum Services in Accra, Ghana"; Awal and Paller, "Who Really Governs Urban Ghana?"; Bénit-Gbaffou, "Party Politics, Civil Society and Local Democracy"; Fox, "Political Economy of Slums"; Gandy, "Planning, Anti-Planning and the Infrastructure Crisis Facing Metropolitan Lagos"; Levenson, "Precarious Welfare States"; Paller, "Informal Institutions and Personal Rule in Urban Ghana"; Paller, "Informal Practices of Accountability in Urban Africa"; Paller, "Contentious Politics of African

Urbanization"; Rajack et al., "Political Economy of Urban Land Management"; Robins, *From Revolution to Rights in South Africa*), and in Latin America and the Caribbean (e.g. Álvarez-Rivadulla, *Squatters and the Politics of Marginality in Uruguay*; Auyero, "Logic of Clientelism in Argentina"; Coates and Nygren, "Urban Floods, Clientelism, and the Political Ecology of the State in Latin America"; Gay, "Even More Difficult Transition from Clientelism to Citizenship"; Gray, *Demeaned but Empowered*; Herrera, *Water and Politics*; Holland, *Forbearance as Redistribution*; Koster and Eiró, "Clientelism in Northeast Brazil"; Murillo, Oliveros, and Zarazaga, "Most Vulnerable Poor"; Shefner, "Do You Think Democracy Is a Magical Thing?"; Weitz-Shapiro, "What Wins Votes.")

9. Bussell (*Clients and Constituents*) argues that constituency service plays an important but underappreciated role in clientelistic democracies. Her research in India demonstrates that nonpartisan, noncontingent but nevertheless individualized (i.e., nonprogrammatic) constituency service in the form of favors provided by high-level officials serves as an attractive alternative for constituents who are not favored by clientelistic or partisan distribution of benefits at the local level. This also allows the politician to reach additional potential voters and develop a personal reputation for responsiveness and generosity. In this manner, clientelism at the local level necessitates the granting of nonclientelistic favors by higher-level politicians.

10. Auerbach et al., "Rethinking Electoral Politics in India."

11. Aspinall and Berenschot, *Democracy for Sale.*

12. Aspinall and Berenschot, 144.

13. Sharma et al., "Land, Politics, and Insecurity in Slums."

14. Hicken and Nathan, "Clientelism's Red Herrings."

15. Gans-Morse, Mazzuca, and Nichter, "Varieties of Clientelism."

16. Álvarez-Rivadulla, *Squatters and the Politics of Marginality in Uruguay*, 57.

17. Auerbach and Thachil, "Capability, Connectivity, and Co-Ethnicity," 3–4.

18. Aspinall and Berenschot, *Democracy for Sale*, 1.

19. Álvarez-Rivadulla, *Squatters and the Politics of Marginality in Uruguay*, 157.

20. Koster and Eiró, "Clientelism in Northeast Brazil," 9.

21. Auyero, "Logic of Clientelism in Argentina."

22. Perlman, *Myth of Marginality.*

23. Burgwal, *Struggle of the Poor.*

24. Björkman, "You Can't Buy a Vote," 621.

25. Auyero, "Logic of Clientelism in Argentina:," 70.

26. Álvarez-Rivadulla, *Squatters and the Politics of Marginality in Uruguay*, 26–27.

27. Awal and Paller, "Who Really Governs Urban Ghana?," 8.

28. Mitlin, "Politics, Informality and Clientelism," 3.

29. Brusco, Nazareno, and Stokes, "Vote Buying in Argentina," 84.

30. Nelson, *Access to Power*, 211.

31. Gay, "Rethinking Clientelism."

32. Watson, "Co-Production and Collaboration in Planning," 70.

33. Benjamin, "Touts, Pirates and Ghosts"; Nelson, *Access to Power*; and Coates and Nygren, "Urban Floods, Clientelism, and the Political Ecology of the State in Latin America."

34. Aspinall and Berenschot, *Democracy for Sale*; Fergusson, Larreguy, and Riaño, "Political Competition and State Capacity"; Goodfellow, "State Effectiveness and the Politics of Urban Development in East Africa"; Herrera, *Water and Politics*; and McCaffery, *When Bosses Ruled Philadelphia.*

35. Keefer and Vlaicu, "Democracy, Credibility, and Clientelism"; Larreguy, Marshall, and Trucco, "Breaking Clientelism or Rewarding Incumbents?"; and Paller, *Democracy in Ghana*.

36. Roy, *City Requiem, Calcutta*.

37. Coates and Nygren, "Urban Floods, Clientelism, and the Political Ecology of the State in Latin America," 1314.

38. Davis, "Modernist Planning and the Foundations of Urban Violence in Latin America."

39. Gandhi, "'Informal Moral Economies' and Urban Governance in India."

40. Satterthwaite and Mitlin, *Reducing Urban Poverty in the Global South*.

41. Fawaz, "Exceptions and the Actually Existing Practice of Planning."

42. Pethe et al., "Re-Thinking Urban Planning in India"; Rajack et al., "Political Economy of Urban Land Management."

43. Roy, *City Requiem, Calcutta*, 154.

44. Satterthwaite and Mitlin, *Reducing Urban Poverty in the Global South*.

45. De and Nag, "Dangers of Decentralisation in Urban Slums."

46. Shami and Majid, "Political Economy of Public Goods Provision in Slums."

47. Keefer and Vlaicu, "Democracy, Credibility, and Clientelism."

48. Yıldırım, "Clientelism and Dominant Incumbent Parties."

49. ICF Consulting Services, *Urban Governance and Services in Ghana*, 129.

50. Satterthwaite and Mitlin, *Reducing Urban Poverty in the Global South*, 63.

51. Bénit-Gbaffou and Oldfield, "Claiming 'Rights' in the African City."

52. Robins, *From Revolution to Rights in South Africa*.

53. Levenson, "Precarious Welfare States."

54. McCaffery, *When Bosses Ruled Philadelphia*, 109.

55. Burgwal, *Struggle of the Poor*; Álvarez-Rivadulla, *Squatters and the Politics of Marginality in Uruguay*.

56. Satterthwaite and Mitlin, *Reducing Urban Poverty in the Global South*, 64.

57. de Wit and Berner, "Progressive Patronage?," 931.

58. Wood, "Staying Secure, Staying Poor," 456.

59. Syagga, Mitullah, and Karirah-Gitau, "Rapid Economic Appraisal of Rents in Slums and Informal Settlements", cited in Fox, "Political Economy of Slums."

60. Land grabbing has been defined as "the control—whether through ownership, lease, concession, contracts, quotas, or general power—of larger than locally-typical amounts of land by any persons or entities—public or private, foreign or domestic—via any means—'legal' or 'illegal'—for purposes of speculation, extraction, resource control or commodification at the expense of peasant farmers, agroecology, land stewardship, food sovereignty and human rights." European Coordination Via Campesina, "How Do We Define Land Grabbing?"

61. Inskeep, *Instant City*, 105.

62. Burgwal, *Struggle of the Poor*.

63. Khan, "Orangi Pilot Project Programs."

64. Björkman, "Becoming a Slum."

65. Buckley and Kalarickal, *Thirty Years of World Bank Shelter Lending*.

66. Owens, Gulyani, and Rizvi, "Success When We Deemed It Failure?"

67. Buckley and Kalarickal, *Thirty Years of World Bank Shelter Lending*.

68. Cromwell, "Over 1,000 Slum Dwellers Homeless After Demolishing Exercise at Old Fadama."

69. Banerji, "Court Order to Clear Delhi's Railway Slums Will Cause 'Great Distress,' Activists Warn"; Thirumurthy, "Chennai Residents Forcibly Evicted by Slum Clearance Board in the Midst of Pandemic."

70. Bhalla, "Forced Evictions Leave 5,000 Kenyan Slum Dwellers at Risk of Coronavirus."

71. Bahl and Martinez-Vazquez, "Property Tax in Developing Countries"; Franzsen and McCluskey, *Property Tax in Africa.*

72. Davis, "Modernist Planning and the Foundations of Urban Violence in Latin America," 386.

73. Perlman, *Myth of Marginality*, 166–67.

74. Holland, *Forbearance as Redistribution.*

Chapter 2

1. For example, Álvarez-Rivadulla, *Squatters and the Politics of Marginality in Uruguay*; Benjamin, "Occupancy Urbanism"; and Fox, "Political Economy of Slums."

2. Roy et al., "Emergence of Slums." The only model to incorporate politics is Amit Patel, Andrew Crooks, and Naoru Koizumi's agent-based model, named Slumulation, which incorporates the impact of politicians who aim to benefit electorally from a concentration of informal settlements (Patel, Crooks, and Koizumi, "Slumulation"). Alexander McGrath modifies the Slumulation model to incorporate electoral cycles, such that rents are lower and the enforcement of laws in informal settlements is more lax during election periods (McGrath, "Modified Agent-Based Model of Slum Formation").

3. A full discussion of the statistical models and results mentioned in this chapter is available in Deuskar, "Informal Urbanisation and Clientelism," and Deuskar, "Clientelism and Urban Growth."

4. All the models described in this chapter are ordinary least squares (OLS) models. Here, I only report results of models for the period 1990–2015, but I also analyzed the periods 1990–2000 and 2000–2015 separately, data permitting, with similar results.

5. Coefficients are expressed as a percentage change of the previous value here and elsewhere because the dependent variable is log-transformed.

6. These were the original set of two hundred cities minus a few outliers and a few more for which control variables were not available.

7. GDP per capita figures in this chapter are in constant 2011 international dollars. An international dollar has the same purchasing power as the U.S. dollar has in the United States.

8. Post, "Cities and Politics in the Developing World."

9. For a discussion of the relationship between state capacity and clientelism, see Bustikova and Corduneanu-Huci, "Patronage, Trust, and State Capacity."

10. Agyemang and Morrison, "Recognising the Barriers to Securing Affordable Housing Through the Land Use Planning System in Sub-Saharan Africa."

11. Levenson, "Precarious Welfare States."

12. Syagga, Mitullah, and Karirah-Gitau, "Rapid Economic Appraisal of Rents in Slums and Informal Settlements," cited in Fox, "Political Economy of Slums".

13. Inskeep, *Instant City*; Khan, "Orangi Pilot Project Programs."

14. Fox, "Political Economy of Slums"; Gillespie, "From Quiet to Bold Encroachment."

15. Álvarez-Rivadulla, *Squatters and the Politics of Marginality in Uruguay*; Björkman, "You Can't Buy a Vote"; Burgwal, *Struggle of the Poor*; De and Nag, "Dangers of Decentralisa-

tion in Urban Slums"; de Wit and Berner, "Progressive Patronage?"; Gandy, "Planning, Anti-Planning and the Infrastructure Crisis Facing Metropolitan Lagos"; Herrera, *Water and Politics*; Inskeep, *Instant City*; Perlman, *Favela*; and Weinstein, *Durable Slum*.

16. Álvarez-Rivadulla, *Squatters and the Politics of Marginality in Uruguay*.

17. Burgwal, *Struggle of the Poor*.

18. Hasan and Mohib, "Case of Karachi, Pakistan."

19. Álvarez-Rivadulla, *Squatters and the Politics of Marginality in Uruguay*; Burgwal, *Struggle of the Poor*.

20. Björkman, "Becoming a Slum."

Chapter 3

1. Sparling, *Political Corruption*, 106.

2. Aspinall and Berenschot, *Democracy for Sale*.

3. Nathan, *Electoral Politics and Africa's Urban Transition*.

4. ICF Consulting Services, "Urban Governance and Services in Ghana."

5. Nathan, *Electoral Politics and Africa's Urban Transition*.

6. Aspinall and Berenschot, *Democracy for Sale*.

7. Zinnbauer, "Leveraging the Role of the Urban Planning Profession for One of the Central Policy Challenges of Our Times"; Klopp, "Pilfering the Public."

8. Aspinall and Berenschot, *Democracy for Sale*, 250.

9. Aspinall and Berenschot, 21; Larreguy, Marshall, and Trucco, "Breaking Clientelism or Rewarding Incumbents?," 2.

10. Riis, *Battle with the Slum*, 427.

11. Nathan, *Electoral Politics and Africa's Urban Transition*, 282–84.

12. Shannon, "Political Machine I"; Lapomarda, "Maurice Joseph Tobin"; Hays, "Changing Political Structure of the City in Industrial America"; Nelson, *Access to Power*; Flanagan, "Progressives and Progressivism in an Era of Reform"; and Nathan, *Electoral Politics and Africa's Urban Transition*.

13. Pasotti, *Political Branding in Cities*.

14. Gay, "Even More Difficult Transition from Clientelism to Citizenship"; Gay, *Popular Organization and Democracy in Rio de Janeiro*.

15. Herrera, *Water and Politics*.

16. Larreguy, Marshall, and Trucco, "Breaking Clientelism or Rewarding Incumbents?"

17. Dyzenhaus, "Patronage or Policy?"

18. Pasotti, *Political Branding in Cities*.

19. Holland, *Forbearance as Redistribution*.

20. Holland, *Forbearance as Redistribution*. Clientelism in informal settlements in Turkey did not completely disappear. Recent research documents active clientelistic ties between the AKP and settlements that are, or at least were when they first formed, informal; Yıldırım, "Clientelism and Dominant Incumbent Parties."

21. Mitlin, "Politics, Informality and Clientelism"; Satterthwaite and Mitlin, *Reducing Urban Poverty in the Global South*; Weru, "Community Federations and City Upgrading"; and Lines and Makau, "Taking the Long View."

22. Mitlin, "Politics, Informality and Clientelism."

23. Appadurai, "Deep Democracy," 29.

24. Mitlin, "Politics, Informality and Clientelism," 21.

25. Weru, "Community Federations and City Upgrading."

26. Mitlin, "Politics, Informality and Clientelism."

27. Mitlin.

28. Patel, Arputham, and Bartlett, "We Beat the Path by Walking."

29. Datta, *Illegal City*, 96–97.

30. Álvarez-Rivadulla, *Squatters and the Politics of Marginality in Uruguay*; Burgwal, *Struggle of the Poor.*

31. Mitlin and Mogaladi, "Social Movements and the Struggle for Shelter"; Mitlin, "Beyond Contention"; and Mitlin, "With and Beyond the State."

32. Satterthwaite and Mitlin, *Reducing Urban Poverty in the Global South*, 197.

33. Flanagan, "Progressives and Progressivism in an Era of Reform."

34. Álvarez-Rivadulla, *Squatters and the Politics of Marginality in Uruguay*, 64–65.

35. Davidoff, "Advocacy and Pluralism in Planning."

36. Mitlin, "With and Beyond the State."

37. Mitlin, "Class Act."

38. Mitlin.

Chapter 4

1. Yeboah and Obeng-Odoom, "We Are Not the Only Ones to Blame," 78, 80.

2. Cobbinah and Darkwah, "Urban Planning and Politics in Ghana," 1229.

3. E. Gbeckor-Kove, interview with the author, June 12, 2019.

4. Arku et al., "Non-Compliance with Building Permit Regulations in Accra-Tema City-Region, Ghana."

5. Owusu-Ansah and Braimah, "Dual Land Management Systems as an Influence on Physical Development Outcomes Around Kumasi, Ghana."

6. Owusu-Ansah and Braimah.

7. Ghana Statistical Service, *Ghana Living Standards Survey 6—Main Report*; World Bank, *Enhancing Urban Resilience in the Greater Accra Metropolitan Area.*

8. Gaisie, Kim, and Han, "Accra Towards a City-Region."

9. World Bank, *City of Accra, Ghana, Consultative Citizens' Report Card.*

10. I conducted interviews for this study over a total of three months in Ghana, mostly in Greater Accra, across multiple visits in 2018 and 2019. The interviewees, some of whom I interviewed more than once, were: eight physical (i.e., spatial) planners in local governments, two other local government officials, one former mayor, one physical planner at a regional government, four physical planners at the national Land Use and Spatial Planning Authority (LUSPA), one representative of the Ghana Institute of Planners, four other national government officials, four representatives of Ghanaian NGOs, two representatives of international organizations, two private planning consultants, seven academic researchers, one researcher at a think tank, one private real estate developer, and an architect. More casual meetings with other experts, including political party "foot soldiers" who were active in informal settlements in Accra, provided additional material. My fieldwork also involved a visit to Kumasi; site visits to indigenous and informal settlements in Accra, including Ga Mashie, Old Fadama, and Agbogbloshie; and visits to outlying areas of Greater Accra.

11. Coppedge et al., "V-Dem Country-Year Dataset 2018."

12. *Urban population* here refers to the population in urban centers, towns, and suburbs per the Global Human Settlements data set (see Chapter 2) in 2015. *Recent urban population*

growth refers to change between 2000 and 2015 (the equivalent figure for 1990–2015 is nearly identical).

13. Fage et al., "Ghana."

14. Economist Intelligence Unit, "Democracy Index 2018."

15. Fage et al., "Ghana."

16. Stacey, *State of Slum*; McDonnell, *Patchwork Leviathan*.

17. Nathan, *Electoral Politics and Africa's Urban Transition*, 77.

18. Andrews, "Navigating Land Rights Institutions in the Greater Accra Region of Southern Ghana."

19. Nathan, *Electoral Politics and Africa's Urban Transition*, 75.

20. United Nations, "World Urbanization Prospects 2018."

21. European Commission, Global Human Settlement Layer (database): Country Fact Sheets Based on the Degree of Urbanisation.

22. Ghana Statistical Service, *Ghana Poverty Mapping Report*.

23. Nathan, *Electoral Politics and Africa's Urban Transition*, 49.

24. Ghana Statistical Service, *Ghana Living Standards Survey 6—Main Report*.

25. Mensah and Birch, "Powering the Slum."

26. Ghana Statistical Service, *Ghana Living Standards Survey 6—Main Report*; World Bank, *Enhancing Urban Resilience in the Greater Accra Metropolitan Area*.

27. World Bank, *City of Accra, Ghana, Consultative Citizens' Report Card*.

28. Bartels, "Uneven Waters of Accra and the Concept of Environmental Justice"; Gaisie, Kim, and Han, "Accra Towards a City-Region."

29. Bartels, "Uneven Waters of Accra and the Concept of Environmental Justice."

30. Gaisie, Kim, and Han, "Accra Towards a City-Region."

31. World Bank, *City of Accra, Ghana Consultative Citizens' Report Card*.

32. Accra Metropolitan Assembly and 100 Resilient Cities, *Accra Resilience Strategy*.

33. Ghana Statistical Service, *Ghana Poverty Mapping Report*.

34. Nathan, *Electoral Politics and Africa's Urban Transition*, 49.

35. Maoulidi, "A Water and Sanitation Needs Assessment for Kumasi."

36. Water and Sanitation for the Urban Poor, "Improving the Quality of Public Toilet Services in Kumasi."

37. J. E. Dadson, interview with the author, July 1, 2019.

38. J. Gyanfi, interview with the author, June 24, 2019.

39. Andrews, "Navigating Land Rights Institutions in the Greater Accra Region of Southern Ghana."

40. E. Gbeckor-Kove, interview with the author, July 16, 2019.

41. J. E. Dadson, interview with the author, July 1, 2019.

42. Boamah and Amoako, "Planning by (Mis)Rule of Laws."

43. Gillespie, "Real Estate Frontier."

44. Njoh, "Urban Planning as a Tool of Power and Social Control in Colonial Africa," 301.

45. "Christiansborg Castle (Osu Castle)."

46. Paller, *Democracy in Ghana*.

47. Jackson, "Sharing Stories from Jamestown."

48. Government of the Gold Coast, "Gold Coast—Report for 1910."

49. Jackson, "Sharing Stories from Jamestown."

50. Government of the Gold Coast, "Annual Report on the Social and Economic Progress of the People of the Gold Coast, 1931–32." This passage is also repeated in the equivalent reports for 1932–33, 1934–35, and 1936–37.

51. Fuseini and Kemp, "Review of Spatial Planning in Ghana's Socio-Economic Development Trajectory."

52. Jackson, "Sharing Stories from Jamestown."

53. Fuseini and Kemp, "Review of Spatial Planning in Ghana's Socio-Economic Development Trajectory."

54. Watson, "Seeing from the South."

55. Trevallion and Hood, "Accra—a Plan for the Town."

56. Government of Ghana, "Greater Accra Regional Spatial Development Framework"; Jackson, "Sharing Stories from Jamestown."

57. Paller, *Democracy in Ghana*, 104.

58. d'Auria, "From Tropical Transitions to Ekistic Experimentation."

59. Acheampong, *Spatial Planning in Ghana*; Fuseini and Kemp, "Review of Spatial Planning in Ghana's Socio-Economic Development Trajectory."

60. Paller, *Democracy in Ghana*, 104–5.

61. Accra Planning and Development Programme, United Nations Development Programme, and United Nations Centre for Human Settlements (Habitat), *Strategic Plan for the Greater Accra Metropolitan Area*; Larbi, "Spatial Planning and Urban Fragmentation in Accra."

62. E. Gbeckor-Kove, interview with the author, July 23, 2018.

63. Amoateng, Cobbinah, and Owusu-Adade, "Managing Physical Development in Peri-Urban Areas of Kumasi, Ghana."

64. Acheampong, *Spatial Planning in Ghana*.

65. Government of Ghana, "Greater Accra Regional Spatial Development Framework."

66. Graphic Online, "Govt Engages Singaporean Planner to Redevelop Accra into Modern City."

67. Ministry of Tourism, Arts and Culture and Adjaye Associates, "Marine Drive Accra, Concept."

68. Japan International Cooperation Agency et al., "Study on the Comprehensive Urban Development Plan for Greater Kumasi in the Republic of Ghana."

69. B. Arkhurst, interview with the author, June 28, 2019.

70. Duho, "790 LUSPA Staff Migrated to Local Government Service."

71. Accra Metropolitan Assembly, *2018–2021 Medium Term Development Plan*.

72. Government of Ghana, Land Use and Spatial Planning Act.

73. P. Owusu-Donkor, interview with the author, July 8, 2019.

74. Adom, "Tackling Informal Entrepreneurship in Ghana"; Osei-Boateng and Ampratwum, "Informal Sector in Ghana"; Obeng-Odoom, "Informal Sector in Ghana Under Siege"; Paller, "Informal Institutions and Personal Rule in Urban Ghana"; and Stacey and Lund, "In a State of Slum."

75. World Bank, *Rising Through Cities in Ghana*, 13.

76. Obeng-Odoom, *Governance for Pro-Poor Urban Development*.

77. Baah-Boateng and Vanek, "Informal Workers in Ghana."

78. Accra Metropolitan Assembly and 100 Resilient Cities, *Preliminary Resilience Assessment Summary*.

79. Japan International Cooperation Agency et al., "Study on the Comprehensive Urban Development Plan for Greater Kumasi in the Republic of Ghana."

80. Government of Ghana, "Greater Accra Regional Spatial Development Framework"; World Bank, *City of Accra, Ghana, Consultative Citizens' Report Card.*

81. Accra Metropolitan Assembly, *2018–2021 Medium Term Development Plan.*

82. Government of Ghana, "Greater Accra Regional Spatial Development Framework."

83. Daum, Stoler, and Grant, "Toward a More Sustainable Trajectory for E-Waste Policy."

84. Accra Metropolitan Assembly, *2018–2021 Medium Term Development Plan.*

85. Accra Metropolitan Assembly and 100 Resilient Cities, *Preliminary Resilience Assessment Summary.*

86. People's Dialogue et al., *City Wide Informal Settlement.*

87. Angel et al., *Atlas of Urban Expansion*, vol. 2.

88. The *Atlas* reports shares of 47% for informal subdivisions and 48% for atomistic settlements in Accra from 1990 to 2015 in the main data set, but 48% and 45%, respectively, for the 1991–2014 period in the historical data set. The values may have been projected to match the 1990–2015 period used in the larger data set (Angel et al., *Atlas of Urban Expansion*, vol. 2.)

89. Adjei Mensah, Antwi, and Acheampong, "Behavioural Dimension of the Growth of Informal Settlements in Kumasi City, Ghana."

90. Owusu-Ansah and Braimah, "Dual Land Management Systems as an Influence on Physical Development Outcomes Around Kumasi, Ghana."

91. Government of Ghana, *Ghana National Urban Policy Action Plan.*

92. Government of Ghana, *National Employment Policy.*

93. Government of Ghana, *National Housing Policy.*

94. Government of Ghana, *National Spatial Development Framework (2015–2035).*

95. Government of Ghana, *Greater Accra Regional Spatial Development Framework.*

96. Accra Metropolitan Assembly, *2018–2021 Medium Term Development Plan.*

97. Accra Metropolitan Assembly and 100 Resilient Cities, *Preliminary Resilience Assessment Summary.*

98. Accra Metropolitan Assembly and 100 Resilient Cities, *Accra Resilience Strategy.*

99. Japan International Cooperation Agency et al., "Study on the Comprehensive Urban Development Plan for Greater Kumasi in the Republic of Ghana."

100. Obeng-Odoom, "Informal Sector in Ghana Under Siege."

101. People's Dialogue et al., *City Wide Informal Settlement.*

102. GhanaWeb, "We'll Eject Agbogbloshie Squatters despite Protest."

103. GhanaWeb, "Ablekuma North Municipal Embarks on Demolition Exercise"; GhanaWeb, "Glefe Slums Go Down as Demolition Leaves Hundreds Homeless"; and GhanaWeb, "Unauthorised Structures Along Odorkor Highway Demolished."

104. Amnesty International, "When We Sleep, We Don't Sleep."

105. Oteng-Ababio and Grant, "Ideological Traces in Ghana's Urban Plans."

106. Cromwell, "Over 1,000 Slum Dwellers Homeless After Demolishing Exercise at Old Fadama."

107. Chasant, "Agbogbloshie Demolition."

108. McTernan, "Accra Slum Dwellers Suspect Cholera Demolitions Are a Pretext for Profit."

109. G. Owusu, interview with the author, July 19, 2018.

110. Gillespie, "Real Estate Frontier."

111. Obeng-Odoom, "Informal Sector in Ghana Under Siege"; Anyidoho, "Informal Economy Monitoring Study"; and Okoye, "Tourist-Friendly Informality Doesn't Always Tell the Whole Story."

112. Resnick, "Politics of Crackdowns on Africa's Informal Vendors," 9.

113. Crentsil and Owusu, "Accra's Decongestion Policy."

114. GhanaWeb, "AMA to Decongest Accra."

115. Resnick, "Politics of Crackdowns on Africa's Informal Vendors."

116. Broadbent, "Research-Based Evidence in African Policy Debates."

117. Obeng-Odoom, "Informal Sector in Ghana Under Siege."

118. Amedzro, "Expulsion of the Informal Sector Through Decongestion Exercises in Accra Metropolitan Area."

119. Gillespie, "From Quiet to Bold Encroachment."

120. Obeng-Odoom, "Informal Sector in Ghana Under Siege"; Anyidoho, "Informal Economy Monitoring Study."

121. Obeng-Odoom, "Informal Sector in Ghana Under Siege"; Ghana Trade Union Congress, "Case Law Involving Street Vendors in Accra."

122. Owusu-Sekyere, Amoah, and Teng-Zeng, "Tug of War."

123. Resnick, "Politics of Crackdowns on Africa's Informal Vendors."

124. Bob-Milliar and Obeng-Odoom, "Informal Economy Is an Employer, a Nuisance, and a Goldmine"; Gillespie, "From Quiet to Bold Encroachment."

125. Bob-Milliar and Obeng-Odoom, "Informal Economy Is an Employer, a Nuisance, and a Goldmine."

126. Owusu-Sekyere, Amoah, and Teng-Zeng, "Tug of War."

127. GhanaWeb, "Chaos at Amasaman as Traders Protest 'Unannounced Demolition' Exercise."

128. Oteng-Ababio and Grant, "Ideological Traces in Ghana's Urban Plans."

129. Brady and Hooper, "Redefining Engagement with Socio-spatially Marginalised Populations."

130. Amorse, "Akufo-Addo's Inner City and Zongo Development Ministry a Threat to NDC's Survival"; Brady and Hooper, "Redefining Engagement with Socio-spatially Marginalised Populations."

131. Ministry of Inner-City and Zongo Development. Official website.

132. Brady and Hooper, "Redefining Engagement with Socio-spatially Marginalised Populations."

133. Nyabor, "Akufo-Addo's 2019 State of the Nation Address."

134. GhanaWeb, "Nima Redevelopment Project."

135. GhanaWeb.

136. Stacey, *State of Slum.*

137. Gillespie, "From Quiet to Bold Encroachment."

138. People's Dialogue et al., "City Wide Informal Settlement."

139. Anyidoho, "Informal Economy Monitoring Study"; Okoye, "Tourist-Friendly Informality Doesn't Always Tell the Whole Story."

140. Kumar and Barrett, *Stuck in Traffic.*

141. Amoako and Cobbinah, "Slum Improvement in the Kumasi Metropolis, Ghana."

142. UN-Habitat, "UN-Habitat Provides Water and Handwashing Facilities for Tens of Thousands in Ghana's Informal Settlements."

143. Stoquart and Majale, "Mid-Term Evaluation of the Participatory Slum Upgrading Programme II."

144. Amoako and Cobbinah, "Slum Improvement in the Kumasi Metropolis, Ghana."

145. Grant, Oteng-Ababio, and Sivilien, "Greater Accra's New Urban Extension at Ningo-Prampram"; UN-Habitat, "Ningo-Prampram Planning Authority Approves Accra's Planned City Extension."

146. E. Gbeckor-Kove, interview with the author, June 12, 2019.

147. Ghanaian Chronicle, "Ningo-Prampram DCE Goes Tough on Land Fraud."

148. World Bank, "Concept Note."

149. These include: the District Development Facility 2 project, which provided performance-based grants to local governments to implement medium-term development plans (multiple donors, US$230 million, 2014–18); the Local Government Capacity Support Project, which aimed to improve urban infrastructure and services and municipal finance across forty-six local governments in Ghana (World Bank, US$175 million, 2011–18); the Greater Accra Metropolitan Area Sanitation and Water Project (World Bank, US$150 million, 2013–18); the Land Administration Project, which supported land registration and spatial planning (World Bank, US$50 million, 2003–18); the Support for Decentralization Reforms Project, which addressed urban management, urban services, and capacity building (Deutsche Gesellschaft für Internationale Zusammenarbeit, €21 million, 2003–16); and the Greater Accra Spatial Development Framework (World Bank, US$0.65 million, 2016–17). World Bank, *Enhancing Urban Resilience in the Greater Accra Metropolitan Area.*

150. Anyidoho, "Informal Economy Monitoring Study."

151. D. Ansah, interview with the author, July 26, 2018.

Chapter 5

1. African Planning Association and UN-Habitat, "State of Planning in Africa."

2. J. Afukaar, interview with the author, July 9, 2019.

3. Accra Metropolitan Assembly, *2018–2021 Medium Term Development Plan,* 287.

4. Jibao, "Ghana," 221.

5. ICF Consulting Services, *Urban Governance and Services in Ghana,* 46.

6. Accra Metropolitan Assembly, *2018–2021 Medium Term Development Plan,* 287.

7. Jibao, "Ghana," 221.

8. ICF Consulting Services, *Urban Governance and Services in Ghana,* 49.

9. Jibao, "Ghana," 221.

10. ICF Consulting Services, *Urban Governance and Services in Ghana,* 42.

11. E. Gbeckor-Kove, interview with the author, June 12, 2019.

12. J. Gyanfi, interview with the author, June 24, 2019.

13. P. Owusu-Donkor, interview with the author, July 8, 2019.

14. Yeboah and Obeng-Odoom, "We Are Not the Only Ones to Blame," 93.

15. K. K. Amedzro, interview with the author, August 17, 2018; M. Awal, interview with the author, August 17, 2018.

16. Acheampong, *Spatial Planning in Ghana.*

17. E. Gbeckor-Kove, interview with the author, June 12, 2019.

18. Arku et al., "Non-Compliance with Building Permit Regulations in Accra-Tema City-Region, Ghana"; Owusu-Ansah and Braimah, "Dual Land Management Systems as an Influence on Physical Development Outcomes Around Kumasi, Ghana"; and Yeboah and Obeng-Odoom, "We Are Not the Only Ones to Blame."

19. Paller, *Democracy in Ghana.*

20. Khan, "Political Settlements and the Governance of Growth-Enhancing Institutions"; Khan, "State Failure in Weak States."

21. Goodfellow, "Seeing Political Settlements Through the City"; Mitlin, "Politics of Shelter"; Croese, "State-Led Housing Delivery as an Instrument of Developmental Patrimonialism"; Gastrow, "Urban States"; and Jackman, "Dominating Dhaka."

22. Kjær, "Land Governance as Grey Zone."

23. Parks and Cole, "Political Settlements."

24. Khan, "Political Settlements and the Governance of Growth-Enhancing Institutions."

25. Mitlin, "Politics of Shelter."

26. Roy, "Anti-Corruption in Nigeria."

27. Khan, "Political Settlements and the Governance of Growth-Enhancing Institutions."

28. Goodfellow, "Seeing Political Settlements through the City."

29. Andreoni, "Anti-Corruption in Tanzania."

30. Khan, "Political Settlements and the Governance of Growth-Enhancing Institutions"; Mitlin, "Politics of Shelter."

31. Nathan, *Electoral Politics and Africa's Urban Transition,* 21.

32. Nathan, 97–98.

33. Nathan, 195.

34. Nathan.

35. Yeboah and Obeng-Odoom, "We Are Not the Only Ones to Blame," 87.

36. E. Gbeckor-Kove, interview with the author, July 23, 2018; K. Yeboah, interview with the author, July 17, 2018.

37. N. N. Amarteifio, interview with the author, July 2, 2019.

38. F. Tackie, interview with the author, July 30, 2018.

39. GhanaWeb, "Bill for Election of MMDCEs Laid in Parliament."

40. J. Paller, personal communication with the author, December 18, 2019; K. K. Amedzro, personal communication with the author, December 5, 2019.

41. Citi Newsroom, "Government Cancels December 17 Referendum."

42. K. Yeboah, interview with the author, July 17, 2018; G. Muquah, interview with the author, June 27, 2019; and G. Bob-Milliar, interview with the author, July 8, 2019.

43. F. Tackie, interview with the author, July 30, 2018.

44. M. Awal, interview with the author, August 17, 2018.

45. K. K. Amedzro, interview with the author, August 17, 2018; E. Gbeckor-Kove, interview with the author, July 23, 2018.

46. E. M. Tamakloe, interview with the author, July 23, 2018.

47. K. Yeboah, interview with the author, July 17, 2018.

48. Nathan, *Electoral Politics and Africa's Urban Transition,* 76.

49. M. Awal, interview with the author, June 10, 2019.

50. L. Amofa, interview with the author, June 18, 2019.

51. G. Bob-Milliar, interview with the author, July 8, 2019.

52. Westminster Foundation for Democracy and CDD-Ghana, *Cost of Politics in Ghana.*

53. Paller, *Democracy in Ghana*, 164.

54. ICF Consulting Services, *Urban Governance and Services in Ghana*.

55. M. Awal, interview with the author, August 17, 2018.

56. E. Gbeckor-Kove, interview with the author, June 12, 2019.

57. Paller, *Democracy in Ghana*, 140.

58. Nathan, *Electoral Politics and Africa's Urban Transition*.

59. E. Gbeckor-Kove, interview with the author, July 23, 2018; L. Amofa, interview with the author, June 18, 2019; A. Owusu-Afriyie, interview the with author, June 25, 2019.

60. Lindberg, "What Accountability Pressures Do MPs in Africa Face and How Do They Respond?"

61. Paller, "Informal Institutions and Personal Rule in Urban Ghana," 126.

62. Awal and Paller, "Who Really Governs Urban Ghana?," 8.

63. Levy, *Working with the Grain*.

64. ICF Consulting Services, *Urban Governance and Services in Ghana*, 11.

65. Appiah and Abdulai, "Competitive Clientelism and the Politics of Core Public Sector Reform in Ghana," 1.

66. Accra Metropolitan Assembly, *2018–2021 Medium Term Development Plan*, xvi.

67. Nathan, *Electoral Politics and Africa's Urban Transition*.

68. Hirschman, *Exit, Voice, and Loyalty*.

69. Bartels, "Uneven Waters of Accra and the Concept of Environmental Justice"; Gaisie, Kim, and Han, "Accra Towards a City-Region."

70. Abdul-Hamid et al., *SABER Engaging the Private Sector in Education Pilot Country Report*.

71. Jibao, "Ghana."

72. ICF Consulting Services, *Urban Governance and Services in Ghana*.

73. E. Gbeckor-Kove, interview with the author, July 23, 2018.

74. K. K. Amedzro, interview with the author, August 17, 2018; M. Awal, interview with the author, August 17, 2018; and R. Oduro, interview with author, August 8, 2018.

75. L. Amofa, interview with the author, June 18, 2019.

76. N. N. Amarteifio, interview with the author, July 2, 2019; K. Ohene-Sarfoh, interview with the author, July 20, 2018; and G. N. T. Tagoe, interview with the author, August 14, 2018.

77. C. Amoako, interview with author, July 9, 2019.

78. F. Tackie, interview with the author, July 3, 2018.

79. Arku et al., "Non-Compliance with Building Permit Regulations in Accra-Tema City-Region, Ghana."

80. Bartels, "Peri-Urbanization as 'Quiet Encroachment' by the Middle Class."

81. Yeboah and Obeng-Odoom, "We Are Not the Only Ones to Blame," 87.

82. However, Paller argues that politics in "purchased" settlements tend to develop along less narrowly targeted lines, and that these settlements see more provision of public goods through collective decision-making. Paller, *Democracy in Ghana*.

83. Yeboah and Obeng-Odoom, "We Are Not the Only Ones to Blame," 88.

84. Yeboah and Obeng-Odoom.

85. K. K. Amedzro, interview with the author, August 17, 2018.

86. Bussell, *Clients and Constituents*; Iyer and Mani, "Traveling Agents."

87. Aspinall and Berenschot, *Democracy for Sale*.

88. K. Yeboah, interview with the author, July 17, 2018.

89. J. Gyanfi, interview with the author, June 24, 2019.

90. E. Gbeckor-Kove, interview with the author, June 12, 2019.

91. J. Gyanfi, interview with the author, June 24, 2019.

92. A. Owusu-Afriyie, interview the with author, June 25, 2019.

93. M. Gariba, interview with the author, June 17, 2019; J. Afukaar, interview with the author, July 9, 2019.

94. Not all planners have antagonistic relationships with their chief executives or are powerless to enforce plans. One planner in the Greater Accra area who has support from his chief executive, and who also has some legal knowledge and a sympathetic local high court judge, told me that he had taken several developers to court for violating regulations, including twelve within one year. A. Owusu-Afriyie, interview with the author, June 25, 2019.

Chapter 6

1. Jackson, "Sharing Stories from Jamestown."

2. Joireman, *Where There Is No Government*; Obeng-Odoom, *Governance for Pro-Poor Urban Development*.

3. Joireman, *Where There Is No Government*.

4. Watson, "Seeing from the South."

5. Tieleman and Uitermark, "Chiefs in the City."

6. Boamah and Amoako, "Planning by (Mis)Rule of Laws."

7. Owusu-Ansah and Braimah, "Dual Land Management Systems as an Influence on Physical Development Outcomes Around Kumasi, Ghana," 694; Cobbinah, Asibey, and Gyedu-Pensang, "Urban Land Use Planning in Ghana."

8. Berry, "Everyday Politics of Rent-Seeking."

9. Tieleman and Uitermark, "Chiefs in the City."

10. A. Owusu-Afriyie, interview with the author, June 25, 2019; P. Owusu-Donkor, interview with the author, July 8, 2019.

11. S. Ayeh-Datey, interview with the author, July 2, 2019.

12. G. Muquah, interview with the author, June 27, 2019.

13. M. Gariba, interview with the author, June 17, 2019; J. Gyanfi, interview with the author, June 24, 2019; and A. Owusu-Afriyie, interview with the author, June 25, 2019.

14. C. Akyeampong, interview with the author, June 26, 2019; L. Amofa, interview with the author, June 18, 2019.

15. Amoateng, Cobbinah, and Owusu-Adade, "Managing Physical Development in Peri-Urban Areas of Kumasi, Ghana"; ICF Consulting Services, *Urban Governance and Services in Ghana*.

16. Cobbinah, Asibey, and Gyedu-Pensang, "Urban Land Use Planning in Ghana"; J. Afukaar, interview with the author, July 9, 2019; J. Gyanfi, interview with the author, June 24, 2019.

17. Ayee et al., "Local Power Struggles, Conflicts and Conflict Resolution."

18. J. Gyanfi, interview with the author, June 24, 2019.

19. Cobbinah and Darkwah, "Urban Planning and Politics in Ghana," 1239.

20. Boamah and Amoako, "Planning by (Mis)Rule of Laws."

21. Tieleman and Uitermark, "Chiefs in the City."

22. Paller, *Democracy in Ghana*.

23. Paller, "African Slums." By contrast, Joan Nelson distinguishes the relationship between a patron and client from the relationship between a traditional leader and follower in two ways: (1) The patron-client relationship is based on reciprocity and is at least partly voluntary on the part of the client, whereas, in principle, the follower automatically owes loyalty to a traditional leader regardless of whether the latter provides any benefits. (2) The patron-client relationship is "dyadic" (one-to-one) rather than one-to-many (though as we have seen, in the case of neighborhood-scale clientelism, this distinction does not hold). Nelson, *Access to Power.*

24. J. Gyanfi, interview with the author, June 24, 2019.

25. L. Amofa, interview with the author, June 18, 2019; K. K. Amedzro, interview with the author, June 28, 2019.

26. P. Owusu-Donkor, interview with the author, July 8, 2019.

27. G. Bob-Milliar, interview with the author, July 8, 2019.

28. J. Afukaar, interview with the author, July 9, 2019.

29. Appiah, "Fear Grip Chiefs as Asantehene Destools Two Chiefs, More Cases Pending."

30. G. Bob-Milliar, interview with the author, July 8, 2019.

31. S. Ayeh-Datey, interview with the author, July 2, 2019. Others agreed: G. Bob-Milliar, interview with the author, July 8, 2019; J. E. Dadson, interview with the author, July 1, 2019.

32. J. Afukaar, interview with the author, July 9, 2019.

33. Stacey, "Urban Development and Emerging Relations of Informal Property and Land-Based Authority in Accra."

34. Green, "Patronage, District Creation, and Reform in Uganda."

35. Owusu, "Decentralized Development Planning and Fragmentation of Metropolitan Regions."

36. P. Osei-Nyarko, interview with the author, June 12, 2019.

37. J. Afukaar, interview with the author, July 9, 2019.

38. GhanaWeb, "5 New Districts Coming."

39. GhanaWeb, "AMA Shrinked to Help Develop Accra Better—O.B. Amoah."

40. GhanaWeb.

41. Owusu, "Decentralized Development Planning and Fragmentation of Metropolitan Regions."

42. Green, "Patronage, District Creation, and Reform in Uganda."

43. Not everyone explains the creation of new MMDAs exactly as Owusu does. While most interviewees took for granted that it was politically motivated, each offered a slightly different take on the exact motivations behind it.

44. Unnamed individual, interview with the author; the interviewee preferred not to be quoted by name on this subject.

45. Owusu, "Decentralized Development Planning and Fragmentation of Metropolitan Regions."

46. P. Osei-Nyarko, interview with the author, June 12, 2019.

47. Fridy and Myers, "Challenges to Decentralisation in Ghana."

48. K. K. Amedzro, interview with the author, August 17, 2018; E. Gbeckor-Kove, interview with the author, July 3, 2018; and G. Owusu, interview with the author, July 19, 2018.

49. ICF Consulting Services, *Urban Governance and Services in Ghana.*

50. Accra Metropolitan Assembly, *2018–2021 Medium Term Development Plan*, 2–3.

51. World Bank, "Enforcing Accountability."

52. Accra Metropolitan Assembly, *2018–2021 Medium Term Development Plan*; Government of Ghana, *Greater Accra Regional Spatial Development Framework*.

53. Transparency International, "Corruption Perceptions Index 2020."

54. ICF Consulting Services, *Urban Governance and Services in Ghana*.

55. Ayee and Crook, *Toilet Wars*.

56. Andrews, "Navigating Land Rights Institutions in the Greater Accra Region of Southern Ghana."

57. Gillespie, "Accumulation by Urban Dispossession"; Gillespie, "Real Estate Frontier."

58. GhanaWeb, "Takoradi Residents Petition Mahama over Land Sales."

59. Gillespie, "Real Estate Frontier," 8.

60. ICF Consulting Services, *Urban Governance and Services in Ghana*.

61. Ayee and Crook, *Toilet Wars*; ICF Consulting Services, *Urban Governance and Services in Ghana*; and Owusu and Afutu-Kotey, "Poor Urban Communities and Municipal Interface in Ghana."

62. Westminster Foundation for Democracy and CDD-Ghana, "Cost of Politics in Ghana."

63. Ayee and Crook, *Toilet Wars*; ICF Consulting Services, *Urban Governance and Services in Ghana*; and Westminster Foundation for Democracy and CDD-Ghana, "Cost of Politics in Ghana."

64. Acheampong, *Spatial Planning in Ghana*, 131.

65. C. Amoako, interview with the author, July 9, 2019.

66. Andrews, "Navigating Land Rights Institutions in the Greater Accra Region of Southern Ghana"; L. Amofa, interview with the author, June 18, 2019; J. Gyanfi, interview with the author, June 24, 2019; E. Gbeckor-Kove, interview with the author, July 16, 2019.

67. Cobbinah and Darkwah, "Urban Planning and Politics in Ghana," 1230.

68. ICF Consulting Services, *Urban Governance and Services in Ghana*, 11.

Chapter 7

1. Lu, "Shop Names in Ghana."

2. Housing the Masses, *Final Report to People's Dialogue on Human Settlements on Community-Led Enumeration of Old Fadama Community, Accra, Ghana*.

3. Housing the Masses.

4. S. Ayeh-Datey, interview with the author, July 2, 2019.

5. Chasant, "Agbogbloshie Demolition."

6. Acquah et al., "Processes and Challenges Associated with Informal Electronic Waste Recycling at Agbogbloshie."

7. Daum, Stoler, and Grant, "Toward a More Sustainable Trajectory for E-Waste Policy."

8. Chasant, "Agbogbloshie Demolition."

9. Paller, "Building Permanence."

10. Grant, *Globalizing City*; Paller, "African Slums"; and Stacey, *State of Slum*.

11. Paller, "Building Permanence"; Paller, *Democracy in Ghana*, 194.

12. Amoako and Boamah, "Becoming Vulnerable to Flooding."

13. Paller, "African Slums."

14. Amoako and Boamah, "Becoming Vulnerable to Flooding."

15. N. N. Amarteifio, interview with the author, July 2, 2019.

16. K. Yeboah, interview with the author, July 17, 2018.

17. Paller, *Democracy in Ghana*.

18. Paller, "Building Permanence."

19. Stacey, *State of Slum.*

20. Amoako and Boamah, "Becoming Vulnerable to Flooding."

21. Paller, "Building Permanence."

22. Yeebo, "Bridge to Sodom and Gomorrah."

23. Paller, "Building Permanence."

24. Paller.

25. S. Ayeh-Datey, interview with the author, July 2, 2019.

26. Paller, "Meaning of Party Politics in Ghana's Urban Neighborhoods."

27. Paller, *Democracy in Ghana.*

28. Paller.

29. Yeboah and Obeng-Odoom, "We Are Not the Only Ones to Blame," 88.

30. Paller, "Building Permanence," 450.

31. Paller, *Democracy in Ghana*, 197.

32. Stacey, *State of Slum.*

33. K. Yeboah, interview with the author, July 17, 2018.

34. J. W. Paller, interview with the author, June 18, 2018.

35. Nunoo, "Old Fadama, Agbogbloshie to Get Social Amenities."

36. Bawumia, "Following my visit to Agbogbloshie and Old Fadama [. . .]."

37. Cobbinah, "Inside Ghana's Biggest Slum Residents Lean on Hope to Bear Covid-19."

38. Chasant, "Agbogbloshie Demolition."

39. Frimpong, "Planning Regimes in Accra, Ghana"; Gillespie, "From Quiet to Bold Encroachment"; Oppong, "Slum or Sustainable Development?"; Stacey and Lund, "In a State of Slum"; and Yeebo, "Bridge to Sodom and Gomorrah."

40. K. K. Amedzro, interview with the author, August 17, 2018; G. N. T. Tagoe, interview with the author, August 14, 2018; E. Gbeckor-Kove, interview with the author, July 23, 2018; and A. Y. H. Yakubu, interview with the author, July 16, 2018.

41. K. Yeboah, interview with the author, July 17, 2018.

42. N. N. Amarteifio, interview with the author, July 2, 2019.

Chapter 8

1. Pieterse, *City Futures*, 7.

2. World Bank, *Rising Through Cities in Ghana*, 28.

3. World Bank, *Enhancing Urban Resilience in the Greater Accra Metropolitan Area*, 51.

4. World Bank, 63.

5. Abankwa, United Nations Human Settlements Programme, and Ghana Women Land Access Trust, *Ghana.*

6. Accra Metropolitan Assembly and 100 Resilient Cities, *Accra Resilience Strategy.*

7. Carothers and de Gramont, *Development Aid Confronts Politics.*

8. Carothers and de Gramont, 3.

9. Ferguson, "Anti-Politics Machine."

10. Sarfoh, "Lost in Translation," 93.

11. Pieterse, *City Futures*, 14.

12. Aspinall and Berenschot, *Democracy for Sale*, 257–58.

13. World Bank, *World Development Report 2004*, 58.

14. ICF Consulting Services, *Urban Governance and Services in Ghana.*

15. Amoako and Cobbinah, "Slum Improvement in the Kumasi Metropolis, Ghana," 168.

16. Agyemang and Morrison, "Recognising the Barriers to Securing Affordable Housing Through the Land Use Planning System in Sub-Saharan Africa," 2655.

17. Cobbinah and Darkwah, "Urban Planning and Politics in Ghana," 1243.

18. Amoako, "Brutal Presence or Convenient Absence," 15.

19. Fuseini and Kemp, "Review of Spatial Planning in Ghana's Socio-Economic Development Trajectory," 319.

20. Cobbinah, Poku-Boansi, and Peprah, "Urban Environmental Problems in Ghana," 44.

21. Arku et al., "Non-Compliance with Building Permit Regulations in Accra-Tema City-Region, Ghana," 379.

22. According to UN estimates, 73% of Ghana's population will live in urban areas in 2050, the final year of its current projections. United Nations, "World Urbanization Prospects 2018."

23. Levy, *Working with the Grain*.

24. ICF Consulting Services, *Urban Governance and Services in Ghana*.

25. Nathan, *Electoral Politics and Africa's Urban Transition*.

26. Hays, "Changing Political Structure of the City in Industrial America."

27. M. Awal, interview with the author, August 17, 2018.

28. Nelson, *Access to Power*.

29. Nathan, *Electoral Politics and Africa's Urban Transition*.

30. Pasotti, *Political Branding in Cities*.

31. Larreguy, Marshall, and Trucco, "Breaking Clientelism or Rewarding Incumbents?," 21–22.

32. Aspinall and Berenschot, *Democracy for Sale*, 12.

33. Nathan, *Electoral Politics and Africa's Urban Transition*.

34. Frey, "Cash Transfers, Clientelism, and Political Enfranchisement"; Larreguy, Marshall, and Trucco, "Breaking Clientelism or Rewarding Incumbents?"

Chapter 9

1. K. Yeboah, interview with the author, July 17, 2018.

2. Government of Ghana, Land Use and Spatial Planning Act.

3. UN-Habitat, UN-Habitat Best Practices Database: Award Winners.

4. Asian Development Bank, "Urban Innovations Series."

5. Graphic Online, "Govt Engages Singaporean Planner to Redevelop Accra into Modern City."

6. Watson, "African Urban Fantasies."

7. Sanyal, "Hidden Success."

8. Forester, "Learning the Craft of Academic Writing," 50.

9. E. Ntsiful, interview with the author, June 17, 2019.

10. Ntsiful.

11. P. Osei-Nyarko, interview with the author, June 12, 2019.

12. G. Muquah, interview with the author, June 27, 2019.

13. K. Yeboah, interview with the author, July 17, 2018.

14. E. Gbeckor-Kove, interview with the author, July 23, 2018.

15. Reporters Without Borders, "World Press Freedom Index."

16. Reporters Without Borders, "Ghana."

17. Levy, *Working with the Grain*; Payne, "Interesting times indeed!"

18. Goodfellow, "Political Informality," 291; Pieterse, *City Futures.*
19. Mitlin, "Class Act."
20. Angel et al., *Atlas of Urban Expansion*, vol. 2.
21. Watson, "Ethics of Planners and Their Professional Bodies."

Conclusion

Note to epigraph: More, "Book One," 83–84.
1. Angel et al., *Atlas of Urban Expansion*, vol. 2.
2. Payne, *Informal Housing and Land Subdivisions in Third World Cities.*
3. For example, Burgwal, *Struggle of the Poor*; Holland, *Forbearance as Redistribution.*
4. Cunha, "Informal Land Subdivision and Real Estate Regularization."
5. Björkman, "Becoming a Slum."
6. Goodfellow, "Taming the 'Rogue' Sector"; Klopp, "Towards a Political Economy of Transportation Policy and Practice in Nairobi"; Kumar, "Understanding the Emerging Role of Motorcycles in African Cities"; and Venter, "Lurch Towards Formalisation," among others.
7. Gibbings, Lazuardi, and Prawirosusanto, "Mobilizing the Masses."
8. Nwosu, Nzeadibe, and Mbah, "Waste and Well-Being"; Rosaldo, "Revolution in the Garbage Dump."
9. Karekurve-Ramachandra and Lee, "Can Gender Quotas Improve Public Service Provision?"; Daby, "Gender Gap in Political Clientelism."
10. Wantchekon, "Clientelism and Voting Behavior."
11. Roy, "Urban Informality: Toward an Epistemology of Planning"; Yiftachel, "Theoretical Notes on 'Gray Cities'"; and Banks, Lombard, and Mitlin, "Urban Informality as a Site of Critical Analysis."
12. Müller and Segura, "Uses of Informality"; Herlambang et al., "Jakarta's Great Land Transformation"; Moatasim, "Entitled Urbanism"; and Swapan and Khan, "Urban Informality and Parallel Governance Systems."
13. Sassen, "Global City"; Davis, *Planet of Slums*; and Harvey, "Right to the City."
14. Myers, *African Cities*, 6.
15. Parnell and Robinson, "(Re)Theorizing Cities from the Global South," 603.
16. Parnell and Robinson, 594–96.
17. Chattaraj, Choudhury, and Joshi, "Tenth Delhi."
18. Weinstein, *Durable Slum*, 3.
19. Weinstein, 13.
20. Weinstein, xi.
21. Weinstein, 14.
22. Harvey, "Right to the City," 36–37.

Appendix

1. Florczyk et al., *GHSL Data Package 2019*; Pesaresi et al., "GHS-SMOD R2019A."
2. Florczyk et al., "GHS Urban Centre Database 2015, Multitemporal and Multidimensional Attributes, R2019A"; Florczyk et al., *Description of the GHS Urban Centre Database 2015.*
3. The *Atlas* data are available in the form of interactive charts and maps, as well as downloadable GIS and Excel files, at www.atlasofurbanexpansion.org.
4. Angel et al., *Atlas of Urban Expansion*, vol. 1, 1.

5. Angel et al., *Atlas of Urban Expansion*, vol. 2, 30.

6. Angel et al., 30.

7. Varieties of Democracy. "About V-Dem."

8. Coppedge et al., "V-Dem Codebook V8," 226.

9. Coppedge et al., 56–57.

10. Coppedge et al., 146.

11. Coppedge et al., 91; Sigman and Lindberg, "Neopatrimonialism and Democracy."

12. For a full discussion of the strengths and limitations of the GHS approach, see Roberts et al., "Urbanization and Development"; Deuskar and Stewart, "Measuring Global Urbanization Using a Standard Definition of Urban Areas."

13. Ghertner, *Rule by Aesthetics*; Roy, "Urban Informality: The Production of Space and Practice of Planning"; Yiftachel, "Theoretical Notes On 'Gray Cities'"; and Myers, *African Cities*.

14. Acuto, Dinardi, and Marx, "Transcending (in)Formal Urbanism."

BIBLIOGRAPHY

Abankwa, Victoria, United Nations Human Settlements Programme, and Ghana Women Land Access Trust, eds. *Ghana: Accra Urban Profile.* Nairobi: UN-Habitat, 2009.

Abdul-Hamid, Husein, Donald Rey Baum, Oni Lusk-Stover, Leslie Ofosu Tettey, and Laura Lewis De Brular. *SABER Engaging the Private Sector in Education Pilot Country Report : Ghana 2015.* Washington, DC: World Bank Group, 2017. http://documents.worldbank.org /curated/en/125361500360031594/SABER-engaging-the-private-sector-in-education -pilot-country-report-Ghana-2015.

Accra Metropolitan Assembly. *2018–2021 Medium Term Development Plan.* 2018.

Accra Metropolitan Assembly and 100 Resilient Cities. *Accra Resilience Strategy.* 2019. http:// www.100resilientcities.org/wp-content/uploads/2019/03/Accra-Resilience-Strategy.pdf.

———. *Preliminary Resilience Assessment Summary.* 2018.

Accra Planning and Development Programme, United Nations Development Programme, and United Nations Centre for Human Settlements (Habitat). *Strategic Plan for the Greater Accra Metropolitan Area: Draft Final Report.* Ministry of Local Government, Department of Town and Country Planning, December 1991. http://mci.ei.columbia.edu/millennium -cities/accra-ghana/additional-research-on-accra/.

Acheampong, Ransford A. *Spatial Planning in Ghana: Origins, Contemporary Reforms and Practices, and New Perspectives.* Urban Book Series. Cham, Germany: Springer International Publishing, 2019.

Acquah, Augustine A., Clive D'Souza, Bernard Martin, John Arko-Mensah, Afua Amoabeng Nti, Lawrencia Kwarteng, Sylvia Takyi, Isabella A. Quakyi, Thomas G. Robins, and Julius N. Fobil. "Processes and Challenges Associated with Informal Electronic Waste Recycling at Agbogbloshie, a Suburb of Accra, Ghana." *Proceedings of the Human Factors and Ergonomics Society Annual Meeting* 63, no. 1 (2019): 938–42.

Acuto, Michele, Cecilia Dinardi, and Colin Marx. "Transcending (in)Formal Urbanism." *Urban Studies* 56, no. 3 (2019): 475–87.

Adam, Abdul-Wahid. "Perceptions of Slum Dwellers and Municipal Officials on Factors Impacting the Provision of Basic Slum Services in Accra, Ghana." Master's thesis, Erasmus University—International Institute of Social Studies, 2013.

Adjei Mensah, Collins, Kwabena Barima Antwi, and Peter Kwabena Acheampong. "Behavioural Dimension of the Growth of Informal Settlements in Kumasi City, Ghana." *Research on Humanities and Social Sciences* 3, no. 12 (2013): 1–10.

Adom, Kwame. "Tackling Informal Entrepreneurship in Ghana: A Critical Analysis of the Dualist/Modernist Policy Approach, Some Evidence from Accra." *International Journal of Entrepreneurship and Small Business* 28, no. 2/3 (2016): 216.

African Planning Association and UN-Habitat. "The State of Planning in Africa." UN-Habitat. 2014. http://mirror.unhabitat.org/pmss/getElectronicVersion.aspx?nr=3537&alt=1.

Agyemang, Felix S. K., and Nicky Morrison. "Recognising the Barriers to Securing Affordable Housing Through the Land Use Planning System in Sub-Saharan Africa: A Perspective from Ghana." *Urban Studies* 55, no. 12 (2018): 2640–59.

Álvarez-Rivadulla, María José. *Squatters and the Politics of Marginality in Uruguay.* Latin American Political Economy. Cham, Switzerland: Palgrave Macmillan, 2017.

Amedzro, Kofi Kekeli. "Expulsion of the Informal Sector Through Decongestion Exercises in Accra Metropolitan Area: Response to the Informal Sector by City Authorities." Master's thesis, University College London, 2012.

Amnesty International. "'When We Sleep, We Don't Sleep': Living under Threat of Forced Eviction in Ghana." Index no. AFR 28/003/2011. April 2011.

Amoako, Clifford. "Brutal Presence or Convenient Absence: The Role of the State in the Politics of Flooding in Informal Accra, Ghana." *Geoforum* 77 (December 2016): 5–16.

Amoako, Clifford, and Emmanuel Frimpong Boamah. "Becoming Vulnerable to Flooding: An Urban Assemblage View of Flooding in an African City." *Planning Theory and Practice* 21, no. 3 (2020): 371–91.

Amoako, Clifford, and Patrick Cobbinah. "Slum Improvement in the Kumasi Metropolis, Ghana: A Review of Approaches and Results." *Journal of Sustainable Development in Africa* 13, no. 8 (2011): 150–70.

Amoateng, Paul, Patrick Brandful Cobbinah, and Kwasi Owusu-Adade. "Managing Physical Development in Peri-Urban Areas of Kumasi, Ghana: A Case of Abuakwa." *Journal of Urban and Environmental Engineering* 7, no. 1 (2013): 96–109.

Amorse, Amos Blessing. "Akufo-Addo's Inner City and Zongo Development Ministry a Threat to NDC's Survival." *Ghana Guardian News*, 2017. https://ghanaguardian.com/akufo-addos -inner-city-zongo-development-ministry-threat-ndcs-survival.

Andreoni, Antonio. "Anti-Corruption in Tanzania: A Political Settlements Analysis." Working paper 001, Anti-Corruption Evidence, SOAS, University of London, October 2017. https://ace.soas.ac.uk/wp-content/uploads/2017/09/ACE-WorkingPaper001-TZ -AntiCorruption-171102.pdf.

Andrews, Erin. "Navigating Land Rights Institutions in the Greater Accra Region of Southern Ghana: An Actor Network Theory Approach." Master's thesis, University of Ottawa, 2017.

Angel, Shlomo, Alejandro M. Blei, Jason Parent, Patrick Lamson-Hall, and Nicolás Galarza Sánchez. *Atlas of Urban Expansion: The 2016 Edition.* Vol. 1, *Areas and Densities.* New York: New York University; Nairobi: UN-Habitat; and Cambridge, MA: Lincoln Institute of Land Policy, 2016.

Angel, Shlomo, Patrick Lamson-Hall, Manuel Madrid, Alejandro M. Blei, and Jason Parent. *Atlas of Urban Expansion: The 2016 Edition.* Vol. 2, *Blocks and Roads.* New York: New York University; Nairobi: UN-Habitat; and Cambridge, MA: Lincoln Institute of Land Policy, 2016.

Anyidoho, Nana Akua. "Informal Economy Monitoring Study: Street Vendors in Accra, Ghana." Manchester, UK: WIEGO, July 2013.

Appadurai, Arjun. "Deep Democracy: Urban Governmentality and the Horizon of Politics." *Environment and Urbanization* 13, no. 2 (2001): 23–43.

Appiah, Danial, and Abdul-Gafaru Abdulai. "Competitive Clientelism and the Politics of Core Public Sector Reform in Ghana." Working paper 82, Effective States and Inclusive Development, University of Manchester, UK, 2017. https://nls.ldls.org.uk/welcome.html?ark: /81055/vdc_100058245019.0x000001.

Appiah, Francis. "Fear Grip Chiefs as Asantehene Destools Two Chiefs, More Cases Pending." Modern Ghana, June 25, 2019. https://www.modernghana.com/news/941152/fear-grip -chiefs-as-asantehene-destools-two-chiefs.html.

Arku, Godwin, Kenneth O. Mensah, Nii K. Allotey, and Ebenezer Addo Frempong. "Non-Compliance with Building Permit Regulations in Accra-Tema City-Region, Ghana: Exploring the Reasons from the Perspective of Multiple Stakeholders." *Planning Theory and Practice* 17, no. 3 (2016): 361–84.

Asian Development Bank. "Urban Innovations Series" (series description). Accessed November 3, 2021. https://www.adb.org/publications/series/urban-innovations.

Aspinall, Edward, and Ward Berenschot. *Democracy for Sale: Elections, Clientelism, and the State in Indonesia.* Ithaca, NY: Cornell University Press, 2019.

Auerbach, Adam. "Clients and Communities." *World Politics* 68, no. 1 (January 2016): 111–48.

Auerbach, Adam, Jennifer Bussell, Simon Chauchard, Francesca Jensenius, Gareth Nellis, Mark Schneider, Neelanjan Sircar, et al. "Rethinking the Study of Electoral Politics in the Developing World: Reflections on the Indian Case." *Perspectives on Politics* (2021): 1–15.

Auerbach, Adam, and Tariq Thachil. "How Clients Select Brokers: Competition and Choice in India's Slums." *American Political Science Review* 112, no. 4 (2018): 775–91.

Auyero, Javier. "The Logic of Clientelism in Argentina: An Ethnographic Account." *Latin American Research Review* 35, no. 3 (2000): 55–81.

Awal, Mohammed, and Jeffrey W. Paller. "Who Really Governs Urban Ghana?" Africa Research Institute. January 27, 2016. http://www.africaresearchinstitute.org/publications /who-really-governs-urban-ghana/.

Ayee, Joseph R. A., and Richard Crook. "'Toilet Wars': Urban Sanitation Services and the Politics of Public-Private Partnerships in Ghana." Working paper 213, Institute of Development Studies, Brighton, Sussex, UK, 2003. http://www2.ids.ac.uk/gdr/cfs/pdfs/wp213.pdf.

Ayee, Joseph R. A., Alex K. D. Frempong, Richard Asante, and Kwame Boafo-Arthur. "Local Power Struggles, Conflicts and Conflict Resolution: The Causes, Dynamics and Policy Implications of Land-Related Conflicts in the Greater Accra and Eastern Regions of Ghana." CODESRIA Research Reports. Dakar: CODESRIA, 2011.

Baah-Boateng, William, and Joann Vanek. "Informal Workers in Ghana: A Statistical Snapshot." Statistical Brief. Women in Informal Employment: Globalizing and Organizing (WIEGO), January 2020. https://www.wiego.org/publications/informal-workers-ghana -statistical-snapshot.

Bahl, Roy, and Jorge Martinez-Vazquez. "The Property Tax in Developing Countries: Current Practice and Prospects." Working paper, Lincoln Institute of Land Policy, Cambridge, MA, June 2007. https://www.lincolninst.edu/publications/working-papers/property-tax-deve loping-countries.

Banerji, Annie. "Court Order to Clear Delhi's Railway Slums Will Cause 'Great Distress', Activists Warn." *Reuters*, September 4, 2020. https://www.reuters.com/article/us-india -court-landrights-idUSKBN25V1XU.

Banks, Nicola. "Livelihoods Limitations: The Political Economy of Urban Poverty in Dhaka, Bangladesh." *Development and Change* 47, no. 2 (2016): 266–92.

Banks, Nicola, Melanie Lombard, and Diana Mitlin. "Urban Informality as a Site of Critical Analysis." *Journal of Development Studies* 56, no. 2 (2020): 223–38.

Bartels, Lara Esther. "Peri-Urbanization as 'Quiet Encroachment' by the Middle Class: The Case of P&T in Greater Accra." *Urban Geography* 41, no. 4 (2020): 524–49.

———. "The Uneven Waters of Accra and the Concept of Environmental Justice: Towards New Pathways of Analyzing Water Inequalities." WaterPower working paper, Governance and Sustainability Lab, Trier University, Trier, Germany, 2016. https://www.researchgate .net/publication/328477356_The_Uneven_Waters_of_Accra_and_the_Concept_of _Environmental_Justice_-_Towards_New_Pathways_of_Analyzing_Water _Inequalities.

Bawumia, Mahamudu (@MBawumia). "Following my visit to Agbogbloshie and Old Fadama [. . .]." Twitter. October 3, 2019. https://twitter.com/MBawumia/status/1179706471346589698.

Bayat, Asef. *Life as Politics: How Ordinary People Change the Middle East*, 2nd ed. Stanford, CA: Stanford University Press, 2013.

Bénit-Gbaffou, Claire. "Party Politics, Civil Society and Local Democracy—Reflections from Johannesburg." *Geoforum* 43, no. 2 (2012): 178–89.

Bénit-Gbaffou, Claire, and Sophie Oldfield. "Claiming 'Rights' in the African City." In *The Routledge Handbook on Cities of the Global South*, edited by Sue Parnell and Sophie Old- field, 281–95. London: Routledge, Taylor and Francis, 2014.

Benjamin, Solomon. "Occupancy Urbanism: Radicalizing Politics and Economy beyond Pol- icy and Programs." *International Journal of Urban and Regional Research* 32, no. 3 (2008): 719–29.

———. "Touts, Pirates and Ghosts." In *Sarai Reader 05: Bare Acts*, edited by Jeebesh Bagchi, Geert Lovink, Monica Narula, Shuddhabrata Sengupta, 242–54. Delhi, India: Sarai Pro- gramme, 2005.

Berry, Sara. "The Everyday Politics of Rent-Seeking: Land Allocation on the Outskirts of Ku- mase, Ghana." In *Negotiating Property in Africa*, edited by Kristine Juul and Christian Lund, 107–33. Portsmouth, NH: Heinemann, 2002.

Bhalla, Nita. "Forced Evictions Leave 5,000 Kenyan Slum Dwellers at Risk of Coronavirus." *Reuters*, May 6, 2020. https://www.reuters.com/article/us-health-coronavirus-kenya -homelessness-idUSKBN22I1VC.

Björkman, Lisa. "Becoming a Slum: From Municipal Colony to Illegal Settlement in Liberalization-Era Mumbai." *International Journal of Urban and Regional Research* 38, no. 1 (2014): 36–59.

———. "'You Can't Buy a Vote': Meanings of Money in a Mumbai Election." *American Eth- nologist* 41, no. 4 (2014): 617–34.

Boamah, Emmanuel Frimpong, and Clifford Amoako. "Planning by (Mis)Rule of Laws: The Idiom and Dilemma of Planning Within Ghana's Dual Legal Land Systems." *Environment and Planning C: Politics and Space* 38, no. 1 (2020): 97–115.

Bob-Milliar, George M., and Franklin Obeng-Odoom. "The Informal Economy Is an Employer, a Nuisance, and a Goldmine: Multiple Representations of and Responses to Informality in Accra, Ghana." *Urban Anthropology and Studies of Cultural Systems and World Eco- nomic Development* 40, no. 3/4 (2011): 263–84.

Brady, Colleen, and Michael Hooper. "Redefining Engagement with Socio-spatially Margin- alised Populations: Learning from Ghana's Ministry of Inner City and Zongo Develop- ment." *Urbanisation* 4, no. 1 (2019): 9–28.

Broadbent, Emma. "Research-Based Evidence in African Policy Debates: Case Study of Decongestion in Accra, Ghana." Working paper, Evidence Based Policy in Development Network, 2012. https://cdn.odi.org/media/documents/9119.pdf.

Brooks, Michael P. *Planning Theory for Practitioners*. Chicago: Planners Press, American Planning Association, 2002.

Brusco, Valeria, Marcelo Nazareno, and Susan C. Stokes. "Vote Buying in Argentina." *Latin American Research Review* 39, no. 2 (2004): 66–88.

Buckley, Robert M., and Jerry Kalarickal. *Thirty Years of World Bank Shelter Lending: What Have We Learned?* Directions in Development; Infrastructure. Washington, DC: World Bank, 2006.

Burgwal, Gerrit. *Struggle of the Poor: Neighborhood Organization and Clientelist Practice in a Quito Squatter Settlement*. Latin America Studies 74. Amsterdam: CEDLA, 1995.

Bussell, Jennifer. *Clients and Constituents: Political Responsiveness in Patronage Democracies*. New York: Oxford University Press, 2019.

Bustikova, Lenka, and Cristina Corduneanu-Huci. "Patronage, Trust, and State Capacity." *World Politics* 69, no. 2 (2017): 277–326.

Carothers, Thomas, and Diane de Gramont. *Development Aid Confronts Politics: The Almost Revolution*. Washington, DC: Carnegie Endowment for International Peace, 2013.

"Christiansborg Castle (Osu Castle)." Visit Ghana. Accessed April 6, 2021. https://visitghana .com/attractions/christiansborg-osu-castle/.

Chasant, Muntaka. "Agbogbloshie Demolition: The End of an Era or an Injustice?" Muntaka .com. August 22, 2021. https://www.muntaka.com/agbogbloshie-demolition/.

Chattaraj, Durba, Kushanava Choudhury, and Moulshri Joshi. "The Tenth Delhi: Economy, Politics and Space in the Post-Liberalisation Metropolis." *Decision* 44, no. 2 (2017): 147–60.

Chidambaram, Soundarya. "Welfare, Patronage, and the Rise of Hindu Nationalism in India's Urban Slums." PhD diss., Ohio State University, 2011. https://www.proquest.com /docview/925813415.

Citi Newsroom. "Government Cancels December 17 Referendum." December 1, 2019. https:// citinewsroom.com/2019/12/govt-cancels-december-17-referendum/.

Coates, Robert, and Anja Nygren. "Urban Floods, Clientelism, and the Political Ecology of the State in Latin America." *Annals of the American Association of Geographers* 110, no. 5 (2020): 1301–17.

Cobbinah, Joojo. "Inside Ghana's Biggest Slum Residents Lean on Hope to Bear Covid-19." My-JoyOnline.com. April 23, 2020. https://www.myjoyonline.com/features/inside-ghanas -biggest-slum-residents-lean-on-hope-to-bear-covid-19/.

Cobbinah, Patrick Brandful, Michael Osei Asibey, and Yaa Asuamah Gyedu-Pensang. "Urban Land Use Planning in Ghana: Navigating Complex Coalescence of Land Ownership and Administration." *Land Use Policy* 99 (December 2020): 105054.

Cobbinah, Patrick Brandful, and Rhoda Mensah Darkwah. "Urban Planning and Politics in Ghana." *GeoJournal* 82, no. 6 (2017): 1229–45.

Cobbinah, Patrick Brandful, Michael Poku-Boansi, and Charles Peprah. "Urban Environmental Problems in Ghana." *Environmental Development* 23 (September 2017): 33–46.

Coppedge, Michael, John Gerring, Carl Henrik Knutsen, Staffan I. Lindberg, Svend-Erik Skaaning, Jan Teorell, David Altman, et al. "V-Dem Codebook V8." Varieties of

Democracy (V-Dem) Project, 2018. https://www.v-dem.net/en/data/archive/previous -data/data-version-8/.

———. "V-Dem Country-Year Dataset 2018." Varieties of Democracy (V-Dem) Project, 2018. https://www.v-dem.net/en/data/archive/previous-data/data-version-8/.

Côté-Roy, Laurence, and Sarah Moser. "'Does Africa Not Deserve Shiny New Cities?' The Power of Seductive Rhetoric around New Cities in Africa." *Urban Studies* 56, no. 12 (2019): 2391–407.

Crentsil, Aba O., and George Owusu. "Accra's Decongestion Policy: Another Face of Urban Clearance or Bulldozing Approach?" *International Development Policy* 10 (October 1, 2018): 213–28.

Croese, Sylvia. "State-Led Housing Delivery as an Instrument of Developmental Patrimonialism: The Case of Post-War Angola." *African Affairs* 116, no. 462 (2017): 80–100.

Cromwell, Ama. "Over 1,000 Slum Dwellers Homeless After Demolishing Exercise at Old Fadama." MyJoyOnline.com. April 15, 2020. https://www.myjoyonline.com/news/national /over-1000-slum-dwellers-homeless-after-demolishing-exercise-at-old-fadama/.

Cunha, Alexandre. "Informal Land Subdivision and Real Estate Regularization: A Comparative Study between Colombia and Brazil." *University of Miami Inter-American Law Review* 40, no. 2 (2009): 315.

Daby, Mariela. "The Gender Gap in Political Clientelism: Problem-Solving Networks and the Division of Political Work in Argentina." *Comparative Political Studies* 54, no. 2 (2021): 215–44.

Datta, Ayona. *The Illegal City: Space, Law and Gender in a Delhi Squatter Settlement.* Farnham, UK: Ashgate, 2012.

Daum, Kurt, Justin Stoler, and Richard J. Grant. "Toward a More Sustainable Trajectory for E-Waste Policy: A Review of a Decade of E-Waste Research in Accra, Ghana." *International Journal of Environmental Research and Public Health* 14, no. 2 (February 2017): 135.

d'Auria, Viviana. "From Tropical Transitions to Ekistic Experimentation: Doxiadis Associates in Tema, Ghana." *Positions*, no. 1 (2010): 40–63.

Davidoff, Paul. "Advocacy and Pluralism in Planning." *Journal of the American Institute of Planners* 31, no. 4 (1965): 331–38.

Davis, Diane E. "Modernist Planning and the Foundations of Urban Violence in Latin America." *Built Environment* 40, no. 3 (2014): 376–93.

Davis, Mike. *Planet of Slums.* London: Verso, 2006.

De, Indranil, and Tirthankar Nag. "Dangers of Decentralisation in Urban Slums: A Comparative Study of Water Supply and Drainage Service Delivery in Kolkata, India." *Development Policy Review* 34, no. 2 (2016): 253–76.

de Wit, Joop. *Urban Poverty, Local Governance and Everyday Politics in Mumbai.* First South Asia edition. Cities and the Urban Imperative. Abingdon, Oxfordshire, UK: Routledge, 2017.

de Wit, Joop, and Erhard Berner. "Progressive Patronage? Municipalities, NGOs, CBOs and the Limits to Slum Dwellers' Empowerment." *Development and Change* 40, no. 5 (2009): 927–47.

Deuskar, Chandan. "Clientelism and Urban Growth: A Global Analysis." Unpublished working paper, 2020.

———. "Informal Urbanisation and Clientelism: Measuring the Global Relationship." *Urban Studies* 57, no. 12 (2020): 2473–90.

Deuskar, Chandan, and Benjamin P. Stewart. "Measuring Global Urbanization Using a Standard Definition of Urban Areas: Analysis of Preliminary Results." Paper presented at the Land and Poverty Conference 2016: Scaling Up Responsible Land Governance, Washington, DC, March 14–18, 2016.

Doshi, Sapana, and Malini Ranganathan. "Contesting the Unethical City: Land Dispossession and Corruption Narratives in Urban India." *Annals of the American Association of Geographers* 107, no. 1 (2017): 183–99.

Duho, Rebecca Quaicoe. "790 LUSPA Staff Migrated to Local Government Service." Graphic Online. March 30, 2019. https://www.graphic.com.gh/news/general-news/ghana-news-790 -luspa-staff-migrated-to-local-government-service.html.

Dyzenhaus, Alex. "Patronage or Policy? The Politics of Property Rights Formalization in Kenya." *World Development* 146 (October 2021): 105580.

Economist Intelligence Unit. "Democracy Index 2018: Me Too? Political Participation, Protest and Democracy." 2019. http://www.eiu.com/Handlers/WhitepaperHandler.ashx?fi =Democracy_Index_2018.pdf&mode=wp&campaignid=Democracy2018.

European Commission. Global Human Settlement Layer (database): Country Fact Sheets Based on the Degree of Urbanisation. Accessed April 4, 2019. https://ghsl.jrc.ec.europa.eu/gate .php?waw=708010138021.

European Coordination Via Campesina. "How Do We Define Land Grabbing?" European Coordination Via Campesina, November 23, 2016. https://www.eurovia.org/how-do-we -define-land-grabbing/.

Fage, John D., Donna J. Maier, Oliver Davies, and Ernest Amano Boateng. "Ghana." In *Encyclopedia Britannica*, online ed. Last updated July 12, 2019. https://www.britannica.com /place/Ghana.

Fawaz, Mona. "Exceptions and the Actually Existing Practice of Planning: Beirut (Lebanon) as Case Study." *Urban Studies* 54, no. 8 (2017): 1938–55.

Ferguson, James. "The Anti-Politics Machine." In *The Anthropology of the State: A Reader*, edited by Aradhana Sharma and Akhil Gupta, 270–86. Oxford, UK: Blackwell Publishing, 2006.

Fergusson, Leopoldo, Horacio Larreguy, and Juan Felipe Riaño. "Political Competition and State Capacity: Evidence from a Land Allocation Program in Mexico," 2016.

Flanagan, Maureen A. "Progressives and Progressivism in an Era of Reform." In *Oxford Research Encyclopedia of American History*. Oxford University Press, online ed., 2021. Article published August 5, 2016. https://doi.org/10.1093/acrefore/9780199329175.013.84.

Florczyk, Aneta J., Christina Corbane, Daniele Ehrlich, Sergio Freire, Thomas Kemper, Luca Maffenini, Michele Melchiorri, et al. *GHSL Data Package 2019.* Luxembourg: Publications Office of the European Union, 2019. http://publications.europa.eu/publication/manifes tation_identifier/PUB_KJNA29788ENN.

Florczyk, Aneta J., Christina Corbane, Marcello Schiavina, Martino Pesaresi, Luca Maffenini, Michele Melchiorri, Panagiotis Politis, et al. "GHS Urban Centre Database 2015, Multitemporal and Multidimensional Attributes, R2019A." European Commission, Joint Research Centre (JRC), 2019.

Florczyk, Aneta J., Michele Melchiorri, Christina Corbane, Marcello Schiavina, Luca Maffenini, Martino Pesaresi, Panagiotis Politis, et al. *Description of the GHS Urban Centre Database 2015, Public Release 2019, Version 1.0.* Luxembourg: Publications Office of the

European Union, 2019. http://publications.europa.eu/publication/manifestation_identifier
/PUB_KJ0219103ENN.

Flyvbjerg, Bent. *Rationality and Power: Democracy in Practice*. Morality and Society. Chicago:
University of Chicago Press, 1998.

Forester, John. "Exploring Urban Practice in a Democratising Society: Opportunities, Tech-
niques and Challenges." *Development Southern Africa* 23, no. 5 (2006): 569–86.

———. "Learning the Craft of Academic Writing." In *The Routledge Handbook of Planning
Research Methods*, edited by Elisabete A. Silva, Patsy Healey, Neil Harris, and Pieter Van
den Broeck, 40–54. New York: Routledge, 2014.

———. *Planning in the Face of Power*. Berkeley: University of California Press, 1989.

Fox, Sean. "The Political Economy of Slums: Theory and Evidence from Sub-Saharan Africa."
World Development 54 (2014): 191–203.

Franzsen, R. C. D., and William J. McCluskey, eds. *Property Tax in Africa: Status, Challenges,
and Prospects*. Cambridge, MA: Lincoln Institute of Land Policy, 2017.

Frey, Anderson. "Cash Transfers, Clientelism, and Political Enfranchisement: Evidence from
Brazil." *Journal of Public Economics* 176 (August 2019): 1–17.

Fridy, Kevin S., and William M. Myers. "Challenges to Decentralisation in Ghana: Where Do
Citizens Seek Assistance?" *Commonwealth and Comparative Politics* 57, no. 1 (2019):
71–92.

Frimpong, Jesse. "Planning Regimes in Accra, Ghana." Master's thesis, University of Water-
loo, 2017.

Fuseini, Issahaka, and Jaco Kemp. "A Review of Spatial Planning in Ghana's Socio-Economic
Development Trajectory: A Sustainable Development Perspective." *Land Use Policy* 47
(September 2015): 309–20.

Gaisie, Eric, Hyung Min Kim, and Sun Sheng Han. "Accra Towards a City-Region: Devolution, Spatial Development and Urban Challenges." *Cities* 95 (December 2019): 102398.

Gandhi, Ajay. "'Informal Moral Economies' and Urban Governance in India." In *Urban
Informalities: Reflections on the Formal and Informal*, edited by Colin McFarlane and
Michael Waibel, 51–66. Farnham, VT: Ashgate, 2012.

Gandy, Matthew. "Planning, Anti-Planning and the Infrastructure Crisis Facing Metropolitan Lagos." *Urban Studies* 43, no. 2 (2006): 371–96.

Gans-Morse, Jordan, Sebastián Mazzuca, and Simeon Nichter. "Varieties of Clientelism:
Machine Politics during Elections." *American Journal of Political Science* 58, no. 2
(2014): 415–32.

Gastrow, Claudia. "Urban States: The Presidency and Planning in Luanda, Angola." *International Journal of Urban and Regional Research* 44, no. 2 (2020): 366–83.

Gay, Robert. *Popular Organization and Democracy in Rio de Janeiro: A Tale of Two Favelas*.
Philadelphia: Temple University Press, 1994.

———. "Rethinking Clientelism: Demands, Discourses and Practices in Contemporary Brazil." *European Review of Latin American and Caribbean Studies*, no. 65 (1998): 7–24.

———. "The Even More Difficult Transition from Clientelism to Citizenship: Lessons from
Brazil." In *Out of the Shadows: Political Action and the Informal Economy in Latin Amer-
ica*, edited by Patricia Fernández-Kelly and Jon Shefner, 195–217. University Park, PA:
Pennsylvania State University Press, 2006.

Ghana Statistical Service. *Ghana Living Standards Survey 6—Main Report*. Accra, Ghana:
Ghana Statistical Service, 2014.

———. *Ghana Poverty Mapping Report*. Accra, Ghana: Ghana Statistical Service, May 2015.

Ghana Trade Union Congress. "Case Law Involving Street Vendors in Accra." June 2013. https://www.wiego.org/sites/default/files/resources/files/G09.pdf.

Ghanaian Chronicle. "Ningo-Prampram DCE Goes Tough on Land Fraud." Modern Ghana. August 1, 2018. https://www.modernghana.com/news/872716/ningo-prampram-dce-goes-tough-on-land-fraud.html.

GhanaWeb. "5 New Districts Coming." November 21, 2018. https://www.ghanaweb.com/GhanaHomePage/NewsArchive/5-new-districts-coming-702671.

———. "Ablekuma North Municipal Embarks on Demolition Exercise." August 3, 2019. https://www.ghanaweb.com/GhanaHomePage/NewsArchive/Ablekuma-North-Municipal-embarks-on-demolition-exercise-769076.

———. "AMA Shrinked to Help Develop Accra Better—O.B. Amoah." April 18, 2019. https://www.ghanaweb.com/GhanaHomePage/NewsArchive/AMA-shrinked-to-help-develop-Accra-better-O-B-Amoah-739476.

———. "AMA to Decongest Accra." January 2, 2018. https://www.ghanaweb.com/GhanaHomePage/NewsArchive/AMA-to-decongest-Accra-614072.

———. "Bill for Election of MMDCEs Laid in Parliament." February 20, 2019. https://www.ghanaweb.com/GhanaHomePage/NewsArchive/Bill-for-election-of-MMDCEs-laid-in-Parliament-724873.

———. "Chaos at Amasaman as Traders Protest 'Unannounced Demolition' Exercise." August 2, 2019. https://www.ghanaweb.com/GhanaHomePage/NewsArchive/Chaos-at-Amasaman-as-traders-protest-unannounced-demolition-exercise-768861.

———. "Glefe Slums Go Down as Demolition Leaves Hundreds Homeless." August 21, 2019. https://www.ghanaweb.com/GhanaHomePage/NewsArchive/Glefe-slums-go-down-as-demolition-leaves-hundreds-homeless-774148.

———. "Government to Inaugurate Six New Districts Today." February 19, 2019. https://www.ghanaweb.com/GhanaHomePage/NewsArchive/Government-to-inaugurate-six-new-districts-today-724450.

———. "Nima Redevelopment Project: Residents to Get Free Housing in 'Glamorous Apartments.'" May 14, 2019. https://www.ghanaweb.com/GhanaHomePage/NewsArchive/Nima-redevelopment-project-Residents-will-get-free-housing-in-glamorous-apartments-Atta-Akyea-746189.

———. "Takoradi Residents Petition Mahama over Land Sales." October 17, 2012. https://www.ghanaweb.com/GhanaHomePage/NewsArchive/Takoradi-Residents-Petition-Mahama-Over-Land-Sales-253385.

———. "Unauthorised Structures Along Odorkor Highway Demolished." August 3, 2019. https://www.ghanaweb.com/GhanaHomePage/NewsArchive/Unauthorised-structures-along-Odorkor-highway-demolished-769016.

———. "We'll Eject Agbogbloshie Squatters Despite Protest—AMA." August 17, 2018. https://www.ghanaweb.com/GhanaHomePage/NewsArchive/We-ll-eject-Agbogbloshie-squatters-despite-protest-AMA-677537.

Ghertner, D. Asher. *Rule by Aesthetics: World-Class City Making in Delhi*. New York: Oxford University Press, 2015.

Gibbings, Sheri Lynn, Elan Lazuardi, and Khidir Marsanto Prawirosusanto. "Mobilizing the Masses: Street Vendors, Political Contracts, and the Role of Mediators in Yogyakarta, Indonesia." *Bijdragen Tot de Taal-, Land- En Volkenkunde* 173, no. 2/3 (2017): 242–72.

Gillespie, Tom. "Accumulation by Urban Dispossession: Struggles over Urban Space in Accra, Ghana." *Transactions of the Institute of British Geographers* 41, no. 1 (2016): 66–77.
———. "From Quiet to Bold Encroachment: Contesting Dispossession in Accra's Informal Sector." *Urban Geography* 38, no. 7 (2017): 974–92.
———. "The Real Estate Frontier." *International Journal of Urban and Regional Research* 44, no. 4 (2020): 599–616.
Goodfellow, Tom. "Political Informality: Deals, Trust Networks, and the Negotiation of Value in the Urban Realm." *Journal of Development Studies* 56, no. 2 (2020): 278–94.
———. "Seeing Political Settlements Through the City: A Framework for Comparative Analysis of Urban Transformation: Seeing Political Settlements through the City." *Development and Change* 49, no. 1 (2018): 199–222.
———. "State Effectiveness and the Politics of Urban Development in East Africa: A Puzzle of Two Cities, 2000–2010." PhD diss., London School of Economics and Political Science, 2012. http://etheses.lse.ac.uk/id/eprint/557.
———. "Taming the 'Rogue' Sector: Studying State Effectiveness in Africa through Informal Transport Politics." *Comparative Politics* 47, no. 2 (2015): 127–47.
Government of Ghana. *Ghana National Urban Policy Action Plan.* Accra: Ministry of Local Government and Rural Development, May 2012. http://www.ghanaiandiaspora.com/wp/wp-content/uploads/2014/05/ghana-national-urban-policy-action-plan-2012.pdf.
———. *Greater Accra Regional Spatial Development Framework.* Accra: Ministry of Lands and Natural Resources—Land Use and Spatial Planning Authority, June 2017.
———. Land Use and Spatial Planning Act, 925 Act § (2016).
———. *National Employment Policy.* Ministry of Employment and Labour Relations, 2014. https://www.ilo.org/wcmsp5/groups/public/---africa/---ro-abidjan/---ilo-abuja/documents/publication/wcms_373458.pdf.
———. *National Housing Policy.* Ministry of Water Resources, Works, and Housing, 2015. https://www.mwh.gov.gh/wp-content/uploads/2018/05/national_housing_policy_2015-1.pdf.
———. *National Spatial Development Framework (2015–2035).* Accra: Government of Ghana, February 2015. https://luspa.gov.gh/publications/documents/.
Government of the Gold Coast. "Annual Report on the Social and Economic Progress of the People of the Gold Coast, 1931–32." Colonial Reports—Annual. London, 1933.
———. "Gold Coast—Report for 1910." Colonial Reports—Annual. London, September 1911.
Grant, Richard. *Globalizing City: The Urban and Economic Transformation of Accra, Ghana.* Space, Place, and Society. Syracuse, NY: Syracuse University Press, 2009.
Grant, Richard, Martin Oteng-Ababio, and Jessy Sivilien. "Greater Accra's New Urban Extension at Ningo-Prampram: Urban Promise or Urban Peril?" *International Planning Studies* 24, no. 3/4 (2019), 325–40.
Graphic Online. "Govt Engages Singaporean Planner to Redevelop Accra into Modern City." October 8, 2018. https://www.graphic.com.gh/news/general-news/govt-engages-singaporean-planner-to-redevelop-accra-into-modern-city.html.
Gray, Obika. *Demeaned but Empowered: The Social Power of the Urban Poor in Jamaica.* Kingston, Jamaica: University of the West Indies Press, 2004.
Green, Elliott. "Patronage, District Creation, and Reform in Uganda." *Studies in Comparative International Development* 45, no. 1 (2010): 83–103.

Grindle, Merilee Serrill. *Jobs for the Boys: Patronage and the State in Comparative Perspective*. Cambridge, MA: Harvard University Press, 2012.

Hackenbroch, Kirsten, and Shahadat Hossain. "'The Organised Encroachment of the Powerful'—Everyday Practices of Public Space and Water Supply in Dhaka, Bangladesh." *Planning Theory and Practice* 13, no. 3 (2012): 397–420.

Harvey, David. "The Right to the City." *New Left Review*, no. 53 (2008): 23–40.

Hasan, Arif, and Masooma Mohib. "The Case of Karachi, Pakistan." Understanding Slums: Case Studies for the Global Report on Human Settlements 2003, 2003. https://www.ucl .ac.uk/dpu-projects/Global_Report/pdfs/Karachi.pdf.

Hays, Samuel P. "The Changing Political Structure of the City in Industrial America." *Journal of Urban History* 1, no. 1 (1974): 6–38.

Herlambang, Suryono, Helga Leitner, Liong Ju Tjung, Eric Sheppard, and Dimitar Anguelov. "Jakarta's Great Land Transformation: Hybrid Neoliberalisation and Informality." *Urban Studies* 56, no. 4 (2019): 627–48.

Herrera, Veronica Maria Sol. *Water and Politics: Clientelism and Reform in Urban Mexico*. Ann Arbor: University of Michigan Press, 2017.

Hicken, Allen, and Noah L. Nathan. "Clientelism's Red Herrings: Dead Ends and New Directions in the Study of Nonprogrammatic Politics." *Annual Review of Political Science* 23 (May 2020): 277–94.

Hirschman, Albert O. *Exit, Voice, and Loyalty: Responses to Decline in Firms, Organizations, and States*. Cambridge, MA: Harvard University Press, 1970.

Holland, Alisha C. *Forbearance as Redistribution: The Politics of Informal Welfare in Latin America*. Cambridge Studies in Comparative Politics. Cambridge: Cambridge University Press, 2017.

Housing the Masses. *Final Report to People's Dialogue on Human Settlements on Community-Led Enumeration of Old Fadama Community, Accra, Ghana*. January 2010. https://sdinet .org/wp-content/uploads/2015/04/2009.May3_.2010.Old_Fadama_Enumeration-1_1.pdf.

Hutchison, Jane. "The 'Disallowed' Political Participation of Manila's Urban Poor." *Democratization* 14, no. 5 (2007): 853–72.

ICF Consulting Services. *Urban Governance and Services in Ghana: Institutional, Financial and Functional Constraints to Effective Service Delivery*. Research monograph. Brussels, Belgium: Cities Alliance, 2017.

Inskeep, Steve. *Instant City: Life and Death in Karachi*. New York: Penguin Press, 2011.

Iyer, Lakshmi, and Anandi Mani. "Traveling Agents: Political Change and Bureaucratic Turnover in India." *Review of Economics and Statistics* 94, no. 3 (2012): 723–39.

Jackman, David. "Dominating Dhaka." ESID working paper 127, Effective States and Inclusive Development Research Centre, University of Manchester, UK, 2020; written November 12, 2019. https://doi.org/10.2139/ssrn.3523025.

Jackson, Iain. "Sharing Stories from Jamestown: The Creation of Mercantile Accra, Ghana." Open Science Framework. May 4, 2019. https://doi.org/10.17605/osf.io/54k89.

Japan International Cooperation Agency, Oriental Consultants, CTI Engineering International, and Almec Corporation. "The Study on the Comprehensive Urban Development Plan for Greater Kumasi in The Republic of Ghana, Final Report Summary." Ministry of Environment, Science, Technology and Innovation; Town and Country Planning Department, September 2013. http://open_jicareport.jica.go.jp/pdf/12145777.pdf.

Jha, Saumitra, Vijayendra Rao, and Michael Woolcock. "Governance in the Gullies: Democratic Responsiveness and Leadership in Delhi's Slums." Policy Research Working Papers 3694, World Bank, Washington, DC, September 2005. https://openknowledge.worldbank.org/handle/10986/8601.

Jibao, Samuel. "Ghana." Chap. 14 in *Property Tax in Africa: Status, Challenges, and Prospects*, edited by R. C. D. Franzsen and William J. McCluskey. Cambridge, MA: Lincoln Institute of Land Policy, 2017.

Joireman, Sandra Fullerton. *Where There Is No Government: Enforcing Property Rights in Common Law Africa*. Oxford: Oxford University Press, 2011.

Karekurve-Ramachandra, Varun, and Alexander Lee. "Can Gender Quotas Improve Public Service Provision? Evidence from Indian Local Government." Working paper, University of Rochester, NY, December 26, 2020. https://varun.kr/files/gender-performance7.pdf.

Keefer, Philip, and Razvan Vlaicu. "Democracy, Credibility, and Clientelism." Policy Research Working Papers 3472, World Bank, Washington, DC, 2005. https://doi.org/10.1596/1813-9450-3472.

Khan, Akhter Hameed. "Orangi Pilot Project Programs." IRC. December 1992. https://www.ircwash.org/sites/default/files/822-PKOR92-11567.pdf.

Khan, Mushtaq. "Political Settlements and the Governance of Growth-Enhancing Institutions." School of Oriental and African Studies, July 2010. https://eprints.soas.ac.uk/9968/.

———. "State Failure in Weak States: A Critique of New Institutionalist Explanations." In *The New Institutional Economics and Third World Development*, edited by John Harriss, Janet Hunter, and Colin Lewis, 71–86. London: Routledge, 1995. http://ebookcentral.proquest.com/lib/upenn-ebooks/detail.action?docID=166438.

Kitschelt, Herbert, and Steven I. Wilkinson. "Citizen-Politician Linkages: An Introduction." In *Patrons, Clients, and Policies: Patterns of Democratic Accountability and Political Competition*, edited by Herbert Kitschelt and Steven I. Wilkinson, 1–49. Cambridge: Cambridge University Press, 2007.

Kjær, Anne Mette. "Land Governance as Grey Zone: The Political Incentives of Land Reform Implementation in Africa." *Commonwealth and Comparative Politics* 55, no. 4 (2017): 426–43.

Klopp, Jacqueline M. "Pilfering the Public: The Problem of Land Grabbing in Contemporary Kenya." *Africa Today* 47, no. 1 (2000): 6.

———. "Towards a Political Economy of Transportation Policy and Practice in Nairobi." *Urban Forum* 23, no. 1 (2012): 1–21.

Koster, Martijn, and Flávio Eiró. "Clientelism in Northeast Brazil: Brokerage within and Outside Electoral Times." *Contemporary Social Science*, published online January 26, 2021. https://doi.org/10.1080/21582041.2021.1876244.

Kumar, Ajay. "Understanding the Emerging Role of Motorcycles in African Cities: A Political Economy Perspective." Urban Transport Series. International Bank for Reconstruction and Development/World Bank, 2011.

Kumar, Ajay, and Fanny Barrett. "Stuck in Traffic: Urban Transport in Africa." Working paper, World Bank, Washington, DC, 2008. https://documents.worldbank.org/curated/en/671081468008449140/pdf/0Urban1Trans1FINAL1with0cover.pdf.

Lapomarda, Vincent A. "Maurice Joseph Tobin: The Decline of Bossism in Boston." *New England Quarterly* 43, no. 3 (1970): 355–81.

Larbi, Wordsworth Odame. "Spatial Planning and Urban Fragmentation in Accra." *Third World Planning Review* 18, no. 2 (1996): 193–215.

Larreguy, Horacio, John Marshall, and Laura Trucco. "Breaking Clientelism or Rewarding Incumbents? Evidence from an Urban Titling Program in Mexico." Working paper, December 2018. https://www.dropbox.com/s/y2thc5nzg237sgs/CORETT_v18.pdf?dl =0.

Levenson, Zachary. "Becoming a Population: Seeing the State, Being Seen by the State, and the Politics of Eviction in Cape Town." *Qualitative Sociology* 44 (2021): 367–83.

———. "Precarious Welfare States: Urban Struggles over Housing Delivery in Post-Apartheid South Africa." *International Sociology* 32, no. 4 (2017): 474–92.

Levy, Brian. *Working with the Grain: Integrating Governance and Growth in Development Strategies*. Oxford: Oxford University Press, 2014.

Lindberg, Staffan I. "What Accountability Pressures Do MPs in Africa Face and How Do They Respond? Evidence from Ghana." *Journal of Modern African Studies* 48, no. 1 (2010): 117–42.

Lines, Kate, and Jack Makau. "Taking the Long View: 20 Years of Muungano Wa Wanavijiji, the Kenyan Federation of Slum Dwellers." *Environment and Urbanization* 30, no. 2 (2018): 407–24.

Lu. "Shop Names in Ghana." *Unwitting Traveler* (blog). July 17, 2012. Accessed May 7, 2021. https://theunwittingtraveller.wordpress.com/2012/07/17/shop-names-in-ghana/.

Maoulidi, Moumié. "A Water and Sanitation Needs Assessment for Kumasi." MCI Social Sector Working Paper Series. Millenium Cities Initiative—The Earth Institute at Columbia University, New York, September 2010. https://www.researchgate.net/publication /270703801_WATER_AND_SANITATION_NEEDS_ASSESSMENT_FOR_KUMASI _GHANA.

Mayne, Alan. *Slums: The History of a Global Injustice*. London: Reaktion Book, 2017.

McCaffery, Peter. *When Bosses Ruled Philadelphia: The Emergence of the Republican Machine, 1867–1933*. University Park, PA: Pennsylvania State University Press, 1993.

McDonnell, Erin Metz. *Patchwork Leviathan: Pockets of Bureaucratic Effectiveness in Developing States*. Princeton, NJ: Princeton University Press, 2020.

McGrath, Alexander. "A Modified Agent-Based Model of Slum Formation." *Berkeley Planning Journal* 28, no. 1 (2016): 68–99.

McTernan, Billie Adwoa. "Accra Slum Dwellers Suspect Cholera Demolitions Are a Pretext for Profit." *Guardian*, October 20, 2014, sec. Global Development. https://www.theguardian .com/global-development/2014/oct/20/accra-cholera-ghana-mensah-guinea-slums -demolished-commercial-profit.

Mensah, James Kwame, and Eugénie L. Birch. "Powering the Slum: Meeting SDG7 in Accra's Informal Settlements." Kleinman Center for Energy Policy, April 2021. https:// kleinmanenergy.upenn.edu/research/publications/powering-the-slum-meeting-sdg7-in -accras-informal-settlements/.

Ministry of Inner-City and Zongo Development. "MICZD Projects." Accessed March 17, 2020. http://www.miczd.gov.gh/projects.

Ministry of Tourism, Arts and Culture and Adjaye Associates. "Marine Drive Accra, Concept," October 2017.

Mitlin, Diana. "A Class Act: Professional Support to People's Organizations in Towns and Cities of the Global South." *Environment and Urbanization* 25, no. 2 (2013): 483–99.

———. "Beyond Contention: Urban Social Movements and Their Multiple Approaches to Secure Transformation." *Environment and Urbanization* 30, no. 2 (2018): 557–74.

———. "Politics, Informality and Clientelism—Exploring a Pro-Poor Urban Politics." ESID Working Papers. Effective States and Inclusive Development Research Centre, University of Manchester, UK, May 2014. https://www.effective-states.org/working-paper-34/.

———. "The Politics of Shelter: Understanding Outcomes in Three African Cities." ESID working paper 145. Effective States and Inclusive Development Research Centre, University of Manchester, UK, 2020; written June 4, 2020. https://doi.org/10.2139/ssrn.3661561.

———. "With and Beyond the State—Co-production as a Route to Political Influence, Power and Transformation for Grassroots Organizations." *Environment and Urbanization* 20, no. 2 (2008): 339–60.

Mitlin, Diana, and Jan Mogaladi. "Social Movements and the Struggle for Shelter: A Case Study of EThekwini (Durban)." *Progress in Planning* 84 (August 2013): 1–39.

Moatasim, Faiza. "Entitled Urbanism: Elite Informality and the Reimagining of a Planned Modern City." *Urban Studies* 56, no. 5 (2019): 1009–25.

More, Thomas. "Book One." In *Utopia: With Erasmus's the Sileni of Alcibiades*, Thomas More, David Wootton, and Desiderius Erasmus, 56–90. Indianapolis: Hackett, 1999.

Moser, Sarah, Laurence Côté-Roy, and Prosper Issahaku Korah. "The Uncharted Foreign Actors, Investments, and Urban Models in African New City Building." *Urban Geography*, published online April 19, 2021. https://doi.org/10.1080/02723638.2021.1916698.

Müller, Frank, and Ramiro Segura. "The Uses of Informality: Urban Development and Social Distinction in Mexico City." *Latin American Perspectives* 44, no. 3 (2017): 158–75.

Murillo, María Victoria, Virginia Oliveros, and Rodrigo Zarazaga. "The Most Vulnerable Poor: Clientelism among Slum Dwellers." *Studies in Comparative International Development* 56 (2019): 343–63.

Myers, Garth Andrew. *African Cities: Alternative Visions of Urban Theory and Practice.* London: Zed Books, 2011.

Nahiduzzaman, K. M. "Housing the Urban Poor: Planning, Business and Politics—A Case Study of Duaripara Slum, Dhaka City, Bangladesh." Master's thesis, Norwegian University of Science and Technology, 2006. https://www.researchgate.net/publication/279751783_Housing_the_Urban_Poor_Planning_Business_and_Politics_A_Case_Study_of_Duaripara_Slum_Dhaka_city_Bangladesh.

Nathan, Noah L. *Electoral Politics and Africa's Urban Transition: Class and Ethnicity in Ghana.* Cambridge Studies in Comparative Politics. Cambridge: Cambridge University Press, 2019.

Nelson, Joan M. *Access to Power: Politics and the Urban Poor in Developing Nations.* Princeton, NJ: Princeton University Press, 1979.

"Nima Redevelopment Project." *The Pulse.* Joy News, May 15, 2019. https://www.youtube.com/watch?v=_02LYDCRuEg.

Njoh, Ambe J. "Urban Planning as a Tool of Power and Social Control in Colonial Africa." *Planning Perspectives* 24, no. 3 (2009): 301–17.

Nunoo, Chris. "Old Fadama, Agbogbloshie to Get Social Amenities." Graphic Online. September 20, 2019. https://www.graphic.com.gh/news/general-news/old-fadama-agbogbloshie-to-get-social-amenities.html.

Nwosu, Bernard Ugochukwu, Thaddeus Chidi Nzeadibe, and Peter Oluchukwu Mbah. "Waste and Well-Being: A Political Economy of Informal Waste Management and Public Policy in Urban West Africa." *Review of African Political Economy* 43, no. 149 (2016): 478–88.

Nyabor, Jonas. "Akufo-Addo's 2019 State of the Nation Address [Full Speech]." Citi Newsroom. February 21, 2019. https://citinewsroom.com/2019/02/21/akufo-addos-2019-state-of-the -nation-address-full-speech/.

Obeng-Odoom, Franklin. *Governance for Pro-Poor Urban Development: Lessons from Ghana.* Routledge Explorations in Development Studies 6. London: Routledge, 2013.

———. "The Informal Sector in Ghana Under Siege." *Journal of Developing Societies* 27, no. 3/4 (2011): 355–92.

Okoye, Victoria. "Tourist-Friendly Informality Doesn't Always Tell the Whole Story." *Informal City Dialogues* (blog). March 4, 2013. https://nextcity.org/informalcity/entry/tourist -friendly-informality-doesnt-always-tell-the-whole-story.

Oppong, Benjamin. "Slum or Sustainable Development? A Case Study of Sodom and Gomorrah in Accra, Ghana." Master's thesis, Minnesota State University, Mankato, 2016. Cornerstone: A Collection of Scholarly and Creative Works for Minnesota State University, Mankato. https://cornerstone.lib.mnsu.edu/etds/600.

Osei-Boateng, Clara, and Edward Ampratwum. "The Informal Sector in Ghana." FES Ghana, October 2011. http://www.wiego.org/publications/informal-sector-in-ghana.

Oteng-Ababio, Martin, and Richard Grant. "Ideological Traces in Ghana's Urban Plans: How Do Traces Get Worked out in the Agbogbloshie, Accra?" *Habitat International* 83 (January 2019): 1–10.

Owens, Kathryn E., Sumila Gulyani, and Andrea Rizvi. "Success When We Deemed It Failure? Revisiting Sites and Services Projects in Mumbai and Chennai 20 Years Later." *World Development* 106 (June 2018): 260–72.

Owusu, George. "Decentralized Development Planning and Fragmentation of Metropolitan Regions: The Case of the Greater Accra Metropolitan Area, Ghana." *Ghana Journal of Geography* 7, no. 1 (2015): 1–24.

Owusu, George, and Robert Lawrence Afutu-Kotey. "Poor Urban Communities and Municipal Interface in Ghana: A Case Study of Accra and Sekondi-Takoradi Metropolis." *African Studies Quarterly* 12, no. 1 (2010): 1–16.

Owusu-Ansah, Justice Kufour, and Imoro Braimah. "The Dual Land Management Systems as an Influence on Physical Development Outcomes Around Kumasi, Ghana." *Journal of Housing and the Built Environment* 28, no. 4 (2013): 689–703.

Owusu-Sekyere, Ebenezer, Samuel Twumasi Amoah, and Frank Teng-Zeng. "Tug of War: Street Trading and City Governance in Kumasi, Ghana." *Development in Practice* 26, no. 7 (2016): 906–19.

Paller, Jeffrey W. "African Slums: Constructing Democracy in Unexpected Places." PhD diss., University of Wisconsin–Madison, 2014. https://search.proquest.com/docview/1609567187 /abstract/14E0E6391DBB457APQ/1.

———. "Building Permanence: Fire Outbreaks and Emergent Tenure Security in Urban Ghana." *Africa* 89, no. 3 (2019): 437–56.

———. "The Contentious Politics of African Urbanization." *Current History* 116, no. 790 (2017): 163–69.

———. *Democracy in Ghana: Everyday Politics in Urban Africa.* New York: Cambridge University Press, 2019.

———. "Informal Institutions and Personal Rule in Urban Ghana." *African Studies Review* 57, no. 3 (2014): 123–42.

———. "Informal Practices of Accountability in Urban Africa." Oxford Bibliographies. Last modified June 28, 2016. Last reviewed October 26, 2020. https://www.oxfordbibliographies.com/view/document/obo-9780199756223/obo-9780199756223-0172.xml.

———. "The Meaning of Party Politics in Ghana's Urban Neighborhoods." Africa Is a Country. April 19, 2019. https://africasacountry.com/2019/04/the-meaning-of-party-politics-in-ghanas-urban-neighborhoods.

Parks, Thomas, and William Cole. "Political Settlements: Implications for International Development Policy and Practice." Occasional Paper. San Francisco: Asia Foundation, 2010.

Parnell, Susan, and Jennifer Robinson. "(Re)Theorizing Cities from the Global South: Looking Beyond Neoliberalism." *Urban Geography* 33, no. 4 (May 2012): 593–617.

Participatory Slum Upgrading Programme. "Slum Almanac 2015/2016: Tracking Improvement in the Lives of Slum Dwellers." Participatory Slum Upgrading Programme, 2015. http://unhabitat.org/wp-content/uploads/2016/02-old/Slum%20Almanac%202015-2016_EN.pdf.

Pasotti, Eleonora. *Political Branding in Cities: The Decline of Machine Politics in Bogotá, Naples, and Chicago.* Cambridge: Cambridge University Press, 2010.

Patel, Amit, Andrew T. Crooks, and Naoru Koizumi. "Slumulation: An Agent-Based Modeling Approach to Slum Formations." *Journal of Artificial Societies and Social Simulation* 15, no. 4 (2012). https://doi.org/10.18564/jasss.2045.

Patel, Sheela, Jockin Arputham, and Sheridan Bartlett. ""We Beat the Path by Walking": How the Women of Mahila Milan in India Learned to Plan, Design, Finance and Build Housing." *Environment and Urbanization* 28, no. 1 (2016): 223–40.

Payne, Geoffrey. "Interesting Times Indeed!" in *GPA 20Plus20: Reflections on Urban Development,* edited by Geoffrey Payne and Associates, 11–17. 2016. http://newgpa.org.uk/wp-content/uploads/2016/05/GPA20@20-FINAL.pdf.

———. *Informal Housing and Land Subdivisions in Third World Cities: A Review of the Literature.* Oxford: Centre for Development and Environmental Planning, Oxford Polytechnic, 1989.

People's Dialogue, Cities Alliance, Shack/Slum Dwellers International, Accra Metropolitan Assembly, and Ghana Federation of the Urban Poor. *City Wide Informal Settlement: Putting Accra Metropolitan Assembly's Informal Settlements on the Map (Land, Services and Citizenship (LSC) Project II).* September 2016. https://dokumen.tips/documents/city-wide-informal-settlement-city-wide-informal-settlement-putting-accra.html.

Perlman, Janice. *Favela: Four Decades of Living on the Edge in Rio de Janeiro.* Oxford: Oxford University Press, 2010.

Perlman, Janice E. *The Myth of Marginality: Urban Poverty and Politics in Rio de Janeiro.* Berkeley: University of California Press, 1976.

Pesaresi, Martino, Aneta J. Florczyk, Marcello Schiavina, Michele Melchiorri, and Luca Maffenini. "GHS-SMOD R2019A—GHS Settlement Grid, Updated and Refined REGIO Model 2014 in Application to GHS-BUILT R2018A and GHS-POP R2019A, Multitemporal (1975-1990-2000-2015)." June 28, 2019. https://doi.org/10.2905/42E8BE89-54FF-464E-BE7B-BF9E64DA5218.

Pethe, Abhay, Ramakrishna Nallathiga, Sahil Gandhi, and Vaidehi Tandel. "Re-Thinking Urban Planning in India: Learning from the Wedge between the de Jure and de Facto Development in Mumbai." *Cities* 39 (2014): 120–32.

Pieterse, E. A. *City Futures: Confronting the Crisis of Urban Development.* London: Zed Books, 2008.

Piliavsky, Anastasia, ed. *Patronage as Politics in South Asia.* New York: Cambridge University Press, 2014.

Post, Alison E. "Cities and Politics in the Developing World." *Annual Review of Political Science* 21, no. 1 (2018): 115–33.

Rajack, Robin, Abhay Pethe, Peter Ngau, and Shrikant Barhate. "The Political Economy of Urban Land Management: Evidence from Mumbai and Nairobi." Paper presented at the Annual World Bank Conference on Land and Poverty, Washington, DC, April 8–11, 2013.

Reporters Without Borders. "Ghana." Accessed June 19, 2020. https://rsf.org/en/ghana.

———. "World Press Freedom Index: Ranking 2020." Accessed June 19, 2020. https://rsf.org /en/ranking/2020.

Resnick, Danielle. "The Politics of Crackdowns on Africa's Informal Vendors." *Comparative Politics* 52, no. 1 (2019): 21–41.

Riis, Jacob A. *The Battle with the Slum.* 1902. Reprint, Montclair, NJ: Patterson Smith, 1969.

Roberts, Mark, Brian Blankespoor, Chandan Deuskar, and Benjamin P. Stewart. "Urbanization and Development: Is Latin America and the Caribbean Different from the Rest of the World?" Policy Research Working Papers 8019, World Bank, Washington, DC, 2017. http://documents.worldbank.org/curated/en/164251490903580662/Urbanization-and -development-is-Latin-America-and-the-Caribbean-different-from-the-rest-of-the -world.

Robins, Steven L. *From Revolution to Rights in South Africa: Social Movements, NGOs and Popular Politics after Apartheid.* Woodbridge, UK: James Currey, 2008.

Rosaldo, Manuel. "Revolution in the Garbage Dump: The Political and Economic Foundations of the Colombian Recycler Movement, 1986–2011." *Social Problems* 63, no. 3 (2016): 351–72.

Roy, Ananya. *City Requiem, Calcutta: Gender and the Politics of Poverty.* Globalization and Community 10. Minneapolis: University of Minnesota Press, 2003.

———. "Urban Informality: The Production of Space and Practice of Planning." In *The Oxford Handbook of Urban Planning,* edited by Rachel Weber and Randall Crane, 691–705. New York: Oxford University Press, 2012.

———. "Urban Informality: Toward an Epistemology of Planning." *Journal of the American Planning Association* 71, no. 2 (2005): 147–58.

———. "Why India Cannot Plan Its Cities: Informality, Insurgence and the Idiom of Urbanization." *Planning Theory* 8, no. 1 (2009): 76–87.

Roy, Ananya, and Aihwa Ong, eds. *Worlding Cities: Asian Experiments and the Art of Being Global.* Oxford: Wiley-Blackwell, 2011.

Roy, Debraj, Michael Harold Lees, Bharath Palavalli, Karin Pfeffer, and M. A. Peter Sloot. "The Emergence of Slums: A Contemporary View on Simulation Models." *Environmental Modelling and Software* 59 (September 2014): 76–90.

Roy, Pallavi. "Anti-Corruption in Nigeria: A Political Settlements Analysis." Working paper 002, Anti-Corruption Evidence, SOAS, University of London, July 2017. https://ace.soas .ac.uk/publication/anti-corruption-in-nigeria-a-political-settlements-analysis/.

Sanyal, Bishwapriya, ed. "Hidden Success." Unpublished manuscript, version dated (no date).

Sarfoh, Kwadwo Ohene. "Lost in Translation—the Nexus of Multi-layered Housing Policy Gaps: The Case of Ghana." PhD thesis, University of St. Andrews, 2010. https://research -repository.st-andrews.ac.uk/handle/10023/1697.

Sassen, Saskia. "The Global City: Introducing a Concept." *Brown Journal of World Affairs* 11, no. 2 (2005): 27–43.

Satterthwaite, David, and Diana Mitlin. *Reducing Urban Poverty in the Global South.* Hoboken, NJ: Taylor and Francis, 2013.

Shami, Mahvish, and Hadia Majid. "The Political Economy of Public Goods Provision in Slums: Preliminary Results from a Field Study in Urban Pakistan." Working paper, International Growth Centre, London, July 2014.

Shannon, William V. "The Political Machine I: Rise And Fall The Age Of The Bosses." *American Heritage*, June 1969. http://www.americanheritage.com/content/political-machine-i-rise-and-fall-age-bosses.

Sharma, Shafali, Lakshmee Sharma, Anup Malani, and Adam Chilton. "Land, Politics, and Insecurity in Slums: A Photo Essay." *Economic and Political Weekly* 55, no. 4 (2020): 7–8.

Shefner, Jon. "'Do You Think Democracy Is a Magical Thing?' From Basic Needs to Democratization in Informal Politics." In *Out of the Shadows: Political Action and the Informal Economy in Latin America*, edited by Patricia Fernández-Kelly and Jon Shefner, 241–67. University Park, PA: Pennsylvania State University Press, 2006.

Sigman, Rachel, and Staffan I. Lindberg. "Neopatrimonialism and Democracy: An Empirical Investigation of Africa's Political Regimes." V-Dem Working Paper, Series 2017:56, Varieties of Democracy (V-Dem) Institute, University of Gothenburg, Sweden, November 6, 2017. https://papers.ssrn.com/sol3/papers.cfm?abstract_id=3066654.

Sparling, Robert Alan. *Political Corruption: The Underside of Civic Morality.* Haney Foundation Series. Philadelphia: University of Pennsylvania Press, 2019.

Stacey, Paul. *State of Slum: Precarity and Informal Governance at the Margins in Accra.* London: Zed Books, 2019.

———. "Urban Development and Emerging Relations of Informal Property and Land-Based Authority in Accra." *Africa* 88, no. 1 (2018): 63–80.

Stacey, Paul, and Christian Lund. "In a State of Slum: Governance in an Informal Urban Settlement in Ghana." *Journal of Modern African Studies; Cambridge* 54, no. 4 (2016): 591–615.

Steel, Griet, Femke Van Noorloos, and Kei Otsuki. "Urban Land Grabs in Africa?" *Built Environment* 44, no. 4 (2019): 389–96.

Stoquart, Rémi, and Michael Majale. "Mid-Term Evaluation of the Participatory Slum Upgrading Programme II (PSUP II)." August 2015. Report, IBF International Consulting, ECFDC, and NIRAS. https://unhabitat.org/european-union-edf-mid-term-evaluation-of-the-participatory-slum-upgrading-programme-ii-psup-ii-august-2015.

Swapan, Mohammad Shahidul Hasan, and Shahed Khan. "Urban Informality and Parallel Governance Systems: Shaping Citizens' Engagements in Urban Planning Processes in Bangladesh." *International Planning Studies*, published online March 14, 2021. https://doi.org/10.1080/13563475.2021.1899902.

Syagga, P., W. Mitullah, and S. Karirah-Gitau. "A Rapid Economic Appraisal of Rents in Slums and Informal Settlements." Government of Kenya and UN-Habitat Collaborative Nairobi Slum Upgrading Initiative, 2002.

Tait, Malcolm, and Heather Campbell. "The Politics of Communication Between Planning Officers and Politicians: The Exercise of Power Through Discourse." *Environment and Planning A: Economy and Space* 32, no. 3 (2000): 489–506.

Thirumurthy, Priyanka. "Chennai Residents Forcibly Evicted by Slum Clearance Board in the Midst of Pandemic." *News Minute*, September 27, 2020. https://www.thenewsminute.com /article/chennai-residents-forcefully-evicted-slum-clearance-board-midst-pandemic -134029.

Tieleman, Joris, and Justus Uitermark. "Chiefs in the City: Traditional Authority in the Modern State." *Sociology* 53, no. 4 (2019): 707–23.

Tomsa, Dirk, and Andreas Ufen, eds. *Party Politics in Southeast Asia: Clientelism and Electoral Competition in Indonesia, Thailand and the Philippines*. Routledge Contemporary Southeast Asia Series 55. New York: Routledge, 2013.

Transparency International. "Corruption Perceptions Index 2020: Ghana." January 28, 2021. https://www.transparency.org/en/cpi/2020/index/gha.

Trevallion, B.A.W., and Alan G. Hood. "Accra—a Plan for the Town: The Report for the Minister of Housing." Town and Country Planning Division of the Ministry of Housing, 1958.

UN-Habitat. "Ningo-Prampram Planning Authority Approves Accra's Planned City Extension." July 27, 2016. https://unhabitat.org/ningo-prampram-planning-authority-approves -accras-planned-city-extension/.

———. UN-Habitat Best Practices Database: Award Winners. n.d. http://mirror.unhabitat .org/bp/bp.list.aspx.

———. "UN-Habitat Provides Water and Handwashing Facilities for Tens of Thousands in Ghana's Informal Settlements." June 22, 2020. https://unhabitat.org/un-habitat-provides -water-and-handwashing-facilities-for-tens-of-thousands-in-ghana%E2%80%99s -informal.

United Nations. "The New Urban Agenda." Habitat III (website). 2016. http://habitat3.org/the -new-urban-agenda/.

———. "World Urbanization Prospects 2018." United Nations, Department of Economic and Social Affairs, Population Division (website). 2018. https://population.un.org/wup/.

Varieties of Democracy. "About V-Dem." Accessed February 8, 2019. https://www.v-dem.net /en/about/.

Venter, Christoffel. "The Lurch Towards Formalisation: Lessons from the Implementation of BRT in Johannesburg, South Africa." In "THREDBO 12: Recent Developments in the Reform of Land Passenger Transport," ed. David A. Hensher, Jackie Walters, and Ruth Steel. Special issue, *Research in Transportation Economics*, 39, no. 1 (2013): 114–20.

Wantchekon, Leonard. "Clientelism and Voting Behavior: Evidence from a Field Experiment in Benin." *World Politics* 55, no. 3 (2003): 399–422.

Water and Sanitation for the Urban Poor. "Improving the Quality of Public Toilet Services in Kumasi." Practice note, July 2016. https://www.wsup.com/content/uploads/2017/08/PN027 -Improving-the-quality-of-public-toilet-services-in-Kumasi.pdf.

Watson, Vanessa. "African Urban Fantasies: Dreams or Nightmares?" *Environment and Urbanization* 26, no. 1 (2014): 215–31.

———. "Co-Production and Collaboration in Planning—The Difference." *Planning Theory and Practice* 15, no. 1 (2014): 62–76.

———. "Seeing from the South: Refocusing Urban Planning on the Globe's Central Urban Issues." *Urban Studies* 46, no. 11 (2009): 2259–75.

———. "The Ethics of Planners and Their Professional Bodies: Response to Flyvbjerg." *Cities* 32 (June 2013): 167–68.

———. "'The Planned City Sweeps the Poor Away . . .': Urban Planning and 21st Century Urbanisation." *Progress in Planning* 72, no. 3 (2009): 151–93.

Weinstein, Liza. *The Durable Slum: Dharavi and the Right to Stay Put in Globalizing Mumbai.*
Minneapolis, MN: University of Minnesota Press, 2014.

Weitz-Shapiro, Rebecca. "What Wins Votes: Why Some Politicians Opt Out of Clientelism."
American Journal of Political Science 56, no. 3 (2012): 568–83.

Weru, Jane. "Community Federations and City Upgrading: The Work of Pamoja Trust and
Muungano in Kenya." *Environment and Urbanization* 16, no. 1 (2004): 47–62.

Westminster Foundation for Democracy and CDD-Ghana. *The Cost of Politics in Ghana.* Westminster Foundation for Democracy. April 2018. http://www.wfd.org/wp-content/uploads
/2018/04/Cost_Of_Politics_Ghana.pdf.

Wood, Geof. "Staying Secure, Staying Poor: The 'Faustian Bargain.'" In "Chronic Poverty and
Development Policy," ed. David Hulme and Andrew Shepherd. Special issue, *World Development*, 31, no. 3 (2003): 455–71.

World Bank. *City of Accra, Ghana, Consultative Citizens' Report Card.* Report no. 55117-GH.
Washington, DC: World Bank, June 2010. http://documents.worldbank.org/curated/en/540521
468249314253/City-of-Accra-Ghana-consultative-citizens-report-card.

———. "Concept Note: Greater Accra Climate Resilient and Integrated Development Project." Ghana: International Bank for Reconstruction and Development and International
Development Association, May 26, 2018.

———. "Enforcing Accountability: World Bank Debars Ghanaian Company for Sanctionable
Misconduct Relating to a Waste Management Project in Liberia." Press release. September 25, 2013. http://www.worldbank.org/en/news/press-release/2013/09/25/world-bank
-debars-ghanaian-company-sanctionable-misconduct-waste-management-project
-liberia.

———. *Enhancing Urban Resilience in the Greater Accra Metropolitan Area.* Washington, DC:
World Bank, May 2017. http://documents.worldbank.org/curated/en/949241495793834492
/Enhancing-urban-resilience-in-the-Greater-Accra-Metropolitan-Area.

———. *Helping Countries Combat Corruption: The Role of the World Bank.* Washington, DC:
World Bank, September 1997. http://documents.worldbank.org/curated/en/79983153
8245192753/Helping-countries-combat-corruption-the-role-of-the-World-Bank.

———. "Population Living in Slums." World Bank Data. Accessed March 9, 2020. https://data
.worldbank.org/indicator/EN.POP.SLUM.UR.ZS.

———. *Rising Through Cities in Ghana: Urbanization Review—Overview Report.* Washington, DC: World Bank, April 2015. http://documents.worldbank.org/curated/en/6132514
68182958526/Rising-through-cities-in-Ghana-urbanization-review-overview-report.

———. *World Development Report 2004: Making Services Work for Poor People.* Washington,
DC: World Bank, 2003.

Yeboah, Eric, and Franklin Obeng-Odoom. "'We Are Not the Only Ones to Blame': District
Assemblies' Perspectives on the State of Planning in Ghana." *Commonwealth Journal of
Local Governance*, no. 7 (November 2010): 78–98.

Yeebo, Yepoka. "The Bridge to Sodom and Gomorrah." Big Roundtable. November 6, 2014.
https://thebigroundtable.com/the-bridge-to-sodom-and-gomorrah-d80d1ceaf560.

Yiftachel, Oren. "Theoretical Notes On 'Gray Cities': The Coming of Urban Apartheid?" *Planning Theory* 8, no. 1 (2009): 88–100.

Yıldırım, Kerem. "Clientelism and Dominant Incumbent Parties: Party Competition in an Urban Turkish Neighbourhood." *Democratization* 27, no. 1 (2020): 81–99.

Zinnbauer, Dieter. "Leveraging the Role of the Urban Planning Profession for One of the Central Policy Challenges of Our Times." Working paper 1, Cities of Integrity, Centre for Urban Research and Planning and African Centre for Cities, 2019. https://www.africancentreforcities.net/wp-content/uploads/2019/07/GI_ACE_WORKING_PAPER_1_DZ_.pdf.

———. "Urban Land: A New Type of Resource Curse?" In *Corruption, Natural Resources and Development*, edited by Aled Williams and Philippe Le Billon, 163–72. Cheltenham, UK: Edward Elgar Publishing, 2017.

Zoomers, Annelies, Femke van Noorloos, Kei Otsuki, Griet Steel, and Guus van Westen. "The Rush for Land in an Urbanizing World: From Land Grabbing Toward Developing Safe, Resilient, and Sustainable Cities and Landscapes." *World Development* 92 (April 2017): 242–52.

INDEX

Accra Metropolitan Assembly (AMA), 69, 76, 78, 81, 84–87, 89, 91, 93–95, 100, 106, 112–14, 116, 125, 129, 131–35, 144, 160, 194–98, 200, 202–4

administrative fragmentation, 69, 114, 116, 122

Agbogbloshie, 80, 85, 86, 101, 124–26, 129, 130, 133, 135, 193, 196, 203, 204

Amarteifio, Nat Nunoo, 129, 136, 199, 200, 203, 204

Argentina, 24, 177, 189

Asantehene, 68, 111, 113, 202

Ashanti, 68, 77, 93, 99, 111, 113

Asian Coalition for Housing Rights, 59, 61, 165

assembly members, 70, 100–102, 117, 119, 159, 160

Atlas of Urban Expansion, 35–38, 41, 45–47, 69, 81–83, 168, 175, 183, 184, 186, 196, 206, 207

atomistic settlements, 37, 38, 42–46, 81, 82, 168, 184, 196

Bangladesh, 20, 25, 51, 66, 97, 186

Björkman, Lisa, 4, 24, 187–92, 206

Brazil, 17–20, 23, 24, 55, 66, 119, 152, 168, 189; Rio de Janeiro, 17, 24, 32, 55, 61, 180, 181, 188, 192

causality, 29, 41–44

CDD-Ghana, 101, 188, 199, 203

chief executives, 70, 78, 87, 92, 98–101, 106, 107, 116, 117, 120, 123, 129, 132, 133, 135, 152, 157–61, 201

chiefs. *See* traditional authorities

Chile, 58, 59, 61, 151

China, 119, 178, 186

clientelism index, 20, 35, 39, 50, 66, 185

club goods, 21, 22, 26, 32, 98, 102, 165

Colombia, 58, 61, 151; Bogotá, 58, 61

colonialism, 7, 10, 11, 67, 73–76, 95, 96, 110, 126, 167, 187, 194

constituency service, 22, 102, 189

corruption, 4, 13, 20, 55, 61, 96, 108, 110, 118–22, 157, 171, 177, 180, 181, 188, 192, 203

COVID-19 pandemic, 31, 86, 90, 135, 191

customary land, 8, 40, 71, 111, 113, 123, 157, 166, 176; family land, 71, 111; stool land, 71, 75, 111, 112, 167

demolition of informal settlements, 2, 4, 6, 13, 22, 28, 29, 31, 45, 55, 59, 74, 82, 85–88, 106, 107, 126, 131–36, 148, 150, 152, 160, 161, 163, 169, 180–82, 190, 196, 197, 204

District Assembly Common Fund (DACF), 94, 101, 102, 104, 114

Ethiopia, 97, 110

ethnic groups in Ghana, 2, 29, 68, 99, 126

flooding, 1, 5, 66, 70, 90, 102, 105, 126, 131, 132, 136, 154, 189, 190, 203, 204

Forester, John, 11, 157, 187, 188, 205

Ga Mashie, Accra, 69, 80, 105, 112, 125, 193

Gay, Robert, 55, 56, 188, 189, 192

Ghana Federation of the Urban Poor (GHAFUP), 59, 89

Ghana Institute of Planners, 78, 99, 155, 158, 193

Global Human Settlements (data set), 35–37, 40, 41, 68, 175, 183, 193, 194, 206, 207

Harvey, David, 178, 180, 187, 206

ACKNOWLEDGMENTS

This book would not have been possible without the support of Eugenie L. Birch in her roles as director of the doctoral program in city and regional planning at the University of Pennsylvania, where I conducted this research; as chair of my dissertation committee; as codirector of the Penn Institute for Urban Research, where I continued to work on this book as a postdoctoral fellow; and as a series editor of the City in the Twenty-First Century series at the University of Pennsylvania Press, along with Susan M. Wachter. Professor Birch provided opportunities and resources to develop the research that resulted in this book, valuable feedback on my writing, and encouragement at every stage.

My research on Ghana also drew on the insights of Jeffrey Paller, first from his published work and later from my conversations with him, joint research with him in Ghana, and the feedback he continued to provide until the completion of this book. Erick Guerra was also supportive throughout my doctoral studies, and my quantitative analysis in particular benefited from his guidance. Others at Penn's planning department who deserve my thanks are Kate Daniel, Roslynne Carter, and my friends in the doctoral program.

Robert Lockhart from Penn Press has guided the development of this book patiently and provided useful suggestions along the way. Lily Palladino and Gwen Burda brought great professionalism and attention to detail to the production and copyediting of this book. I am grateful to the two anonymous peer reviewers, as well as Drew Austin and Indivar Jonnalagadda, all of whom provided thoughtful and important feedback. Anonymous peer reviewers of drafts of my articles in the *Journal of Planning Literature* and *Urban Studies* also contributed to the development of material that evolved into parts of this book.

The case study of Ghana would not have been possible without the kindness of everyone who took the time to meet and share their knowledge with me during my visits there. I owe a special debt of gratitude to Eden Gbeckor-Kove and

Kofi Kekeli Amedzro, who met with me multiple times during each visit, provided valuable information, put me in touch with other key people, and arranged site visits. Special thanks are also due to David Durban and Campbell Meyer for showing me around Accra. Others who shared their time and knowledge with me were (in alphabetical order): Alhassan Ibn Abdallah, Joe Addo, Janet Adu, Joyce Afukaar, Cecilia Akyeampong, Mohammed Alhassan, Nat Nunoo Amarteifio, Clifford Amoako, Linda Amofa, Kojo Anane, Ruth Leticia Annom, Dorcas Ansah, Benedict Arkhurst, Divine Asafo, Mohammad Awal, Sam Ayeh-Datey, George Bob-Milliar, Jeb Brugmann, Muntaka Chasant, James Ebenezer Dadson, Mustapha Gariba, Joyce Gyanfi, Benoite Labrosse, Louis Lauzer, James Kwame Mensah, Gladys Muquah, Noah Nathan, Kimberly Noronha, Abena Ntori, Ebenezer Ntsiful, Richard K. Oduro, Patience Osei-Nyarko, George Owusu, Akwasi Owusu-Afriyie, Peter Owusu-Donkor, Richard Panda, Nii Kwartelai Quartey, Nii Addo Quaynor, Dagna Rams, Kwadwo Ohene Sarfoh, Martine Sobey, Frank Tackie, Nii Tieko Tagoe, Nada Tandoh, Alhaji Yahaya Hameed Yakubu, and Kwadwo Yeboah. I am also grateful to Perry World House of the University of Pennsylvania for providing partial funding for one of my field visits to Ghana.

Finally, I am grateful to my family for their continuous support, generosity, and encouragement throughout the process of researching and writing this book.